THE WRITINGS OF WILL ROGERS
VI-1

SPONSORED BY

The Will Rogers Memorial Commission
and Oklahoma State University

THE WRITINGS OF WILL ROGERS

RADIO
BROADCASTS
OF
WILL
ROGERS

STEVEN K. GRAGERT, *Editor*

OKLAHOMA STATE UNIVERSITY PRESS
Stillwater, Oklahoma
1983

Illustrations courtesy
Will Rogers Memorial
Claremore, Oklahoma

Printed in the United States of America
Library of Congress Catalog Card Number 82-61001
International Standard Book Number 0-914956-24-8

CONTENTS

GOOD GULF SHOW

INTRODUCTION

Commercial radio programming began in the United States on November 2, 1920, in the KDKA shack atop a six-story building in Pittsburgh, Pennsylvania. During the next decade the popularity of the new medium increased as rapidly as did its technical improvements. Stations and receiving sets proliferated; by 1934 there were 593 broadcasting stations in the country and several million home radios. Crude local programming quickly gave way to coast-to-coast network dramas, situation comedies, news shows, soap operas, and musical entertainment. Performers from the fading world of vaudeville found new glory in the infant industry; actors famed from stage and screen crossed back and forth between the new medium and the old; and new stars were discovered among the hundreds of persons who appeared before studio microphones.

Among the famous personalities who "discovered" radio in the 1920s was Will Rogers. He made occasional appearances on the medium throughout the second half of the decade, although like many performers accustomed to audience reaction, he was never fully at ease behind a microphone in an empty studio. Following one of his first nationwide broadcasts, he wrote that he "was as nervous as [he] ever was on a first night." Missing were the laughter and applause of a theater full of people. He felt intimidated by a microphone that did not react to his humor, did not give him a clue as to whether his remarks had struck a funny bone or had fallen flat. "It's made to order for a singer, and a person making a straight forward speech," he wrote. "But to have to line up there and try to get some laughs, . . . its [sic] the toughest test a Comedian has."

Nevertheless, in early 1930 Rogers began his own regular program, sponsored by E. R. Squibb & Sons. From that date until shortly before his death in August of 1935, he performed on the air, most often before a studio audience, as the political and social wit of the nation. He delivered twelve radio broadcasts for Squibb in 1930, fifty-three for Gulf Oil Company between 1933 and 1935, and made other air appearances in between, including an especially memorable broadcast for President Herbert Hoover's Organization on Unemployment Relief in 1931. His radio work consumed much of each year; indeed, he was taking a well-earned hiatus from studio microphones when he perished with pilot Wiley Post in an airplane accident in Alaska on August 15, 1935. Before leaving on the flight, Rogers had signed a long-term agreement to continue the Gulf broadcasts in the fall of that year.

Rogers' radio career is the focus of this the twenty-first—and final—volume of *The Writings of Will Rogers*, a cooperative effort of Oklahoma State University and the Will Rogers Memorial Commission of the State of Oklahoma to edit, annotate, and publish the definitive collection of the public works of the famed humorist/philosopher. Some persons acquainted with this project may question the appropriateness of including Rogers' radio broadcasts in a collection of his writings, but the decision was made primarily on the basis of accessibility. The radio broadcasts are the least available to scholars and laymen of any of Rogers' public works. His newspaper and magazine writings can be gathered from the original sources by any industrious, persistent researcher working in the collection of a public library. On the other hand few complete recordings of Rogers' air work have survived, and fewer still are available for use by the general public. Thus, when an opportunity arose to put in book form the broadcasts of Rogers—to make them accessible to everyone—the editors of this project seized the chance.

Radio Broadcasts of Will Rogers offers readers the humorist's twelve essays for Squibb, his depression-era talk for the Organization on Unemployment Relief, and sixteen of the fifty-three shows that he made for Gulf Oil Company. Of the latter we chose to include only those for which sound recordings were available. Typed transcripts, which apparently had been prepared soon after each performance, were available for the remaining thirty-seven broadcasts, but their doubtful reliability necessarily precluded their inclusion in this volume. A complete listing of all of the broadcasts of the "Good Gulf Show" may be found in the APPENDIX preceding the NOTES section. The transcripts of the same are on file at the Will Rogers Memorial in Claremore, Oklahoma.

Followers of our series will find the subject matter and the style in this latest and last volume familiar. Politics, foreign relations, domestic affairs, prohibition, motion pictures, economics, lifestyles, and a myriad assortment of other topics became the foci of Rogers' insightful humor. And, because he gathered his own material for each radio program and worked without a script, his on-the-air comments were spontaneous and impromptu, resembling on paper the style of his newspaper and magazine writings. To preserve the naturalness of the radio material, Rogers' thought and speech patterns—all of his pauses, acknowledgments of audience reaction, natural stammering, and momentary diversions afield—are left untampered and intact.

One major difference, however, exists between this and earlier volumes. With Rogers' published works, the purity of the material that appeared in print remains in doubt, for often newspaper and magazine editors who disagreed with him made manuscript changes or omitted passages in part or in whole. The spontaneity of Rogers' live radio performances, however, precluded any form of editing. Network censors found it impossible to preview his remarks, and sponsors refused to censor his material. Thus, more than one-half of the material in this volume is among the most purely Rogers as can be found anywhere.

Radio did force Will to make some changes in his style, however. On the lecture circuit and on the stage, he never really felt the constrictions of time. He often continued a monologue well beyond the hour set by a schedule. Radio, he discovered, was geared to the clock; if his one-hour show was scheduled to end at 9:30 that was when it ended. To adapt his free-wheeling style to the new medium, Rogers used an alarm clock to signal the end of a program. The clock became a trademark of his show and helped to generate a few extra chuckles.

In preparing this volume for publication, we faced a few problems, not the least of which was in transcribing the broadcasts. The Squibb essays proved no great hardship. The text contained herein was taken from a printed collection of the broadcasts published in 1930 by E. R. Squibb & Sons. A more difficult task confronted us when we began working with the radio address for the President's Organization on Unemployment Relief and with the Gulf broadcasts. Fortunately, the capable staff at the Will Rogers Memorial, especially Mr. Gregory Malak, proved indispensable in making relief and useful typescripts of the sound recordings on file at the Memorial. These new typescripts, with some minor changes in capitalization, spelling, and punctuation, form the body of material recorded here. The headings that accompany each Squibb piece comes from the 1930 published edition of the broadcasts. The title for the unemployment speech derives from a reprint of that broadcast published in *The Survey* magazine in November of 1931. Because the Gulf broadcasts had never previously been published, we headed each with the title of the radio program, "The Good Gulf Show," and the date of the respective broadcast. As with our previous volumes, we have added brief annotations in which we have indentified persons and events mentioned that may be unfamiliar to present-day readers.

The publication of *Radio Broadcasts of Will Rogers* culminates a fourteen-year-plus effort to offer scholars and other readers the public works of America's Cowboy Philosopher in a readily available, complete collection. A chance conversation many years ago between the late Dr. Irving Fisher of the Will Rogers Memorial Commission and

Dr. Robert B. Kamm, then president of Oklahoma State University, gave birth to what became known as the Will Rogers Research Project. Since beginning operations in 1968 the project has collected thousands of pages of documents related to Will Rogers, has conducted extensive research into the man's public life and his times, and has produced twenty-one volumes of his works, totaling 5,202 pages of printed material. The project ends with the publication of this book, but its legacy—the twenty-one books—hopefully will provide, well into the future, a complete treasury of the wisdom and wit of a most remarkable man.

Certainly, after so many years, the project's debts of gratitude are owed to many individuals and groups. Perhaps the greatest of these obligations is due Dr. Kamm for his work in founding the project and seeing it through its formative years. No less beneficial has been the encouragement and advice offered by his successor to the university presidency, Dr. Lawrence L. Boger, whose unwavering support has proven significant at critical moments.

Three persons, in addition to myself, have held the title of director/editor of the project since 1968. The first, Dr. Theodore L. Agnew, undertook the difficult task of establishing operational guidelines, collecting manuscript and research material, arranging for funding, formulating criteria for publishing, and preparing for print a significant portion of the *Daily Telegrams*. Under the direction of Dr. Agnew's immediate successor, Dr. Joseph A. Stout, Jr., the first seven volumes of *The Writings of Will Rogers* were edited, annotated, and published and a format established for succeeding volumes. Work continued under Dr. James M. Smallwood, who became head of the project in 1976. During his leadership another seven books were published, including the long-awaited *Daily Telegrams* series and the first three volumes of *Weekly Articles*. The final one-third of *The Writings of Will Rogers* collection has appeared since the last change in directorship in 1981. I can unhesitatingly and gratefully acknowledge that the work on these last books was made less arduous by the efforts of the previous directors and their staffs.

Appreciation also is extended to numerous other persons and offices at Oklahoma State University that have made worthy contributions to the project through the years. Included among them has been the College of Arts and Sciences, the Edmon Low Library, the Departments of History and English, the Public Information Office, the Graphic Arts Department, and the Oklahoma State University Foundation. The members, past and present, of the Will Rogers Advisory Committee, most recently under the chairmanships of Drs. George

A. Gries and W. David Baird, have been most generous and kind in their collective attention to the success of the project.

Equally helpful during the past many years has been the staff of the Will Rogers Memorial and the members of its state commission. The first director of the memorial, the late Mrs. Paula McSpadden Love, a niece of Will Rogers, took a devoted interest in the Will Rogers Project and fortunately lived to see the first volume of *The Writings of Will Rogers* issue from the press in 1973. Her successor, Dr. Reba N. Collins, likewise has given generously of her time to assist in the publication of the volumes, offering advice, proofreading manuscripts, loaning documents, and running interference when critics appeared. Of her highly competent staff, Mr. Elwyn Isaacs and Mr. Gregory Malak have been particularly outstanding. Mr. Malak has been especially helpful in the publication of the present volume. He voluntarily undertook the task of listening to and preparing a transcript of each Gulf broadcast. He continued to assist our work by proofreading and correcting annotations and by loaning illustrations.

Funding for the editorial work of the project has been provided in large measure by the State of Oklahoma with the cooperation of the Oklahoma Historical Society and the Regents of Higher Education. Mrs. T. S. Loffland made a significant early contribution to the publication of *The Writings of Will Rogers* and has continued to show support for the volumes. Mr. Sylvan Goldman, the Kerr-McGee Foundation, Phillips Petroleum Corporation, and the late Mr. and Mrs. Robert W. Love also have made donations to the financial and research needs of the project.

I would be remiss if I did not recognize several other persons who gave of their labors, skills, and expertise to help produce the Will Rogers books. I wish especially to thank Dr. John Hamilton, former director of the Oklahoma State University Press, who established and persistently upheld a high standard of quality in the publication of these volumes and continues to take an abiding interest in them; Mr. Glenn Shirley, who as the press's first publications specialist acted as liaison with the project and contributed greatly to the design of the books; Dr. Peter C. Rollins, a former associate editor of *The Writings of Will Rogers*, who lent a literary flair to the project; the three past directors/editors for not only being earnest administrators and scholars, but also—and at times most necessarily—capable diplomats who strove to keep the project alive until its goals had been reached; and, not least of all, the score or more persons who staffed the project's office through the years and lent their own special and individual talents to its work. The aforementioned people served well the project in the past. By the same token, Ms. Judy G. Buchholz, the present publications specialist for the Oklahoma State University Press, and Ms. Marina C. Pepper, secretary for the project, have been the instrumental forces in the more recent work of the project. Industry, dependability, and creativity have been their hallmarks. To all the foregoing, past and present, I am most deeply indebted.

No volume of this nature—indeed, no collection of this kind—could possibly conclude without a final, admiring word of acknowledgment for the person who in fact made it all possible: William Penn Adair "Will" Rogers. The way in which people's eyes "smile" when they reminisce about him provides me a vivid understanding of what he meant to more than a generation of Americans. He was more than a simple comedian, a countryfied humorist, an urban cowboy, a motion-picture star, a radio performer, or a theatrical entertainer. He was much more. He was believable and dependable; he could be trusted; he was a neighbor. His countrymen relied on him to expose the "bunk"—the "applesauce," as he would have said—of everyday existence and to explain life and to expound on it in an easily understood vernacular. He was not always accurate or roaringly funny, but he was consistently honest and sincere. His death, so unexpected, stunned his admirers and detractors alike. With his passing they lost a part of their daily routine; daily telegrams, weekly articles, and radio monologues no longer spung from his quick mind. While we certainly—but most regrettably—cannot resurrect Will Rogers, the living man, we have striven to offer his extensive legacy, his writings and broadcasts, for the use and pleasure of present and future generations. May they enjoy.

Steven K. Gragert
Editor

E. R. Squibb & Sons Broadcasts

Arms Conference

Just when I was bragging on the radio and thought there was such a wonderful entertainment here they had to lower themselves by resorting to giving a little outline of the story of my life. That shows you how hard up they are for entertainment, when anybody would be interested in anything I—they did have it right about appearing on the stage in 1905.[1] I was carried on as a baby. They took me on there—they wanted a baby in the scene and they took me on and that is my first appearance on the stage.

I started with Mr. Ziegfeld in 1914 as a child prodigy.[2] I was just a little feller, and went in the Follies first on account of chewing gum. I chewed gum for Ziegfeld for twelve years, and never dropped a cud or anything. I was better than a cow that way.

Now tonight all I know is this—just what little I read in the papers during the day. I have been reading an awful lot here lately about other—every editorial you pick up is discontented with the way the disarmament conference is going and they think that Europe is very warlike and that they ought to go on and disarm and agree to everything that we want them to. Now let's just kind a look it over and put ourselves in their position and see what we would do under similar circumstances to them. Suppose you took Germany, for instance, and you trade places with Mexico and you let Germany be living where Mexico is, and then you took France up with our good friends on the North, your Canadians—why you put France up there and they are living there with all the big army and everything, and they live up there and England, we move them into about where Cuba is now, you know. Then Japan comes into Honolulu, around, around the Hawaiian Islands there, you know. Now just surround us with those four gorillas and see how much disarmament we start hollering about, see if we want any disarmament.

E.R. Squibb & Sons Broadcast, April 6, 1930

3

You know I don't mind telling you brothers that geography has been mighty good to us. It's wonderful to pay honor to Washington and Lincoln, but I want to tell you we ought to lay out one day a year for the old boy that laid out the location of this country. I don't know who he was, but boy he was a sage, that bird was.

Europe, when I was over there lately and then when I was over there two or three years ago, used to ask me, they says, "Rogers, why is it you all are in so bad?" (you know, nobody seems to like America), and so I had to admit that we was in kinda bad. We are sort of the pole-cat of nations, you know. We wasn't hardly what you would call the world's sweetheart, but after they kept this up for quite a while, I used to casually ask them, I says, "Well, now," be it Englishman or Frenchman or Italian or whatever was, I used to say to him, "Well, we are in bad, but will you just kinda, offhand, just casually name me a list of your bosom friends among other nations?"

Say, listen, they, they, they can't hate us as bad as them, you know. All those nations over there have been hatin' each other for years and they can't hate us as bad as they hate each other, you know, and they wouldn't hate us so bad if they really knew and they wouldn't envy us, I mean, as bad if they knew really how we was gettin' along. They think we are doing better than we are. They could be doing just as good as we are if they bought as much on credit as we do. They are an ignorant kind of people. They don't know, they just go and pay for anything when they buy it. They don't know you can have nice radios and automobiles and everything and never pay for it, you know. They are awfully funny that way.

They have got it in for each other, you know, because everyone of them owns land. There is not a piece of land in Europe that every nation over there ain't owned it themselves at some particular time, and everyone of them is goin' to try to get it back just as soon as the other bird is not looking.

These conferences and things they started after this war; after the war the conferences started. When the nations quit fightin' they had nothing to do, so they started in to confer and it's always been a matter of doubt as to whether the fightin' wasn't better than the conferrin' is, you know, because we, we, everybody, in fact I know it is with us, we had more friends when we was fightin' than we have now since we started in, into conferrin', you know.

America, a funny thing about us, we never was very good in conference you know. We are great talkers but we are mighty poor conferers, you know. We have a unique record, America has a unique record. We never lost a war and we never won a conference in our lives, and we never did, you know. We can, I think, without any degree of egotism we can say, with our tremendous resources, we can lick any nation in the world single-handed, I think, and yet we can't confer with Costa Rica and come home with our shirts on. I don't know why it is, you know, we, we, we mean well when we go into these conferences, we don't go over there to try to put it over on anybody or we don't go into wars to get anything out of it, we go in with the best intentions in the world.

You've seen men that had good intentions and yet everybody says, "Well, poor fellow, I don't know, he means well but he is just in wrong." That is the way we are when we go over there, you know. Individually we are not bad, but collectively, as a delegation, we are terrible. I don't know why it is.

Half of the unemployed in this country are people that's goin' or comin' from a conference somewhere. I don't know where they've been or they don't know just so they have been to a conference, that's all!

We get into more things for less reasons than any nation in the world. Not long ago China wanted to have a war. Now China is an awful peaceful nation, they don't bother nobody; China goes along, attends to their own business and they don't mess with nobody else's. We learned an awful lot of useful things from China, you know, and they are poor people and they don't get much pleasure and they wanted to have a civil war, just have a nice little war among themselves to kinda break the monotony of being a Chinaman. Do you think they could have that war alone? No, they couldn't have it; we was there the day it opened, we was right there, we was the first one there; we got there before the Chinamen did, us and England—there's another old busybody nation; they have to horn into everything, too. We was right there. China don't hurt nobody in the war, they don't fight on rainy days. A Chinaman will get his gun and start marching to war, and he comes to a sign that says, "Rain, no war today." He gets his little rain check and goes back home and waits, you know, for a dry day to shoot somebody when he won't get his gun wet, you know.

Then Nicaragua, they was havin' some trouble. Nicaragua wasn't in trouble, they just wanted to have a good time down there among themselves and put on a little civil war and just use home talent; they didn't want no outsiders at all, just take up a few among their own people. Do you think they could have a little war, have their little fun? No, we was right there, we had to be there.

Haiti, just the other day a little island down here, Haiti, they wanted to do something you know, the other day they wanted to have a little shootin' and use each other as targets. Well, the day the shootin' was to come off, before they could fire the opening overture we was there, we was right there, there to get in it. We not only sent the marines down, we said, "What's the big idea of having a war?" and we went in. "Where do you guys get that stuff?" See! We sent a commission down, too. The Haitians or Haitians, I don't know what it is, anyhow they don't mind marines because they have been around these countries and fought with them so much they like the marines, they are likable chaps, you know, and everything, but they told them, "For the Lord's sake send this commission home; we will do anything if you send this commission home." So we got that out of there, you know.

I don't know how we know that all these things are goin' on. We must have scouts out somewhere. It takes a big navy for us and England just to locate somebody else's business.

We are never late; we are always there on opening days; we get right there. We do this, you know, I don't know why. I'll bet you if we ever started taking care of our business once—we, we are awful imitative you know, and we like a thing and it would be such a novelty if we went to takin' care of our own business it would be wonderful, you know, and I guess we would like it, but we are funny people. I bet you right now that they could have, they could have a-a-a-a-an egg layin' contest, we will say, somebody could scare up an egg layin' contest in Czechoslovakia and if America could find out where it was, we would send more delegates and lay less eggs than any nation in the whole hen house.

Good-bye you all. The next time I meet you it will be in a conference somewhere, I don't know. Good-bye.

Charles Lindbergh

It was about 7:30 in the morning at Mexico City and 200,000 people were packed on the field, and on a platform built over a hangar they have got there was the President of Mexico, Mr. Calles, and his staff and his entire cabinet and all the dignitaries of Mexico and Lindy was lost somewhere in the fog.[1] And they waited there all day. He didn't arrive until 3:45 in the afternoon. Yet not a thing was served to eat, not a bite to eat or drink or a thing. You couldn't have walked by and given those Mexicans anything to eat. You know, their minds just wasn't on eating. It was on this boy that was lost in their country coming in to their country—coming in to see them. And that was beautiful and I will never forget Mexico for that.

Now, we won't do it, we won't do it here. I was out on Long Island one time waiting for the Germans and that Irishman to land, and when it come noon, we looked up and we said, "Well, we would like to see the boys come in, but we have got to get a hot dog somewhere."[2] And we went prowling off looking for some.

And when Lindy landed down in Mexico, a funny thing, they didn't have any soldiers to guard his plane. Up here, you know, with these curio hunters, when he landed, we had to have soldiers all around. Somebody would reach in and would get a pocketful of carburetors or take the engine and put it under his coat. But these Mexicans, they didn't touch a thing. The thought never entered their heads to take the plane apart and carry it home at all. They are just ignorant that way, you know. They are awful primitive people. They haven't been educated up to progress at all.

Oh! I must tell you about the bull fight. You know, the people up here didn't want Lindy to go to the bull fight, you know. They wired the Embassy, "Don't let Lindbergh go to bull fight." You know, when I was down there, some of these old ladies' societies wired me

E.R. Squibb & Sons Broadcast, April 13, 1930

and said, "Don't let Lindbergh attend bull fight." Well, you know, I was lucky to talk to Lindbergh, much less tell him where to go. So I wired them back, "What are you worrying about Lindbergh going to the bull fight for? Stop the bull from going. There is the head man in that show, the bull."

And one day, he was going out of the Embassy as I was going in there, and he asked me, he said, "Will, do you want to go with me? I am going out to the field. I will take you up. I am going to take up the Mexican plane."

On the way out, he said, "I won't take you up first. I will take somebody else because it wouldn't look good to come to Mexico and take up an American first."

When we got to the field and I saw him lead out this old Mexican plane—it had bandages on it and it was wrapped up in barbed wire—they didn't allow them to ship them in from this country then—terrible looking old plane—when I saw that plane, I was willing that he take all of Mexico before he got to me.

So he finally hollered. "Come on in." I was the third one, and he took me up. I was certainly scared to get in that plane, honest I was. It was awful for an American to say he is scared to fly with Lindbergh, it is almost sacrilegious. My only claim to fame, you know what I mean, would have been to have fallen with Lindbergh, but I was too big a coward to even want to fall with him. We got in there, and we was flying this old plane around and them wings looked every minute like they was going to fold right up and say, "Brother, we are with you."

When we was driving back that night, I said, "Colonel, that was a pretty sick sister we was in there today, wasn't it? I never rode in an old plane like that."

Here is the only undiplomatic remark I ever did hear that fellow make. He said to me, "I just wanted to fly that plane to see if a plane that old would fly."

Mr. Morrow told me this little story over in London this trip.[3] Lindbergh had been entertained by the Morrows two or three weeks, and he flew to Guatemala, and the first they heard from him—and I made a little copy of it right here—the first they heard from him, it says, "Dear Mr. and Mrs. Morrow, I left Mexico City this morning at six o'clock.[4] I arrived at Guatemala at 7:13. I was 13 hours and 13 minutes in the air. It will take this letter 12 days to reach you. If we had air mail, it would reach you tomorrow night. Yours respectfully, Charles Lindbergh."

Wasn't that just like him, you know? All for aviation. He didn't even thank them for his visit there. He was just thinking of this air line to Guatemala. Didn't even thank them for the buggy ride or firecrackers or nothing, just interested in getting an air line to Guatemala. And, Lord, we ain't got nobody in Washington can find Guatemala on the map.

First time I rode with him was coming out of Long Beach. We was flying up to Los Angeles in a big, three-motored Ford plane and was going to land in a field near Englewood, and there wasn't no sock blowing to show which way the wind was blowing. I was sitting in the seat by him, and I said, "Colonel, how can you tell how to land when you can't tell what way the wind is blowing."

He said, "Didn't you see the way those clothes was blowing on that line back there a while ago?" Didn't I see the way some washing was blowing down around Hoya or somewhere? I didn't even notice to see what kind of clothes was on the line at all. So I thought I would pull one of my Smart Alec remarks, so I said, "Well, what would you do if it wasn't Monday?"

And he said—to show you this guy has a good sense of humor, he come right back at me and he said, "I wouldn't fly over such a dirty place."

The other day, I said, "Colonel, what is the most amusing thing ever happened to you?"

"The most amusing thing happened a while ago. I was hurt in a parachute leap, have a bum shoulder and have to go to a doctor once in a while to get it fixed up. I went to one, and the doctor fixed it up, and the papers heard about it, and they had it in there, 'Lindbergh near crash in big airplane accident. He goes to doctor to get patched up'."

And he told me how he did it. He was playing with the dog, a little old dog they had, and the dog ran under the bed and he went under the bed to scare the dog out and hit his shoulder. He said, "Ain't that a fine thing for a big, able-bodied American aviator to make a forced landing under a bed and knock his shoulder down." He has a good sense of humor, you know. A great guy!

I never liked to hear him called "Lucky"—he ain't lucky. Yes, I'll take that back, he is lucky—I met his wife. Now I will say he was lucky. He was never lucky in flying, that was premeditated, but landing a girl like he did was really lucky. She is really the Grace Coolidge of prominent men's wives.[5] Good night.

9

President Hoover

There is Orthodox Quakers and then the modern Quakers. The Orthodox stayed in Philadelphia and the modern ones got out. The further away from Philadelphia they got, the more modern they was. Mr. Hoover's is about the most modern of all of them.[1] They got to Iowa. Of course, there was no California in those days. The motion picture camera hadn't been invented, and then climate was only a condition and not a sales commodity.

Mr. Hoover, he was left an orphan when he was a little boy, at a very early age, and he went to live for a while with an uncle. This uncle lived down in Pawhuska, Indian Territory, now Oklahoma, Pawhuska, Oklahoma.[2] Pawhuska, to give you an idea—now of course maybe you never heard of it—Pawhuska is just fifty-five miles from Claremore, and it is near Tulsa, too, but it is fifty-five miles from Claremore, and he used to come to Claremore. People did from Tulsa, too. Pawhuska and Tulsa people used to come over to Claremore for their mail and to find out what time it was. We had a clock there.

Well, it has always been credited that this splendid association with these fine people that he met down in that country has really molded Mr. Hoover's future character. I mean, I think that is where he got his wonderful character, was in meeting those people. Just this touch of kind of artistic environment that he got in our country there, that has made him what he is, you know. He wouldn't have developed anything like that if he had stayed anywhere else. If he had stayed in Iowa or gone directly to California, he would have just turned out to be another real estate salesman, that is about all he would have been.

The next big step in Mr. Hoover's career, as I picture it and read about it, after having his character formed in Rogers County, Oklahoma, was to go to Leland Stanford School. It wasn't hardly

E.R. Squibb & Sons Broadcast, April 20, 1930

known in those days because Pop Warner was still coaching the Carlisle Indians.[3] They brought him away from Carlisle, and of course the Carlisle Indian School had to close, and Stanford become a university. There is no college now that has got a higher standing than Stanford has. Their stadium is just as big as anybody's stadium, and they can afford to pay as much for a good full-back or end as Harvard or Yale or Princeton or any of them.

In the days of course when Mr. Hoover went there, there was no football, so if you wanted to work your way through school you had to work, you couldn't just play for it. You had to work, and that is what Mr. Hoover did. He worked his way through school and was really a self-made man that way. If there had been football in his day he would never have been president; he would have just turned out to be another coach.

Well, he not only picked up an education at Stanford but a wife, too, which is an education in itself. There was a mighty fine girl going to school there. Her name was Lou Henry.[4] She was studying flowers and plants. She fell in love with Mr. Hoover. Now, if that strikes you as kind of strange, that is nothing. Look at Mrs. Coolidge, she was a teacher in a deaf and dumb school when she fell in love with Calvin.[5]

He graduated, Mr. Hoover did, in 1895. The year he graduated there wasn't any filling stations for a college man to work in, so he took up engineering. He wasn't a stationary engineer; he was a locomotion engineer, I guess that is what you would call it, for he was always moving. He couldn't seem to make a go of it in any one place. He just prowled around all over the world.

The first job he got was in Australia. Well, he thought Australia was too wild a country to get married and take a wife to, that is, a new wife, so he decided to wait until he got to a more civilized place to go before he married. Then he figured, too, that after he got back from Australia, why he wouldn't have to go in debt for the license. So he waited until he finished this job in Australia, and he got a job in the interior of China. It was quiet and nice and fine there. He got married and went there. China give him a wonderful reception. They put on the Boxer Rebellion for him when he arrived. They was barricaded in the town of Zin Zin or Tin Tin, or something like that, or Sen Sen, I don't know the name of it, one of those names, they all sound alike besides Hongkong.[6] They was barricaded there for a long time, and the Chinamen shot at them for three months. That was for a honeymoon.

He went to South America and Siberia and Africa and Alaska and once in his early days he got as far away from civilization as to do some government surveying in Arkansas. That is my wife's state, I pulled that for her.[7]

Through all these years of travel, Mrs. Hoover stuck right with him and she helped him out in his work. He would think up new places to go, and she would look up the time table and see how to get there. If they stayed two weeks in any one place, why Mr. Hoover joined the Old Settlers Club.

Mrs. Hoover is not only a charming woman but a very brilliant woman. She helped him translate an old book on engineering that was written some four hundred years ago, and nobody knew what the book said, and they figured it out, and of course we don't know whether they figured it out right or not because nobody knows what the book said.

That brings him up to the war in 1914. He was chairman of the American Relief Association, and he helped feed Belgians, and a little later it was found we was worse off than the Belgians, so they brought him home to feed us. He is always feeding somebody. Now he is feeding the Republicans. No Armenian that ever lived can eat more than one of them can.

I always did want to see him elected. I wanted to see how far a competent man could go in politics. It has never been tried before.

Women have always been very strong for Mr. Hoover. When his picture appeared on the screen, all the time the women have always applauded him. Even during the war, the women would drop their knitting to applaud for Mr. Hoover. Of course, they would be knitting on a sock that the soldier afterwards wore for a sweater, but, you know, their patriotism was better than their knitting, but they meant well.

He really won the war for us. Did you ever figure that out? He was our food dictator.[8] He won the war for us, but he ruined our stomachs. He gave us liberty with indigestion.

You remember all the slogans we had during the war. Well, he is the inventor of all of them—"Butter it thin and you're bound to win;" and "Drink your coffee black and give the enemy a whack," and all of them. Mr. Hoover thought of all those things, you know.

One time I was down in the flooded area in the Mississippi Valley. I was shown around down there during the flood, and I saw some of the splendid work Mr. Hoover did. He really saved people's lives in that flood, he honestly did, he saved their lives. Out on a raft, he really pulled people out of the water with his own hands, you know, and then after he got them out and wrung them out, they was Democrats.

Well, that was wonderful, you know. Suppose you swam in and

laid yourself liable to some personal injury and dragged something out and find it was only a Democrat, you would have a tendency to shove him back in again you know. But he didn't, you know, he didn't. He kept them out, you know, and that showed that he was really a humanitarian at heart, you know, because Congress ain't going to do nothing about the floods at all. Just before they closed the last session, they passed a resolution denouncing floods. They come out against them then. So if you have got any friends down in the Mississippi Valley, why, you had better advise them to get a row boat. I would put more dependence in a skiff during a flood than I would in the whole of the Senate or Government and all, you know.

Mr. Hoover, you know, he was originally a Democrat himself when he come back. When we was going to run him in 1920, we had him all framed up to run on our side. A lot of people tell you that Mr. Hoover ain't a politician. Well, he ain't a politician in a way, but he is a smart fellow all right, you know. You didn't see him running with the Democrats, did you? No, he liked us all right, but he didn't run with us. He waited until he got on the right side before he run, you know.

The politicians, you know, they have all been against him. That is really what elected him. The minute the people found out the politicians didn't want him, the whole nation said, He is the kind of fellow we want.

Of course, we kid about his commissions and all that, but I tell you in this late Wall Street crisis, I really believe that the way he got all those big men together, really saved a very delicate situation there, and you know there is quite a psychology in getting a lot of big men on commissions with you. You have just got that many more men working with you, you know. Any time you tell a fellow you will put him on some committee or something, he thinks, you know, it kind of makes him do a little better, you know, and I think that is one thing that Mr. Hoover did about that.

Of course, they talk about how everything is getting along and everything. He has only been in a year, and it all depends on what we do the last year. You know, the memory of a voter—you can give him three years of prosperity and then if you give him the last year and he ain't doing very well, a voter just goes to the polls and if he has got a dollar you stay in, and if he ain't got a dollar, you go out, you know. The memory of a voter is about as long as a billy goat. So it is all going to depend on how Mr. Hoover makes out the last year.

I guess I ought to say something about his recreation. Most men's recreation is golf, and their business is talking about it, talking about the golf, but he hasn't golfed in a long time, in years, in fact. He trad-

13

ed his niblick and putter for a can of worms, and now he goes to Virginia, you know. They used to raise presidents in Virginia, and now they just raise the fish that the presidents catch.

You know, when Mr. Coolidge was in and just let everything go along, that was wonderful. Nobody ever asked Coolidge to fix a thing. We just let everything go, and everybody grabbed off what he could and all, never fixed anything. We are great people to go to extremes. We just jump from one thing to another. Now Mr. Hoover is elected and we want him to fix everything. Farm relief—we want him to fix the farmer. Now, the farmer never had relief. You know what I mean. He never had it even under Lincoln, he never had it. But he wants it under Hoover. He thinks Mr. Hoover ought to give him some relief.

Prohibition—they think Mr. Hoover ought to fix prohibition. Well, my goodness, Mr. Hoover can't—I don't know, but if I remember right, the boys had a couple of nips under Calvin's administration, I think they did.

Prosperity—millions of people never had it under nobody and never will have it under anybody, but they all want it under Mr. Hoover.

Women—women in this country, they think that Mr. Hoover, my goodness, he ought to come in and wash the dishes, you know, and help take care of the baby or something. They are all wanting something from Mr. Hoover. If the weather is wrong, we blame it on Hoover. So all in all, I believe he is doing a pretty good job, and I only claim one distinction, and that is that I am the only person that I know of that is not on one of his commissions. And so good night.

Vice-President Curtis

I don't know about communing with you all here on this beautiful Sunday afternoon. I don't know how I am going to make out because all I can hear are airplane propellers buzzing around. I used to joke the army about only having one airplane and trying to get them to get another, and yesterday they flew in here with 150 of them. General Fechet wanted me to go up in every one of them, it looked like.[1]

Night before last we flew over and bombed the city of Los Angeles and in where I was standing, in the place in this big bomber, was a place for 4,000 pounds of explosives that drop on anybody, you know, drop right out of this place.

They drill with those things just like soldiers. It is wonderful to see a formation of one of those things. We are getting along wonderful with our airplanes. That reminds me of years ago, when an army officer took me up first—General Mitchell.[2] Do you remember General Mitchell they had all the trouble over after the war about criticizing the boys? I was down in Washington one time. He said, "Will, would you like to see Washington?" Lord, I had seen Washington; I didn't care anything about seeing Washington. I had been around there with all the Senators and Congressmen for years. I thought, "Maybe he knows some place they don't," but I doubted it very much. So we went out and he was going to show me. He took me to the aviation field. He threw me a suit of clothes and said, "Here, slip these things on." It was like a pair of overalls. I said, "Wait a minute; I am not going up." I had never been up before; I had never been off the ground. He said, "Come on; get in here."

I said, "No, I ain't going to go up."

He said, "You are just as safe here as on the ground."

That is what worried me, was why I didn't want to go up. Finally they kept on kidding me, all these army officers, and got me in

E.R. Squibb & Sons Broadcast, April 27, 1930

15

the plane. I didn't even look over when we started. I don't know whether we ever did start. He might have been on the ground and the engine going for all I know. I picked out one cloud up in the air and I was sitting there looking at this one cloud all the time. We took off. He was in the front seat in an open cockpit. Finally he hollered back at me and said, "Washington's home, Mount Vernon." Lord, it might just have been Clara Bow's home in Brooklyn for all I cared.[3] It didn't matter to me. It could have been Al Capone's home in Miami.[4] The Father of our Country had lost all interest for me then; I didn't know anything about it. We were flying around and he banked the plane, twisted around right quick. Now he was going around Washington's monument. I wish I could fly one of those right around Washington's monument. Boy, if that monument had had handles on it, he would have lost a customer right then. Off there I would have gone. Well, sir, we came down and landed. Walking over across the field he said, "Will, I don't know whether you know it or not, but you know they have demoted me, they have taken my commission away from me as a general," or whatever it was, some high office, and that night at twelve o'clock his old commission was to go out and he was to be given some other one. He said, "You are the last person that ever flew with me as a major-general," or something. That was wonderful. Here is a fellow who had gone over there; he had commanded our air forces during the war and everything, and it was a wonderful thing. I told him, "Major, I certainly appreciate it very much, the idea that I was the last one to fly with you." I had to say something in return, so I told him, "If it is any consolation to you, you are the last one that I ever will fly with at all."

But after that I got so I knew a whole lot and now I am crazy about it; I am going everywhere; I flew over to Oklahoma last week and my boy flew over there and he flew back with me. You know we are flying around all the time.

I have been trying to get Brisbane.[5] Arthur Brisbane is a great booster for aviation. I have been kidding him through the papers for the last few days about not flying. I got a cute telegram from him. I told him I would hold his hand if he would go up with me and we would fly. He sent back this telegram. He said, "Will, we couldn't go up together. If something happened to the plane, there would be nobody to tell the world the truth, if you and I went down together."

This ain't got nothing to do with what I am here for, you know. I am picking prominent men to talk about all the time, and I want to talk about Charlie Curtis.[6] So I wired Charlie. He is an Indian, you know. I said, "Charlie, I am going to talk about you."

He wired and said, "Will, if you talk about me, be sure and mention that I am Vice-President." So I thought I would. I think it is a patriotic duty that I ought to perform, or somebody ought to perform every once in a while, and let the people of this country know who is Vice-President in every administration. I think it would be good just to have that. So I will take that on myself. No matter who is President, I will always keep you all informed as to who is Vice-President. Charlie Curtis is Vice-President, and he is a good one, too, he really is. That is not flattery, that is really sincere. Charlie is making a good Vice-President.

Vice-President Marshall was a great old fellow.[7] He was Vice-President under Mr. Wilson, you know.[8] He had a lot of humor, too. Marshall was a funny old fellow. He was a Democrat. You have got to be funny to be a Democrat. It takes more humor to be a Democrat than it does a Republican anyhow. One time the Senate was sitting there doing nothing, as usual. Somebody suggested that they make Marshall permanent Vice-President. He was an awfully good presiding officer, and everything, so they wanted to make him Vice-President for life—no matter who is in, he is Vice-President. So all of them made speeches on it, and everything. Finally, old John Sharpe Williams, a great old Senator from down in Mississippi, got up and said, "Tom would make a mighty fine Vice-President; he is a splendid character, this Tom Marshall.[9] He handles the office with dignity and understanding, but there is just one little thing that worries me about him being permanent Vice-President. Suppose something would happen to the President? Where would the country be?" That kind of knocked Tom out of a permanent job.

I always liked Mr. Coolidge because he liked Marshall. Every time I ever had a chat with Mr. Coolidge we were always talking about what a very human and fine man Tom Marshall was, and he told me some great stories about Mr. Marshall and how he helped him while he was Vice-President. You know Mr. Coolidge followed Marshall in as Vice-President and he gave him some very wonderful tips and it brought out kind of a human side to Mr. Coolidge that a lot of you don't get just from the outside, and I have always loved him just for that thing, because he liked Tom Marshall.

You know I am an Indian. My folks are Cherokees and I am very proud of the fact and us Injuns are mighty proud of Charlie Curtis. He is a leader of the Senate and was the most able man in there. Of course that don't give you much of an idea of his ability, but he is at least the best they had in there. A Senate leader is a very important position. Then they elected him Vice-President, and he lost his standing then and he is down at the bottom now and has to work up again. The Vice-President, you know, don't have any vote on anything unless

17

it is a tie, and there never was but one tie in the history of the Senate and that is when Dawes was Vice-President.[10] Do you remember when Dawes was in? That tie came at a time when Dawes was asleep, and he didn't get to vote on it after all. Curtis don't wait for a tie to go to sleep; he just sleeps in there any time whether there is any tie or not. He makes an awfully good presiding officer in that way. He is to be envied; any man who can sleep in the Senate really is to be envied. The President gets $75,000 a year just to argue with the Senate, and the Vice-President only gets $12,500 to have to listen at them all the time. I tell you there is no justice in the world at all.

The Senate is a body of men entirely surrounded by Senator Grundy.[11] They can talk for two weeks on the duty on hairpins, even when women ain't using them, but that don't matter; they will talk for two weeks on them and there is no way stopping them. I suggested a plan one time to shorten the Senate debate. Every time a Senator tells all he knows, make him sit down. That will shorten it. Some of them wouldn't be able to answer roll call. They are a pretty tough bunch of hyenas, those Senators, but they are likable rascals. Every time we let one of them out, a worse one gets in. So I am in favor of keeping this same bunch we have got now. We are kind of used to them now, and I think we should just keep them.

Our record with the Indians is going to go down in history. It is going to make us mighty proud of it in the future when our children of ten more generations read of what we did to them. Every man in our history that killed the most Indians has got a statue built for him. The only difference between the Roman gladiators and the Pilgrims was that the Romans used a lion to cut down their native population, and the Pilgrims had a gun. The Romans didn't have no gun; they just had to use a lion.

The Government, by statistics, shows they have got 456 treaties that they have broken with the Indians. That is why the Indians get a kick out of reading the Government's usual remark when some big affair comes up, "Our honor is at stake."

Every time the Indians move the Government will give them a treaty. They say, "You can have this ground as long as grass grows and water flows." On account of its being a grammatical error, the Government didn't have to live up to it. It didn't say "flown" or "flew" or something. Now they have moved the Indians and they settled the whole thing by putting them on land where the grass won't grow and the water won't flow, so now they have it all set.

Charlie's mother was a half-breed Indian.[12] She is a Kaw Indian. It really means Kansas Indian, but they couldn't spell Kansas, I guess, and they called it Kaw. The ones that couldn't spell it included Charlie

18

himself. He was born in Topeka, Kansas. Kansas was not in the Union at that time. In fact, there is still a dispute as to whether it is. Kansas was the first state to adopt prohibition and the last one to practice it. He was born in 1860. That is the year they took the census; otherwise, we wouldn't have known anything about his birth at all.

Lincoln was elected President that same year that Curtis was born. Charlie's mother read so much about Lincoln's early life that she started Charlie to splitting rails when he was six months old.

South Carolina seceded from the Union that year, and then they found that they wasn't missed, and they came back.

Charlie had the usual life of a child born in Kansas. He grew strong from shoveling the grasshoppers off the sidewalk, so they could go to town and get Capper's Weekly. That is a catalogue printed in Topeka telling the farmers how to order relief. He owes his early life to the fact that his people had a storm cellar. There were other great children born in Kansas, but they were blown over into adjoining states.

He was a jockey in his early days. The only thing more shady than horse racing is politics. Charlie worked himself up and he was a leader in that, too. His recreation is attending Republican conventions and his profession is betting on horse races. Charlie will bet you on a horse race quicker than Hoover will appoint you on a commission. When he is not asleep in the Senate, he is at the races. When Kansas stopped horse racing along with snoring and deep breathing, Charlie left there and went to Washington where he could be near the races at the Maryland tracks so he wouldn't lose much time. He was elected to the Senate in the usual underhand methods, the usual way, by going to Congress first. Kansas sentenced him to Congress. They really sentenced him there because he didn't move to Oklahoma like all the other Kansians did. His hobby is farm relief. He has always fought for it, which has given him a perpetual cause through life. He thinks it is still in its infancy.

Coolidge has the best idea on this farm relief. He went out and spoke to the farmers one time in Minneapolis. He said, "Farmers, you are in a hole. I can't help you, but I will get in with you." He did. That made it fine so the farmers were satisfied as long as Coolidge was going to get in with them.

Charlie had a little trouble not long ago about sitting at a table.[13] So as to eliminate any setting table, the whole of Washington has just eliminated having any more dinners now. They don't have any dinners. They all go to Child's restaurant. They feel more at home and can get more to eat there, too. Charlie didn't care anything about where they seated him at the table. He didn't care if he had to stand up but they put him with the Senators. He said, "I get paid for sitting with these Senators in the daytime, and I will be blamed if I am going to sit here at night with them for nothing."

His daughter, I will always remember, made the best nominating speech of any woman I ever heard at the Kansas City Convention.[14] She just said, "I have been asked to second the nomination of my father." Wasn't that wonderful? Never said anything else. Anybody else would have tried to tell where they were speaking and spoiled the whole thing.

In speaking of Indians, do you know that Claremore, Oklahoma, is going to open the only Indian hospital in the United States? That is no lie, no kidding or anything. It isn't boosting Claremore. But we have the only one, built by the Government entirely for Indians. You know Columbus discovered this country about 400 years ago or something, and it took 400 years for the Government to build a hospital for the Indians. Look what the Indians have got to look forward to in the next 400 years. They are liable to build us a cemetery or something, I guess.

If Charlie were president, I would run for Vice-President under him. Here are some of my qualifications if I were Vice-President. I could go to all the dinners when the President couldn't come; if a speaker got up he would say, "We are very sorry the President couldn't come. He got a better offer, that is why he didn't come. But we have with us the Vice-President," and he tries to think of the name. I could go to the dinners. I am a fair eater. I don't eat correctly, but I eat a lot. Then I could make a speech, not a good speech but good for a politician. Any audience who would gather to hear a politician speak wouldn't know a good speech if they heard one. Of course they would have to get me a dress suit. I ain't got any dress suit and I couldn't go in a hired one because they would mistake me for a Congressman. It is hard to get a man to take the Vice-Presidency. It is a job that doesn't have a nice future. I would take it and trust to luck. I would say to the Lord, "I am Vice-President, do your duty." And I have enough faith in the Almighty to believe he would get me somewhere. You know Charlie didn't want this job as Vice-President. He took it as a patriotic duty. It was forced on him. It really was. Charlie Curtis wasting his time in there is just like having Henry Ford spend four years in a filling station.[15] So good luck to you, Charlie, old Injun, and I hope you are elected President some day and we will run the White House out of this country. That is what we will do. Good night.

20

Alfred E. Smith

We are right at home tonight, folks. We are talking about the Democrats. Yeh, I am going to talk about the Democrats, the Lord's chosen people. He loves the Democrats. He wanted to keep them exclusive, that is why he made so few of them. The Republicans, they are common. They are not only common because there's lots of them, but I don't know, they are just naturally common anyhow, you know. Why is there more Republicans than there's Democrats anyhow? Well, because the Republicans pay more for the votes, and the reason they can pay more is because there's more in office all the time and they have more to pay than the Democrats do, and the reason they are in office more is because the Democrats can't buy enough to git into office.

But tonight we are going to take the most popular hero the Democrats has had in years, and of course he didn't get elected, but he got more votes than other Democrats that did git elected. We will talk about a man that has got more personality and color in his big toe than all the other politicians in both parties combined, that is since the days of Roosevelt.[1] Of course there was the king of all of 'em. But without Roosevelt, Smith has got the most personality.[2] I've had more letters to talk about Al Smith than I've had to talk about all the other one hundred and twenty million people in the country combined. So if there ever was a speech that is made by request and popular demand, it's this one. People would walk further to see Al Smith just put on his derby hat and pronounce the word radio, raddio, than they would to hear Mr. Hoover and Mr. Coolidge on a joint debate of Farm Relief with the Senate refereeing and Congress acting as the ushers. Al is a bear. He beat the Republicans in New York so long for Governor that they offered to make the office permanent. The man that was nominated against Smith in New York, he wasn't a candidate, he was

E.R. Squibb & Sons Broadcast, May 4, 1930

just a victim, that was all. This guy Smith has an uncanny way of holding the affections of the people of the country. Some way or another, during the Democratic uprising in Madison Square Garden in the summer of '24 and '25 and part of '26—you see the Democrats, we always have great conventions, us Democrats, we have good conventions but we don't get any further than that.[3] We only see the inauguration in the movies, but we do put on some awful nice conventions, you know. I have known Smith for years, and he has been a great friend of the stage and all of its people. Well, as the convention dragged along and I used to come back to the theatre at night in the Follies, the door man, the stage hands, would all ask, "Will, how about it? How about the last vote? Has he got a chance?" A big, tough-looking cop used to stop me on the corner with pretty near tears in his eyes and he would ask me, "How is it going, is he going to make it?" The newsboys, when they had to announce that Smith was behind in the balloting, they didn't act like they wanted to sell the papers. Barbers, elevator boys, everywhere you went, it was the same real downright heartfelt anxiety. You can't get that on nothing, you know. The delegates from down home in Oklahoma, a lot of old friends from Texas around, they used to ask me up there at the convention, "Will, what manner of fellow is this fellow Smith that these people all worship so?" Well, tonight, we are going to look him over and see how he got that way.

You talk about being born under the shadow of the Brooklyn Bridge. He was born while they was building the bridge. I don't know what year it was, I never looked it up, but he's just as old as the bridge is, however old that is, and they're both strictly products of New York, in fact Al is better known than the bridge. There has been a lot of other bridges built since, but never any more Als. He lived in South Street, not Oliver Street, he didn't move there until later. He used to live near a firehouse, Engine Company Number Two. In those days they used to work horses on these fire wagons. He was a great favorite with all the firemen, he spent the first ten years of his life just chasing the fire wagon to fires. He was so keen, he could tell by the smell of the smoke whose house was on fire, that is he could tell the nationality of the house anyhow. At the age of eleven, somebody invented a fireproof house, and on account of them burning so much quicker and faster, why it just wasn't physically possible for him to attend all of the fires. In fact, the Department got so they couldn't do it with horses any more. They had to get automobiles to make all of these, after fireproofing came in. Fireproofing and insurance have caused more fires than going to bed with a lighted cigarette.

This running to fires is where Smith got the idea of running for office. He said, "Why run for nothing, why not run for a job and then have something easy when the race is over?" He used to sell newspapers on the street, and naturally became a politician. All newsboys become politicians and all bootblacks become bankers. He quit selling newspapers and went to work in the Fulton Street Fish Market. He was always keen and alert. He soon discovered that there was a hundred people in New York City that ate fish to every one that could read a paper. He says, let us fill up their stomachs, never mind the New Yorkers' minds. At the age of twelve he studied elocution, and at thirteen his father died, and he left him the sole support of his mother and sister. His father was a truckman, and Al could have gone in his father's business and drove the truck, but the horses wouldn't stand for the elocution, he was practicing then. So he went to work with the fish. Fish would listen to him recite. They are like political audiences, they are not very discriminating that way. As a matter of fact, Al has been talking to strange fish ever since.

In the Garden that year at the convention, we had fathered the queerest collection ever assembled in the annals of fish-ology. That is why they held it in a swimming pool that year. There were suckers from the West, and flounders from the South, and bullheads from the North and eels from the East, and every one that got up to make a speech was a big-mouthed bass. At an early age he won a solid gold medal in a debating contest, and that kept him busy for the next two years just polishing that medal to keep it from tarnishing. Once you win a debate you're lost for physical work the rest of your life. So he started in loafing right away, started in acting in amateur theatricals, that's the worst kind of acting there is. It is bad enough to act for money, but when you ain't good enough to get paid for it, it's terrible. By the way, I want to tell you a joke about that. One night I introduced Smith at a dinner in New York, and I told that little joke about him, about him acting for nothing, and when he got up he says, "Yes, Will, I was a ham actor, and I acted for nothing, but at least my conscience is clear." Boy, he knocked me in the creek with that one. He certainly got a big laugh on that. He's fast on his feet, Al is, and if he could come back at me tonight, I would take to the woods as soon as I get through.

Did I ever tell you the one about the time in the Legislature in Albany, they was discussing colleges, and what ones the members had come from. One dignified statesman said, "Cornell;" another one said "P. S. meaning Penn State;" another said, "W. & J., Washington & Jefferson." Finally, someone said, "Al, why don't you get up and say what your old alma mater is?" Al said, "F. F. M., Fulton Fish Market."

After he got to be an actor, of course the next thing he did was fall in love with an Irish girl named Catherine Dunn.[4] That was in the long ago when people married into their own tribe. Well, when the Dunns heard that Al, an amateur actor, was hanging around, they moved to the Bronx. Now, to lots of my hearers here tonight, I will have to explain exactly what the Bronx is. It is the northeast boundary of Palestine. That's where all on the east side of New York "Passover" to the north side to escape the Irish persecution. Well, the Dunns moved to the Bronx, they are the first and last Irish family to go Semitic. The Dunns thought by going there, they would be done with Al, but as he was training for a theatrical career, he walked clear up there and found her. So the family had to practically sacrifice Catherine, just to get rid of Al. So finally one night they all went down to see Al act. The family did, and they objected to him being an actor, but after they saw the show, they says, "Daughter, we were wrong about accusing your sweetheart of being an actor."

They never figured there might be something worse as a profession than acting, and there is, and Smith found it. It's politics. He served seventeen times in the New York Legislature. Only one other man served more, another man served eighteen terms in there. He's in Matteawan now. Al got out just in time. He was Sheriff of New York City, but the crooks got so bad he couldn't walk out on the streets alone, and he couldn't find a cop to go with him, so he had to resign. He was Governor so long that it looked like the State was a monarchy instead of a republic. He was just beat once for Governor, and that was the only time he was ever beat up to this last time. That was the year everybody had it in for Wilson, because he was right, and so Al, when he was beat, went out and started a trucking company, and two years later he took his trucks and moved the Governor who had beat him out with his own trucks, and took his trucks and moved himself in again.

I used to be asked during the election, "Will, how about a Catholic running the country?" Well, he was a lifetime in there as Governor of New York, and any time these Jewish people trust you with a State where they own ninety per cent of the stock, there's no reason why Protestants can't trust him with what little we have got left of the United States. If he took everything we got and he moved it to the Vatican, we wouldn't be much the loser anyhow.

When they used to ask me, "Do you think on account of his being a Wet that the South will be against him?" Well, I never did think that it would be, I really didn't. I told them I says, "No, I don't think they will. I don't think they'll be sober enough to notice it." I don't mean by that the South drinks any more. Drinking in America is not

24

in any part, the North or South, or the East or the West; they all drink the same. Drinking is not regulated by any section, it's regulated by capacity, that's all. The ones that don't want to drink, don't drink, no matter what part of the country they live in, they just don't drink. The ones that do drink, they drink all they can hold, no matter where they are at. So section ain't got nothing to do with it. So I really don't think, I can say in all truthfulness, I don't think Al's defeat was due to liquor, or religion, or Tammany Hall, or a brown derby, or raddio—there was just one thing that defeated Smith, and that was being a Democrat, that's all, just being a Democrat was all that beat him. It just wasn't our year in '28. It wasn't our year. We are a good party, and we have got some good ideas, but we just need some more votes, that's all. We are just a little short of votes.

You see, I always advised that Al shouldn't have run in '28. I wrote in the *Saturday Evening Post*, and with all seriousness and conviction, I said, it wasn't his year. It wasn't in the cards for Smith or anybody else to beat Mr. Hoover. You couldn't have beat him with anybody. Of course, later on now if he had waited, it might be a different thing. We are a people that get tired of a thing awful quick, and I believe this continual prosperity will begin to get monotonous with us. We can't go through life just eating cake all the time, you know. Of course, we like prosperity, but we are having so much of it that we just can't afford it. I don't know if Al wants another crack at the nomination or not, I don't know. We got awful good men, in fact we have always had good men. We've had as many good men beat as they've had elected. We got Al, we got Joe Robinson.[5] I want to tell you about Joe some time too, we got Joe Robinson, and we got Owen D. Young, great, all of them.[6] All in the world we need is just some more votes, that's all. Our slogan will be "Elect a Democrat and Let's Get Poor Again." Of course, I personally think Mr. Hoover is going to come through, and if he does, I'm in favor of not starting a Democrat against him in '32, just save up all our money to buy votes in '36. Then there's Calvin. I don't know what is going to happen to us. We've just got to wait until those two get too old to run, and we've got to get Mellon out of the way—that is the fellow that us Democrats has got to get out.[7] That's the fellow that has kept both of those other fellows in there.

Good night.

Mother's Day

All of you know that this is Mother's Day, but did all of you know that tomorrow is Hospital Day? The only way that we know that our civilization has advanced in this country is by our splendid hospitals. It is the birthday of Florence Nightingale, the founder of modern nursing.[1] It is fine to remember the well, but it is the sick that really need it, so do something for somebody tomorrow at a hospital.

I was to talk today on the Prince of Wales, but I have received so many letters to me to talk on Mothers and various women that I am going to put the Prince off until next Sunday and talk on Mothers.[2] Of course, he is a wonderful little fellow and Americans think an awful lot of him and he has got a great many accomplishments, but after all he was never a mother.

The thing that makes Mother's Day so appropriate this year is reading so much in the papers of these Gold Star Mothers on their way to Europe. They are going over there to visit the graves of their sons at the expense of our Government. That seems just about the finest thing that our Government has ever done. It will make up for a lot of the fool things it does. Think of giving those wonderful old ladies a chance to have their sons' final resting place imprinted on their memories. Just imagine if none of us knew where our father's or mother's grave was, what it looked like or where it was located. What a welcome they will get, what reverence and respect will be showered on them over there. France will get a new view of America—those white-haired old souls with a constant tear in their eyes, but a brave smile on their faces. Then France will see what has made us what we are. She will see the mold from which America was carved.

What possible group could more thoroughly really typify America? They won't need any interpreter, those mothers. Mothers

E.R. Squibb & Sons Broadcast, May 11, 1930

26

Will Rogers in a studio at radio station KDKA in Pittsburgh, Pennsylvania, in 1922. With him are several fellow performers appearing in Pittsburgh with the Ziegfeld Follies. Left to right: Peggy Udell, son of Pearl Eaton, Pearl Eaton, Olive Osborne, Eva Clark, Rogers, an unknown, Betty Rogers (seated at the piano), Annette Bade, John Hope (manager of the troupe), and an unknown.

are the only race of people that speak the same tongue. A mother in Manchuria could converse with a mother in Nebraska and never miss a word. We wish and pray for every one of them to have a safe return. We can't wish them happiness but we do wish them contentment.

And when they close their eyes on this earth, we know what will be pictured. It will be that cross they saw in France, that cross with a name on it, and they can visualize every blade of grass about that grave, and they will go with a satisfied smile to join them.

Great artists say that the most beautiful thing in the world is a little baby. Well, the next most beautiful thing is an old lady, for every wrinkle is a picture.

My own mother died when I was ten years old. My folks have told me that what little humor I have comes from her. I can't remember her humor but I can remember her love and her understanding of me. Of course, the mother I know the most about is the mother of our little group. She has been for twenty-two years trying to raise to maturity four children, three by birth and one by marriage.[3] While she hasn't done a good job, the poor soul has done all that mortal human could do with the material she has had to work with.

You know, there ought to be some kind of a star given to any woman that can live with a comedian. Now, that little compliment ought to repay for the flowers that I forgot to get today.

I have had so many suggestions on what woman to talk on. Most of them I knew personally and some I didn't. I just last night wrote a letter to Helen Keller telling her how fortunate it was she couldn't see me—and they don't make them much more remarkable than Helen is.[4]

Mrs. Coolidge—you all know what I think of her. I have shouted her praises from the tariff-bound shore of New England to the poverty-stricken farms of the Pacific slope.

Mrs. Hoover is graciousness and charm personified. My wife knows her better than I do. She says she is marvelous.

Alice Longworth—I look to Alice for all my political knowledge, like a Senator looks to see which side the American Federation of Labor is on before he will vote.[5] She is tremendously keen.

All these I mention are mothers.

Lots of letters have asked me to talk on Anne Lindbergh. Yes, it is so, it is not a rumor but it is really true. Yes, Anne has got her pilot's license and she will soon have her mother's license. I can see Anne and Charlie when they take the little rascal out for an airing, towing him in a glider instead of a baby buggy. They will give him a parachute instead of a rattle.

Mrs. Morrow—that's Anne's mother—is worth an evening all to

28

herself. She not only has raised those fine girls, but she has kept Mr. Morrow from going out without his shirt on and with his shoes tied every morning.

Ruth Hanna McCormick, one of our best political minds, a mother every inch of her.[6] But the one I am picking out tonight you perhaps have read more about than any of these, and that is Lady Astor.[7]

It has been my good fortune to have seen a great deal of her on my trips over to England. She has been awful nice to me; in fact, I pretty near boarded at her house. It was the only place in London I could get good coffee. It will be a long time before the female of the species, or whatever you call it, before we produce another like her. She is one of those things that come along every few generations among breeds of people or horses or something, one of those things you call a freak.

She combines more different qualities than any woman I ever saw. Just think of the achievement of the American woman who is the first to sit in the stately old House of Parliament. That is not a Senate seat, you know; you don't buy that. You buy titles over in England, but you have got to get into Parliament on the level.

This fellow, Lord Astor, that she is married to, you know, he is one of the finest, most modest, likable chaps you ever saw.[8] Their married life seems to be perfectly ideal.

I had been to the town house a lot, but I had never seen their country place. It is about an hour, I guess, out from London, and this last trip I went out. It is just a modest little bungalow, some eighty or ninety rooms, rambling, but kept within the bounds of good taste and on the British Isles.

There is a landing field in each wing of the house so you can take off and make the dining-room by lunch time. The ceilings give you plenty of altitude.

It was a lovely Sunday afternoon, and she was out playing tennis, going like a Helen Wills.[9] A day in Lady Astor's life is just like perpetual motion. Following her through one day is like going to a circus.

She left the game and come out to show me about the place. We went out in front of the house, and she told me, "Right here, Will, where we are standing, is where I stood when I arrived here the first time and had my old Virginia colored woman, the old maid with me. She took one wild-eyed look at this house and said 'Miss Nancy, is here where you-all going to live?'

"'Why, yes, Cynthia, here is our future home.'

"'My Lord, Miss Nancy, you certainly done out-married yo'self'."

29

She can tell that like it ought to be told. She still retains her darky dialect from Virginia crossed with English.

It is a beautiful estate on a bluff that overlooks the Thames River. We came to a beautiful monument, very high, out on the place. It was erected in honor of the men that was killed that worked on their estate.

Then we walked on down the side of a wonderful wooded hillside. We suddenly come up, you know, on the most beautiful spot I ever laid my eyes on, a kind of a sunken garden effect, oblong-shaped with a marble balustrade around it, and standing over this was a beautiful statue, done by some famous artist. It typified mother love, a statue with arms outstretched. She was looking through a clearing of great trees down over the Thames, looking towards the west, and in this beautiful little garden down there at the statue's feet was buried maybe seventy-five boys from all over the world.

You know, they turned their place into a hospital during the war, and the Canadian Red Cross had charge of it. The stones were not standing up like we have them in the graveyards. They was all laying down and had the addresses and the names of the boys on each one of them.

"I knew every boy in here personally, Will. I knew lots of them. I held their hands when they went West." She told me funny little stories and characteristics of each.

She is a great soldier. She used to come into the hospital and say, "Now you boys have either got to get well or die. I am not going to have you lay around here sick all the time."

That sounds terrible, you know, to hear anybody say that, but when she says it it is great—just what they wanted, you know. They would kind of lose courage and get down in the mouth, and she would come in and jolly them along.

She told me of this case, about a boy—she says to him, "Now, listen, you are going to die. Get ready. You are going to die."

"Oh, Lady Astor, please don't. How do you know I am going to die?"

"Because you don't want to get well. You are a Scotchman. If you was a Canadian you would be well and get out of here."

Well, sir, she told me he almost jumped out of the bed—"What do you mean, the Scotchmen are the greatest and nerviest people on earth. What do you mean, the Canadians are more nervy!"

And sure enough, she told me, the fellow got well.

One boy was terribly sick, and she was worried about him, you know. They knew he was going to go, and what worried him was that he didn't have any wrist watch. The other boys had wrist watches. She told him, "Jack, if you live until I get back from London, I will go there and get you the finest there is," and she did. And he had it on, smiling as he passed on. "And he is laying right here under me now, Will, right here, him and the wrist watch."

A lot of our boys was buried in there. She has the ground all consecrated for the religion that asks that. Long before our Government thought of it, she paid the way of mothers to come there and visit their sons' graves. One old ranch lady from out in Canada she brought over that wanted to move her son back, and after she got there, she told me, she said, "Lady Astor, I didn't think a place could be so beautiful. I wouldn't move him for nothing."

There she stood, telling me all these things with tears in her eyes—this same woman that can stand up in the House of Parliament, hard boiled, and give better than she can receive.

Here was the famous Lady Astor—a wit and a statesman and the center of every drawing-room crowd, but here she was, just a mother, all the fight and all the social graces gone. There, in the very shade of this great house of hers, lie buried what she calls "her boys." So don't let anybody say evil of her in my presence.

When we got back to the house, she wanted to order some tea. I said, "No, I don't want no tea. I have got to have me some port wine."

She said, "How dare you not be a Prohibitionist?"

I said, "I have always read that it was the custom of the old, landed gentry after looking over the estate, to come in and have a sip of port, and I am strong on tradition."

I got my port. She is a Prohibitionist, you know, not by preaching but by practice. She is a great Christian Scientist.

I introduced her one time in a London audience in the theater where I was playing and I couldn't get her to stand up. Afterwards she came to New York and came to my little show. Last year, I got her to stand up. I said, "Lady Astor, I couldn't get you to stand up in London in the theater, and in the House of Parliament they can't get you to sit down.

She took me to see Lloyd George, and we spent an awful nice two hours with him.[10] There they was—him and her was kidding each other. That is a human fellow for you, that Lloyd George.

She was the one that arranged my meeting with George Bernard Shaw.[11] She thinks a lot of Shaw, but Shaw keeps her worried to death, the same as he does all England. You know, England wonders what he is going to pull on them every minute.

Lady Astor says she can't think of anything worse than a man-ruled world unless it was one ruled by women.

An Irish member of Parliament, seeing her for the first time, said,

31

"So you are the grand Lady Astor. Why, you are just a plain, homely-looking woman."

They were discussing the navy one time when an opposition member shouted at her, "What do you know about the navy? You stick to milk and babies."

She replied, "If you stuck to milk instead of Scotch whiskey you would not only know more about the navy, but you would know more about how to be decent to women."

She was campaigning one time, talking about child welfare, when an old, gray-haired bird jumped up out of the audience and interrupted her. You know, they are great on interrupting over there in England. He shouted at her, "What does your ladyship know of children? I am a man that has raised five, and you are going to stand up there on the platform and tell me about children?"

She hollered back at him, "I am a woman that has got six, and I am not through yet. What do you think of that?" She set that bird right down.

Say, those children of hers come first, before Parliament, speeches, dinners, or anything, so when you speak of mothers, she is one of them. If she had stayed in this country she would have been President by now. Good night.

H. R. H. the Prince of Wales

If they showed pictures on the screen of all the world's famous people, it is a funny thing, but the two best-known ones all over the world would both be Englishmen. They would be Charlie Chaplin and the Prince of Wales.[1] They would know Charlie by his baggy pants and they would know the Prince because his are not. Then, besides, the Prince rules over (that is, some day he will be ruler over) a country that embraces about one-fourth of the entire land of the country, to say nothing about the waters. Of course, England has four-fourths of that.

Most every country on the face of the globe has seen him personally. He has visited all these different places. You know the woods has been full of Princes since this Prince business started, but they just came and went as a matter of routine. You know there is one around in almost every Royalist country, but nobody couldn't tell or remember who it was. Of course, they date time from when old Henry VIII was prowling around.[2] England was organized and then you didn't hear no more of England 'til Henry started messing about. Then you didn't hear no more about Princes until it got clear on down to this lad's grandfather, King Edward.[3] There was a bear—that fellow. When he was Prince he had great popularity and had some of the women practically locoed. Then the prince business settled back into its humdrum routine again, you know, kind of dropped off again, until this present boy came along. Say, he showed them really how to be a Prince. He introduced humaneness, you know (he is a regular human) into the prince business, and to stand out above all other Princes of other times you have to have something. The title will get you in, and the way you act will get you back in again. This lad can play a return date anywhere.

The War come pretty near ruining royalty. It was pretty near as

---

E.R. Squibb & Sons Broadcast, May 18, 1930

hard to get a King after the War as a three-minute speaker. Kings went out about as quick as silk shirts. Well then, you might say, "How come he is not known as the Ex-Prince of Wales, now?" Well, that gets you back to the individual. The War really strengthened England's Royalists in their hold, instead of weakening it. If you could have been in the great hall and heard the King make his speech to the late London Disarmament Conference (his first public appearance, by the way, since his severe illness) and had watched the anxiety with which the Englishmen would meet you on the street or somewhere and ask you, "How did the King look? Is he all right again? Did he look fine?" you felt like wiring Russia, "Boys, you are wasting your time trying to break up a country like this!"[4]

And the Prince—oh Lord!—what do they think of him? He is their royal Lindbergh over in England. You know, it's a funny thing, but those two fellows have a lot that reminds you of each other. Of course, Lindbergh arrived by achievement, and the Prince by birth, but they both got a quiet reserve and dignity that is exactly alike. There is some inborn intuition in both of these fellows that tell them the right thing to do. Popularity is the easiest thing in the world to gain and it is the hardest thing to hold. But these are the only two fellows that I know of that we can feel absolutely sure when we wake up in the morning and pick up our morning paper, that they will be just as popular as they was the day before.

Let me see! Let me kind of take you back to a summer's evening in June, 1894. A baby was born that afternoon. It wasn't a particularly good day for babies to be born but just one of those things that had to happen. The little runt didn't look much like the Prince of Wales— in fact, he wasn't. That grand old lady, Queen Victoria, was living then, and the first time in history that a Queen had lived to see three generations of her line.[5] He was a great-grandchild. He was born in Richmond—that is, not Virginia; he couldn't have been a Virginian for he didn't have enough ancestry. His father paced the floor, with the short-sightedness of all fathers, and prayed for a son, when as a matter of fact, girls cause you less trouble and they stay with you longer. He was a very ordinary baby—had colic from birth. He kept four generations of royalty awake for three months.

The first time I ever met him was about in the summer of '24. I spoke at a dinner given to him at the Piping Rock Club on Long Island, given by the Poultry Association. Nobody watched me when I was speaking—everybody watched to see how he would take my jokes. Englishmen was all anxious because they had never heard royalty kidded right to their face, but he was marvelous. He certainly played straight for me. There was several Englishmen at the dinner, with the title of "Sir," so the Prince got a big laugh out of my opening gag which, if I remember right, run something like this:

"Everybody asked if I was nervous, speaking here tonight before royalty. Say, this is not my first time speaking before royalty. One time I spoke before Sir Harry Lauder.[6] Well, I was all swelled up over that till I found out that a 'Sir' is about the lowest form of royalty there is. It is kind of the Ford of titles.

"Prince, you know we like you over here. You are the first Englishman that didn't come here to lecture. I can't offer you a beautiful home on Long Island like all these other folks has done, but I can give you a cot in my dressing room at the Follies, where I am playing. The accommodations are not so good, but a hundred of the most beautiful girls in the world that Mr. Ziegfeld has ever assembled pass by your door all the time. And say, at that, I bet if the kid here had his way, he would take my offer instead of yours.

"I had no idea you were over here in this country at all until I happened to see a little notice about it way down among the ads this afternoon in the paper. You have made yourself mighty popular, Prince, in spite of your birth. I admire any man that can rise above his surroundings.

"Now, I suppose, according to the usual run of American humor, I am supposed to tell you some jokes here tonight, Prince, about your falling off your horse. Well, I have never seen a picture of you where you had fallen that the horse hadn't fallen too. I am not much of a horseman, but all these people that joke about your falling off, what do they expect a man to do when his horse falls? Is he supposed to remain up in the air until the horse comes back up under him, or just what is he supposed to do? I saw one picture where you had fallen in a creek. We haven't got a comedian in this country that could swim across this creek, much less try to jump it on a horse and we haven't got an editorial writer that could row across it. So I am afraid we are going to have to find something else to kid the Englishman about besides his horsemanship.

"If you want to find comical riding you don't have to go any further than Central Park. If I can't get hold of something funny in an Englishman besides his riding, I am a mighty poor comedian."

You know one time, just getting away from that little act I did there, one time the Prince left his car when he was going to go on a fox hunt, he left his car at the place. A man didn't know who he was. The Prince came back and he got into the car and the man knew the Prince was on the hunt. He asked him, "How did the Prince make out? Did he get his usual fall?" The Prince of Wales said, "Yes, he fell."

35

The fellow said, "He ought to be stopped from that hunting, he is going to break his neck."

The Prince said, "Well, it's his neck, ain't it?"

That is about the way he feels about it.

Look at me, every time I play polo I fall off one of those little Blue-Jay corn pad saddles. The falls I receive don't attract any attention at all. They hurt just as bad. The blood I spill ain't royal, but it's all mine. I don't care how common your blood is, you don't want to waste any of it.

Well, that remark about the horse falling, the Prince liked a lot. I afterwards used it at every performance at the Follies and the papers copied it and it went all over the country and he was nice enough to tell me that he knew it had much to do with stopping the eternal kidding about his falling, for, as anyone that knows anything about it knows, it is the tough races he goes in and the terrible jumps he tries to make that cause it. In fact, he is a very good horseman.

I was over in London a couple of years ago, when the 'phone rang and my oldest boy said, "Dad, it is the equerry to the Prince of Wales."[7] He asked me to come over to see the Prince, and I told him I thought that it could be arranged. I was away from home and had no reputation to uphold, and it didn't matter much where I went. He was living at York House then. When I got to the door, there came a fellow to meet me. I learned from Emily Post that he was a butler.[8] No livery, no lace, no brass buttons—he took me up to the Prince's room and from the time I entered that house until I left (it was over an hour) he was the only servant I saw. Of course, I guess he must have had a cook, but I don't know—he eats out so much—maybe he didn't have.

After having seen and been in a lot of famous Hollywood screen stars' homes, and some oil men's palaces, why this place where the Prince was in looked kind of like a joint. The place was positively simple, compared to some Long Island homes. It looked like an igloo.

He met me at the door of his private room—he and his equerry, General Trotter. I shook hands with him and I said, "Hello, old-timer, how are you falling these days?"

He grinned, and quick as a flash (he has a corking sense of humor) he came back at me, "All over the place." It scares me to see pictures in the movies of some of these fellows going over jumps like he does.

You girls all want to know how he is dressed for he has caused more women to powder their noses and more ambitious mothers to scrub up their daughters than any other person in the history of the world. He was dressed all in brown—just like any other brown suit I ever saw, only this one fit. The room was what made a hit with me.

Just a medium-sized, ordinary living-room, with a fireplace burning and a mantel with pictures on it, and a framed photograph of his mother in the center of the mantel—no great paintings or old family crayons. They were pictures of the family, mostly of his brothers and his sister. They looked like enlarged snapshots they had taken themselves.

The center table had books on it and one I noticed had the wrapper on it of the "Life of Queen Victoria." I guess that was a new book that had just come out. That old lady would have been proud if she had witnessed this boy's popularity at present, wouldn't she? The room gave me the feeling of some boy who was fortunate enough to have his own room and fix it up the way he wanted to. I didn't see a single girl's picture among them. You couldn't help but feel at home in the place.

We talked about the general strike which was on in England at that time—every workingman in England was out then, and yet nobody seemed excited about it. The strike just seemed to settle itself a la Coolidge, and by the way, he asked about Mr. Coolidge and said they had had a charming luncheon. I tried to get him to tell me what him and Calvin had talked about but he couldn't remember—clothes, I guess. He asked me how Prohibition was getting along. I told him the same as ever—we are arguing and drinking yet.

We talked of Canada and his ranch. I know the old ranchman who sold him his ranch—old man Lane, up there—originally came from Texas, but went to Canada.[9] The Prince told me this one on himself. One time, it was out at a round-up where they had a big bunch of cattle rounded when old man Lane said, "Hey, Prince, get out of here; you are scaring these cattle and you are in the way of the cowboys."

He is very fond of Canada, the Prince is, and he likes it there. I said, "I saw you sitting in the gallery of the House of Commons the other day and I wanted to holler at you but I was afraid they might want to revive the old chopping block at the Tower of London, if I did."

He said, "I would like to see you under the block and hear what your last words would be."

He come to the theatre twice while I was playing over there. This time, at the Naval Conference, I didn't see him. He was hunting lions in Africa, with a camera. Fine fellow! Very, very human. No wonder they like him over there, for he is a regular guy. Good night!

Dwight Morrow

Well, how come you all this afternoon? I was going to take my text this evening—my evening sermon was going to be on an old friend, Henry Ford, a parable of transportation. In Exodus it says (that is, the Book of Exodus, in the Bible), "Come unto me all ye who can afford," but this afternoon I was driving in from my little ranch out here in the country, in one of those things of his, and it went "flooey" on me (it is one of the new models, too). So I says, "No, I am not going to talk on Uncle Henry today, feeling like I do. I wouldn't do him justice; I would be biased."

Then I read of another old friend, a man who had received—I don't know, but I think he has received more publicity during the past year, and especially in the last few weeks, than anyone I know of. It is not often that a man can become prominent just because he is a father, you know. But that is what happened to this fellow. He has received more publicity by doing nothing but just running for the Senate than any other man that ever did. That don't get you much publicity, generally, just running for the Senate, because everybody is running for it. But this fellow got it just because he was the father of little Annie Lindbergh. He was just an obscure lawyer before that. His business was raising daughters. He not only kept the wolf from the door by working for J. P. Morgan & Company, but he kept them within the bounds of the law, too. He was born at Huntington, West Virginia, in 1873, on the illiterate side of the Ohio River. His parents were the usual West Virginia type. They owned the coal mine and a still. They made enough out of the still to keep the coal mine going.

West Virginia had seceded from Virginia when they got tired of listening to nothing but ancestry and smoked hams. With West Virginians, you know, they could have bragged about their ancestors, too, only they weren't such big liars as the Virginians were. Really, West

E.R. Squibb & Sons Broadcast, May 25, 1930

Virginia is what you might call the truthful end of the Virginias. Two feuds was about as far as a West Virginian can ever trace any of his ancestors.

Another reason why West Virginia seceded from the old sister state was the right of political freedom. People were voting Republican in Virginia, but they wasn't getting their votes counted. The Slaves got their freedom by war and the Republicans got theirs by secession from old Virginia.

Morrow as I say, was born in 1873, and nothing more was heard of him until the summer Lindbergh fell in love. From then on, of course, you know all about him. His life is an open book. It is on the front pages of pretty near every paper you pick up every morning. We all know him as the world's most famous father-in-law, but it is of the years in between that I want to enlighten you on. I want to show you what he was doing while Lindbergh was carrying the mail. I want to pick out the obscure part of his life from 1873 to 1928—we will say, from the time of his young manhood to the day Anne said "Yes, Lin."

His father was a college professor, and it looked like he would grow up to be the usual college professor's son. Then all at once a change came over him, and he went to work. He grew up to what they call sturdy manhood in those rugged Republican mountains of John W. Davis' state.[1] He reached a total height of 4 ft. 1 2/3 inches. He passed his examination for West Point. They didn't know that he was standing on another West Virginian's shoulders when they measured him. He really did pass for West Point. His brother had gone through West Point, and there was some talk all over the country about the school being conducted entirely just for the Morrows, so Morrow didn't go there—he went to Amherst. There could never be any scandal about entering that school. In fact, there would be practically no publicity at all. All you needed to get into Amherst was just a Republican registration card.

Then he run into another little fellow—Calvin Coolidge. All Coolidge had at that time was a dialect. They went through school together. Calvin, he sat right behind Morrow and could look over his shoulders. They got the same grade. Coolidge never had much to say, even in those days. He was too busy copying down. That is why he always had a warm spot in his heart for Morrow.

When they graduated, the class took a vote. Now, when I speak at any time during the little sermon here this evening on graduation, I am doing it from hearsay—I know nothing about graduation. I never graduated from anything. Yes, I did, I did, too—I graduated from Ziegfeld Follies. I was nine years finishing a four-year course in that.

Mind you, I ain't knocking education. There ain't a day that I don't wish I had stayed in school a couple of days longer. In fact, I have an educational scheme that I wish they would adopt. In a week or so, all these high schools are going to turn out, and I have got an idea. If you take students when they graduate from high school and let half of them go to college and half go to work, just half and half, and then at the end of four years when the ones come out of college they can go to work—the ones that went to college can go to work for the ones that went to work first.

I got to get back to Morrow and Coolidge and Amherst, that is what I am going to talk about.

They took a vote on who was the man in the class who was liable to accomplish more in life (I think these classes do that now) or, in other words, who would perhaps do something to make people think he had come from Amherst. Do you know, out of all that graduating class, Morrow got all the votes—all but two, Calvin got those two. Morrow voted for Coolidge, but they never could exactly locate that other vote.

I am not accusing Calvin, understand, but Morrow told me himself that it did look like Mr. Coolidge started his first vote-receiving career with his own support.

Well, nothing much happened in Morrow's career from then on. I guess we can skip the others right up until the time Anne was born.

Morrow's college friend, Coolidge, drifted along from bad to worse and he landed in the White House. At that time, we were in wrong with the world, and Mexico particularly. Our Marines were enforcing American diplomacy from the Yangtze River, in China, to the headwaters of Lake Managua, in Nicaragua. We were getting soldiers to enlist, but we had to draft ambassadors to go to any foreign country. We had sent some ambassadors to Mexico, but the more we sent, the madder it seemed to make Mexico, and we had no more Marines to send, so Coolidge happened to think of Morrow. He always had it in for him, I think, ever since he got those votes at that school.

By the way, when they graduated at Amherst, Morrow won a scholarship to a college. He chose Columbia. That is where he met Nicholas Murray Butler.[2] You know him, the wet old thing. It was this sordid association with President Butler that decided Morrow to leave Pittsburgh and move to Englewood, New Jersey. He moved there so Anne could be near Roosevelt field, where if she ever wanted to, she could be married right before forty newspaper reporters' eyes and they wouldn't suspicion that she was doing it.

When Morrow was appointed to Mexico, it looked like just another rich man passing into oblivion. He immediately resigned his position with Morgan & Company, where they had him there to add to the moral tone of the organization that was just about then flirting with financial indecency, but he resigned. That resignation from Morgan & Company made the first big impression on the whole country, for that showed right away that this man Morrow was not a politician, for it was not customary to give up one job to work for the Government. A man don't have to quit work just because he is going to start drawing a pension, you know. It is generally understood that you won't do so much for the Government that it will interfere with your original position, but here he was taking this ambassadorship seriously.

I met him in Mexico about two weeks after that. He had got down there just before I did, and he told me of Coolidge's instruction to him. He kept sitting around waiting for Coolidge to tell him what to do when he got to Mexico. Finally Morrow had to ask him, "What am I to do down there, Calvin?"

Mr. Coolidge told him, "Dwight, don't jump on Mexico, just keep Mexico from jumping on us."

I claim that is a pretty smart thing to tell an ambassador. That is about the best thing he can do. And do you know, that is exactly what he did in Mexico.

If it hadn't been for Morrow, they would have jumped on us, and we would have been at war with them. I had not been with this fellow a day in Mexico when I could tell this fellow is no more of a diplomat than he is a politician. He was displacing this diplomacy and etiquette and doing away with all that, and replacing it with just plain old human nature. He was doing everything that an ambassador had never done, including getting along with the people who was running the Government. They went on a two weeks' trip all over Mexico, him and the President. They had never heard of such familiarity, an American Ambassador traveling with a Mexican President. He left rich old social families flat and spent his time with the President and his Cabinet. He was criticized, of course. Some said he was lowering the social standards, and that the President and his crowd was all nothing but just revolutionists. Morrow told me about it. He said, "I come here accredited to this Government, to the men who are at present running this Government, not to the aristocracy."

You see he wasn't there to bat any .300 in the Dinner League. He figured that the men running the Government at the very moment, you know they may not have known a demi-tasse from an hors d'oeuvre, and they might have scabbards on their knives to keep them from cutting their mouths, but they was the people that he was there to deal with. He was there to do business with Mexico and not lead

41

a cotillion. It didn't matter to him if some of these Mexican Presidents could show more bullet holes than they could diplomats. One day I was talking to him and he said, "Will, I don't know who these men shot to get into this office or how they got in, but they are in, and why they are in I don't know, but they are in and they are the babies that I have got to deal with."

He is the most down-to-earth little rascal you ever saw in your life, and his wife—gee! She was a great help to him in his work in Mexico! She was a Grace Coolidge, and that is the last word in help.

I knew what Anne would be before I ever met her. Show me the mother and I will give you a pretty good line on the girl! They are an awful lot alike—Mrs. Morrow and Anne—both full of life and pep, and great personalities.

He did a great work for us in Mexico. He has been a great inspiration, you know, for other rich men to get out and do something worth-while for the country. Did you ever figure it out, Morrow is Wall Street's sole contribution to public career?

Of course, these are just a few little obscure things that I dug up in his career, these ones I have spoken to you about, things that you people didn't know nothing about. Of course, his later exploits in Mexico, and his work at the London Conference, and his race for the Senatorship of New Jersey—they are well known.

I have been speaking tonight on what he did B. A. M. L., *Before Anne Married Lindbergh*. I don't care to deal with a man after he has become famous. I am interested in what he was doing when he was nobody. He is a great fellow, you can't help like him. You know, Morrow is really one father-in-law that is trying to make good on his own. Good night!

Henry Ford

You know, I was going to talk on Henry Ford last week, and I told you about mine going "Flooey" on me when I started to drive in here last Sunday evening, and I was afraid I wouldn't give Mr. Ford a fair deal.

Well, the next morning I got a wire from Mr. Ford himself, saying "What was the matter? Was the tank empty?"

I know he has got quite a sense of humor. A few years ago I was out to his home in Dearborn. I was playing there with the Follies, and I went out to his home and it was the time when the Star car was supposed to be going to cut quite a dash in the Ford sales, so I asked him, "Mr. Ford, I know it is rather inquisitive, but in case these opposition things get to cutting the prices and all, just how cheap could you sell your car?"

He said, "Well, Will, that is kind of personal but if the worst comes to the worst, I could give it away, as long as we retain the selling of the parts. You know, Will, one of these things will shake off enough in a year to pay for itself."

Did you ever figure out, no man in our time or in anybody else's time has ever had as much influence on the lives of people as Henry Ford has? Think what he has done for beasts! Even if he has been a detriment to man, he has sure converted horses from a burden of toil and made them kind of objects of curiosity.

Now, take George Washington—of course, he was great—he was the Father of our Country on account of having no children. He was a surveyor and he owned half of Virginia, because he surveyed his own lines. He was a general on our side because England wouldn't make him one on theirs. He was a politician and a gentleman—that is a rare combination. But you know a lot of his stuff has been overestimated by history. It is like a lie—the longer you tell it, the

E.R. Squibb & Sons Broadcast, June 1, 1930

bigger it gets. He got a reputation for truthfulness when his father caught him with a tree down and a hatchet in his hand and in perspiration—well, I would even go as far as to say that he had sweat streaming down his brow. What did he say? He said, "Father, as much as I detest circumstantial evidence, here is one time when it is true; I cut it down and if I had it to do over again, I wouldn't do it, for that is without doubt the dullest hatchet in the state of Virginia."

Lincoln was great. He freed the slaves and put the Southern whites in bondage for the duration of their natural lives. He furnished General Grant with cigars to smoke and poor Lee had no gas mask so he had to surrender. Lincoln tried his best to prevent that war between the Democrats and the Republicans. Since then, they have been settling their difficulties at the polls, with about the same results.

Those men never started, as history-makers, in comparison to Henry Ford. Why, he has run over more people in one month than either Washington or Lincoln disposed of in both wars. He has changed the mode of living and the habits of more people than Caesar or Mussolini or Chaplin or Daniel Webster or Clara Bow or Xerxes or Amos 'n' Andy or Bernard Shaw.[1]

You know Brigham Young originated mass production, but Henry Ford was the guy that improved on it.[2] You must get this into your head—he alone is absolutely responsible for this great era of transportation in which we half-way live. If there had never been a Ford car, there never would have been a cheap car. It would always have been classed as just a rich man's luxury. You can remember when we all had it in for the men that come along our roads honking for us commoners to get out of the road. We was sore at them and hated the guys that was in them, but the minute that Ford built a cheap one, and we could get in one and we was the ones that was doing the honking—that made it different. Had the poor man never been able to get a car, he never would have voted with the rich man on good roads, and without roads, the thing would have passed right out like Mah Jong, Eskimo Pie or some of those things.

He is responsible for more buildings than any man living. There is more garages and filling stations built than there is homes, churches, schools, and all those. If there was a single bed in every filling station in America, it would give every man and woman and child a home to themselves.

I have always wanted to see Ford elected President—I really have. Compared to the business he runs, our Government affairs would be a kind of a branch office for him. He has got his own ideas on farming. He says that a farmer spends half of his time raising a half-dozen things to feed an old cow to eat, and all he gets in return from the cow is milk and half the time it is clabber. His theory is to learn the people to eat those things and then I think he is going to do away with the cow—I don't know. He believes that a farmer ought to work part of his time on his farm and the other part in the factory. The farmer claims that when you get through working on the farm and asking your Congressman for relief, there ain't no time to even visit a factory. If he ever runs for President we are going to call his party the "Old Roads Party." I would like to see him get in there. When Congress got to stalling around, he would go around and lift up the hood of Congress or the Senate to see what was the matter with it. He would arrange the Government so that it went by one of these trolleys, you know, on one of these overhead trolleys, and every Congressman and Senator would throw something on as the thing went by.

A lot of wise guys have had a lot of fun joking about Ford because he admitted one time that he didn't know history. He don't know it—but history will know him! He has made more history than his critics has ever read.

Uncle Henry is the very boy that knows our problems. Our problem is paying for one of his problems—that is our problem. He has drove more people in debt than the War. Disarmament ain't worrying this country near as much as parking space is. Congress has argued over the tariff since Washington wore satin knee breeches—golf breeches, only they didn't have golf then—but they have never lowered any taxes. Taxes, not tariff is what we are interested in. There's two mortgages in this country to every vote. We are operating on $10 down and a dollar a week. If we get $30 a week, we are paying on 30 things.

If I wanted to put an object on the market today I would advertise, "It will last until it is paid for." Nothing could be better than that.

Mr. Ford believes in Prohibition and he won't let a man work for him that drinks. Before you go to work every morning, he smells your breath. You can't blame him because the stuff they are drinking nowadays would rust the bolts out of the machines. He don't say the buyer must not drink—in fact, he encourages that, because the more drinking, the more turnover, and they have the largest turnover of any business in the world.

Do you know that Ford used to work for Edison?[3] Did you know that? Well, he did. He used to work for Edison for $100 a month. This is when he built the first automobile—he built it on Edison's time and with Edison's tools. For a time in the year he used one of Edison's factory clocks, and the flywheel was off of one of Edison's electric question-askers. The steering apparatus was a kind of straight-handled

45

affair then. Well, it was a handle of a spade, also appropriated from Mr. Edison, and the funny part about the whole thing was the thing run but it took him over a year before he got it to run. That started Ford in the automobile business. It come pretty near putting Edison out of the electrical business. Mr. Ford had to give him a dinner at Dearborn last year to square himself. By the way, at that dinner more prominent men was gathered there to honor Mr. Ford and Edison than had ever gathered in one place. If a man worked in Ford's factory and carried out as much junk as Henry did out of Edison's it would put the whole Ford factory out of commission. Just dropping one bolt will stop 10,000 men in his place now.

When Mr. Ford first made his car, he had it in the house (yes, it was in the bedroom) and Mrs. Ford made him take it out and put it in the backyard.[4] It made so much noise in the house that it kept Edsel awake.[5] He took it out in the backyard and it keeps the whole world awake.

Ford's success is due to the fact that he uses common sense in his business instead of a board of directors. He shames a lot of the other concerns in paying high wages. He believes in giving a man a job, at least giving him a hand-out.

When he found he was wrong in his argument with the Jewish people, he apologized.[6] He saw them in a Chevrolet and he says, "Boys, I am wrong! I am wrong!" But he is responsible for more things than any man living.

Hoover fed the Belgians, but Ford took them for a ride. About 193,000 people is just fixing punctures on those things every minute of every day and 432,000 is just advising them how to fix them. There is 3,000 Ford radiators boiling over the hills of this country every minute of every day; 21,000 people just holding up the hoods and looking at the radiators; 20,000 with the same expression. Preachers, statesmen and great orators will have made speeches but no man has ever moved this country like Henry Ford.

The Ford car is the best-known object in the world. You can take a Chinaman in the heart of China that don't know where his next missionary is coming from but he knows how to pour a couple of quarts of rice in the thing and it will run. An Englishman knows it like he does his teapot. A Zulu can take one apart and get enough back so it will run. There is more jokes told about it than any other thing. A Ford car and a Democratic Convention has kept a lot of us comedians alive. He is the first man to realize that every joke sold a car and every joke bought one.

I like him because he sees more music in an old-time fiddler than he does in a long-haired one with a foreign name. He has caused more

46

dirty dishes to be left in the sink after supper than all the leading men on the screen put together. He has broken more wrists than all the osteopaths combined. He has caused more profanity than a Senate investigation. He has given more value for the least money. A Ford car and a marriage certificate is the two cheapest things there is. We no more than get either one than we want to trade them in for something better.

He is a great old fellow and he is very, very human. I always liked Mr. Ford. I think he is a great man, and I wish we had a lot more like him. Good night.

Will Rogers (far right) and members of the Eveready Orchestra at radio station WEAF in New York City on election night in 1924.

48

Prohibition

Down here in the room where we are gathered—it is the main studio in New York, and there is a lot of folks around here, too. We don't have this many people in Los Angeles, even according to the census. We don't have as many as are in here, do you know? I have got a lot of friends here—Bill Fields that used to be in the Follies with me and Brandon Tinnan and a bunch of them here.[1] If you want to laugh at it, go ahead. The folks out in Claremore won't mind.

I left Beverly Hills Friday morning and flew to my home in Oklahoma and spent that night with my folks, and here I am in here today, and all this was not any special plane. It was on an ordinary, regular passenger line and on regular passenger ships, for about the same fare as you would pay, you know, on a train, including your Pullman fare. Of course, I never took one, always slept on my neck.

I have received more letters in the last few weeks to talk on Prohibition than on any other subject. I haven't said a word about it. I was really ashamed. So many was talking and arguing over it that I wanted to be original and just let it alone. Can you name me one subject in the entire world that there has been as much time and energy wasted on? If you took all the Prohibition talk out of the Congressional Record, you could mail the rest of it out on a post card. Congress has cost us more talkin' about Prohibition than it has tryin' to enforce it, and I have yet to hear anybody talk on it that wasn't some kind of a fanatic, no matter which side they was on. But of course a fanatic is always the fellow that is on the opposite side.

But with all the shoutin' and ravin' and all their investigations and all this straw votin', I will bet you there hasn't been a single soul converted to the other side. They haven't changed a vote. It's one of those things like religion—you have your mind made up and you don't want anybody coming around trying to tell you what to think.

E.R. Squibb & Sons Broadcast, June 8, 1930

49

I have often said that I wish the wets would become so soused they would be speechless and couldn't say anything, and that the drys would become so perfect that the Lord would come down and take them away from here, and that would leave the country to the rest of us who are tired of listening to both of them.

So I got to wondering if it wasn't possible for a fellow to talk on it without being a nut on either side. I think if I could do that I would be speaking in behalf of practically millions of people.

Now, it is not so terribly serious, this Prohibition. It is not a life or death problem with us. If it was repealed tomorrow, the lives and habits and morals of the whole country, they wouldn't be ruined; the country would drag along just about the same. Taxes and parking space would hit us in the face just the same. Henry Ford wouldn't leave the country if it was repealed. You couldn't run him out of here.

Then, on the other hand, if it is never repealed, we will still drag along. The country won't go to the dogs. We lived with the eighteenth amendment and we have lived without it and we are still here under both systems, so you see there is perhaps problems greater.

We kill thousands of people every year with automobiles, yet all we do about it is write an editorial; every once in a while, we see one in the papers. We didn't argue over going into war near as much as we have argued over Prohibition.

America is getting so big, you know, it really is, this country is getting so big that no matter what it is, it don't bother us any more. We just struggle along in spite of ourselves. It takes more than a drink to really interest us any more. It is not undermining—you know they always say it is undermining the moral fibre of a great nation. That's a lot of hooey. Neither is it our greatest experiment. If we wasn't trying it, we would be trying some other experiment. We are just like a monkey, we can't let anything alone. We have got to feel of it and see what it is.

Some folks on both sides have just kidded themselves it is our greatest problem. The real wet is going to drink I don't care what your laws are, and a real dry is going to lecture to him while he is drinking, no matter what your laws about it are. You can't change human nature. But while those two are fighting it out, there will be 500 passing by tending to their own business, living their own lives, and doing exactly what they think is best for them.

The Literary Digest sent out 20,000,000 votes and 5,000,000 answered, showing that there was 15,000,000 that is about three-quarters of the people, that didn't care what happened to either side.

The wets have always claimed that the law has made a lot of dry people mad and made them drink. Well, if they was dry and got sore because it went wet, why if you made it wet, they are liable to get sore and go back dry again. So that wouldn't leave anybody to drink after you had already got everything all wet for them.

We are trying to settle something here that has been going on since way back in Bible times. Those old prophets couldn't even settle it and you can't tell me that Moses of New Hampshire and his gang of Senators know any more than Moses of Palestine and his troupe did.[2] Right in the first book of Genesis, you don't read but just a few pages until Noah was lit up like a pygmy golf course. Here is just how it started. Wait a minute, I got it right here on the paper; I will read it to you. Right in the start of Genesis, the ninth chapter and the twentieth verse it says, "And Noah became a husbandman and planted a vineyard." The minute he became a husband he started in raising the ingredients that goes with married life. So you can trace all drink to marriage, see. What we got to prohibit is marriage.

In the very next verse, the twenty-first verse, it says, "And he drank of the wine and was drunk." Now that was Noah himself, our forefather. Practically all of us can trace our ancestry back to him. That is where we all join and get even with the D.A.R.'s. We started life on an equality with the D.A.R.'s, but they left us in '76. The Bible says, "Thou shalt not take up arms against thy neighbor," and the D.A.R.'s did and became famous. We didn't take up anything and we don't amount to nothing.

Now you see Noah drank and he didn't drink water and he was a man that knew more about water than practically any man of his time. He was the Water Commissioner of his day. Old Noah was an expert on water, but the Lord is very far-seeing, and everything He does is for the best. Through Noah partaking of too much wine and going on this little spree, that is just why the Lord picked on him to pick out these animals to take in to the Ark. He was the only man that had even seen all of them. So if Noah hadn't drunk, today we would be without circuses and menageries. Of course, other men since Noah's time have claimed that they have seen animals that Noah didn't put into the Ark, but they were drinking from a different vineyard.

Noah took in two kinds of every animal, two of every kind, all but a Democrat and its mate. He forgot the mate. That is why the Democrats have never increased and prospered.

Noah lived—you know this wine had such ill effects on Noah that he only lived to be 950 years old. That is just 19 years short of Methuselah, who held the longevity record of his and all times. So Prohibition is not a new problem by any means. There is no need for this generation to feel conceited enough to think that they can settle it. It is like stopping war. We are always going to do something that no other generation has even been able to do. If you could take politics out of Prohibition, it would be more beneficial to this country than if you took the alcohol out of our drinks.

The fuss raised over Prohibition has done twice as much harm as the drinking has. The drys wanted it in the Constitution and they got it in there. The wets wanted to drink and they got it. So what is all this shooting about anyhow? It is in the Constitution and it is going to stay there as long as there is a bottle left.

I have told Prohibition jokes on both sides of this question all over the country, in every town hall and every hay barn and in lots of the churches all over the country I have spoke in, and people have laughed at the little jokes, and then they would go right out the next day and elect a dry.

Now here is something that I want you all to remember, a wet makes more noise, but a dry votes the oftenest. And don't get the idea that Prohibition is staying in the Constitution on account of its moral grounds; it is economics. It has got to stand or fall on economics. Big business don't care about what your morals are, but they do care about how much work you can turn out in a day's time. If somebody invented an alcoholic stimulant tomorrow whereby everyone taking a swig of it would start right in working right hard and keep it up for eight hours, the country would vote wet in a month.

Of course, they are drinking some terrible stuff. They are making an ingredient, they are putting together some stuff now that puts courage into you without breathing, they really do. You know, in the old days you had to be born courageous. Your father had to be courageous, or your mother. You had to inherit it. But now they bottle courage. You take one dram of this White Mule and you go out and meet a street car head on purposely. Europe is even trying to find out how we make it. They have found that this liquid weapon of ours carries more authority than a hogshead of beer or a flacon of wine. They have never experienced, they never had before up to the time they tried this, the sensation of unconsciousness without an anaesthetic before.

So they have been taking it back over home to Europe and having it diagnosed, and their scientists and their chemists have looked to see what it contains but at last we got even with Einstein.[3] They know no more about our theory than we do about his. The minute they would find out what one bottle contained, the next one they would examine, it wouldn't have any of the ingredients of the first bottle, so at last we have made an article that Europe couldn't duplicate cheaper. After assaying hundreds of bottles, the only thing they found out that each bottle held in common with the other bottle was that it all flowed and death was inevitable.

So now our liquor has become one of their principal imports. Just one bottle of this mountain dew fell into the hands of the Riffs and they declared war on Spain immediately. Mussolini ordered a case and now he wants to take on the world.

I claim we will never get a true test of the Prohibition vote until they invent a machine, a kind of machine that registers your breath as well as your vote. You have a thing like this microphone is here; that is, at every voting booth you put one of these and you drop your vote in the box and you breathe in this, and your vote and your breath has got to correspond. You can't vote one way and breathe another.

I would hate to think that this country has arrived in such a state that we are worrying over whether to drink or not to drink. I really would, I would hate to think that we had got to such a state where our whole future depended on whether we drink or not.

City people seem to be more excited about Prohibition. Country folks are more excited over making a living.

America ain't as bad off as it might seem. The young are not drinking themselves to death and the old are not worrying themselves to death over the condition of whether the young are drinking or not. Chain stores are worrying this country a lot more than chain saloons are. Turkey is the only other Prohibition country in the world, us and Turkey. There's a fine gang to be linked up with, ain't it? If we enjoyed some of the other privileges, things wouldn't be so bad. We enjoy them, but they are not legal.

Now listen here, folks, honest, this is what I want to get over to you tonight, let's not all get excited about it and break friendship with our neighbors and fall out with our brother over this Prohibition. Nothing is going to be done about it during our lifetime. There ain't anybody hearing me tonight who will live to see the time when anything is done about it, so don't let's all worry and get all het up about it, get all hot and bothered. Don't let's take it so serious. The drys and wets both combined can't hurt this country. Talking about Prohibition is like whittling used to be, it passes away the time but don't settle anything.

Now go to bed and forget about it and let's hope that some day our country will be as dry as the speeches made by both the wets and the drys.

You know, you think we got troubles. Say look at Roumania. Carol is back and brought all his harem with him.[4] Now there's a country that has got trouble. Good night!

Boston

Well, here we are up here in Boston! They call it up here "Bosting." You do, don't you? Oh, yes, we have got a lot of folks here in the studio. They sent out invitations and we have some very exclusive people here tonight, so they say. Oh, a lovely studio, too! This ain't like any of these I have been talking in. This is WNAC in Boston, and it is more like a home or something, you know. Oh, it is fine! I don't know how to act in a place like this. We are in Boston, the home of Harvard, and Harvard is the home of culture and poor football. Everyone in Harvard can speak good English, you know, but nobody can make a touchdown. But we are glad to have you folks here with us tonight. The Governor was coming down, you know, but this is pretty late—it is 10 o'clock here—and that is pretty late for Boston, and he didn't get down.[1] He gave me a little badge yesterday. He come down to the Metropolitan Theatre there and he pinned this little badge on me. Here it is, but I had to take if off; it was tarnishing. The Governor of this State has a very unique record, and he gave me some gloves. He is a glove manufacturer, too. He gave me some gloves—old ones—and imagine, you know, that is the height of New England hospitality—to give you gloves in the summertime!

But he told me a good Coolidge story. He is a great friend of Mr. Coolidge, and he has had about the same political career as Mr. Coolidge. He started in as a town selectman and then he went on up and he has been Congressman from the State of Massachusetts and Senator, and Speaker of the House, and President of the Senate, Lieutenant-Governor, and now he is Governor. They gave him a dinner not long ago and Mr. Coolidge come to the dinner in honor of him. Mr. Coolidge spoke at the dinner and he says, "Governor Allen, your political career has paralleled mine—up to now."

Oh, we have got a great bunch of people here tonight. From all

---

E.R. Squibb & Sons Broadcast, June 15, 1930

these people in the studio it looks like Ben Lyon and Bebe Daniels' wedding, only nobody brought nice presents, that is the only thing.[2] Bebe got married yesterday—her and Ben and this is their freshman wedding. That is unusual in Hollywood, for anybody to get married the first time.

Well, anyhow, everybody says, "What are you doing in Boston?" I am here helping them to celebrate their tercen—ter—I can't say the thing—their 300th Anniversary or something—it would take me 300 years to learn to pronounce the word.

I have got to be honest with you—I don't know what you are celebrating the 300th—anybody come here from the outside, I don't see how they can tell when you are celebrating your 300th and when you ain't. You can't look at the town and tell when it is celebrating. I drove down here in a car tonight and the ruts we hit must have been 300 years old.

They had a big celebration out at Salem yesterday, and everybody was supposed to have on the old-fashioned costumes of the Early Revolutionary Period. I went down there and I couldn't tell the people that was dressed for the thing from the ones that wasn't. But really—all kidding aside—you want to come up here this summer. This is the most beautiful country in the world. Honest, New England is really lovely and we all have a warm spot in our hearts for New England. Here is where all of our learning and culture and everything—whatever we have got—comes from. But it is fine, and they are having this big celebration here and this fall they are going to have the American Legion; all the boys, you know, are coming here, and we have got to take care of those boys because they are the ones we have got to use in another war; you know, because we can't dig up new ones.

But really, it is a great old place. Every house in New England is where some old Revolutionary man slept, every one of them. Some of them old generals must have done nothing but sleep. They must have just slept in one house, then got up and moved over and slept in another.

Oh, they got historical spots here. This country is mangy with history. You never saw so much history scattered around. Out in California, if we just had the lower end of Bunker Hill, we could sell enough lots to pay for moving the hill out there. That would be marvelous, you know, because California should have something named "Bunker."

I had a great visit just the other day—I must tell you about going out to the Coolidges! I went out there and had a lovely visit with Mrs. Coolidge—Mr. Coolidge wasn't there (I knew that before I went.) I knew he wasn't there and me and Mrs. Coolidge sat down and we had the finest time—just gossiping. I had just come from Washington and we had all the scandal. I had seen Admiral McLean down there and I had all the latest dope.[3] She showed me all over the grounds, and the dogs, and everything. We had a dandy visit!

I was awfully sorry Mr. Coolidge wasn't there, but I didn't miss finding out anything—you know what I mean. He wouldn't have told me nothing if he had been there.

Here is what I wanted to tell you. I had wired up the day before, and I says, "Mr. Coolidge, I am going to come up to Boston tomorrow and I would like to come by Northampton and drop by and say hello to you." I asked him if I could come up.

He wired, "Yes; I will be in New York tomorrow. Come up!"

Boy, is he a bear, you know! He works for some life insurance company and he went down and they pay the directors every time they come down, you know and he was down there getting his fee, you know.[4]

I says to Mrs. Coolidge, "Mrs. Coolidge, does he ever miss one?" and she says, "Not yet! He has never been ill."

You know, he goes down there (I won't mention the name of the company he works for, because that would be a boost; you know what I mean). That would be an advertisement and I don't want to advertise; I won't do it gratis. But it is some big company—I think it is the Beechnut Liability Company. I think that is the insurance company he is with. Either that or Squibb's Dental Indemnity, one of those—I don't know which—maybe it is Bull Durham, or Claremore Radium Water.

Then I had a visit, I must tell you about my visit with Mr. Hoover, during the past week. You see, all I know is what little I read in the paper or what I find out as I bum around the country.

Pat Hurley is Secretary of War—you all know Pat—and he took me over.[5] He says, "Have you seen the President?" Pat comes from Oklahoma, you know.

I says, "No, I haven't seen Mr. Hoover since he has been in office," so he says "come on over."

They won't let a Democrat go in alone. They will either send a Secret Service man with you or another Republican. So Pat took me in and Mr. Hoover was fine.

He asked us to stay for dinner—it was pretty near six o'clock then, and he says, "I would like to have you all have dinner with me."

I had another dinner engagement so I says, "Mr. Hoover, I have got on these old clothes; I can't go to dinner with you, I'm sorry."

He was very nice and he said, "Well, I will wear the ones I have on.'' He paid me a compliment, you know, and he says, ''These look about like yours.''

I had on this same suit I have on now. You folks here can see how it looks. I know I had on this suit—if I didn't have on this suit, I didn't have anything on.

Well, it was fine, and we had a lovely visit there with Mr. Hoover. Then I told him, I says, ''Pat has an engagement; his wife has a dinner and she is going to feed Jim Watson and some Senators.''[6]

He says, ''I am sorry, I would like to have you for dinner.''

So then I happened to think and I says, ''Will this offer hold good, Mr. Hoover? Suppose I don't go with you now; will it hold good?''

He says, ''Yes,'' and I says, ''Can I depend on that?''

He says, ''Yes,'' and I says, ''I would like to have you put it down in writing, if you don't mind.'' I am kind of like the Senate—I don't trust the President, either.

So I didn't stay, but we had a lovely visit.

Somebody had told him about my radio talk on Prohibition, last Sunday, and so something come up about it and I asked Mr. Hoover if he had heard it. He said, ''No.'' He said he had heard several of them but he didn't hear the one last Sunday night. He said he would like to have heard it so I said I would send him a copy. I said, ''I am kind of proud of it because I have talked on Prohibition and I have had no kick from either side.'' He said, ''I would love to see it!''

Mr. Hoover had a good sense of humor. He said, ''I would like to hear anything said by anybody that wouldn't have a kick from somebody. Tip me off as to how you do it.''

I am going to send him that speech.

When we got outside, Pat said to me, ''Do you know what you did?''

I said, ''I don't know.''

He said, ''Why, you refused the President. When the President asks you to do anything, that is not a request, it is a demand.''

And here I had turned down the President, but I didn't know nothing about it. I told Pat, I said, ''Well, I wasn't hungry, I couldn't help it.''

But we had a lovely time. Mr. Hoover is looking fine and he seemed to be in pretty good spirits under the circumstances.

Now, let's see what else we have got in the papers. Everybody has been asking me how I stood on this prize fight thing. I don't know much about these prize fights. It is all I can do to try to keep track of Bishop Cannon and Uncle Joe Grundy.[7] I am worrying about them. But it looks to me like prize fighting has got so in this country that they just have it not to see who is the good athlete, but just for the argument they have after the thing is over. Ever since Tunney knocked Dempsey down and they didn't start counting until the next day, prize fights have nothing but arguments.[8] That is all everybody does. The fighters have their fight and when they are out, the audience starts in. They fight for another year. I know Sharkey is a nice fellow—a good family man, a good boy, and everything.[9] I have never met this German, but he must be a fine, upstanding young boy, but I don't know—the condition that the prize fight game is in now, it strikes me as being very appropriate to have a champion named Schmeling.[10] I know of no sport that gives out a greater odor than it does now. I know that.

Well, sir, Mr. Dwight Morrow comes up for election Tuesday, and you know I honestly think a great deal of that man—I really do—but I don't know but what I want to see him defeated because I don't want to see him get in that Senate with the group of hyenas they have got in there. I was down to the Senate the other day and met them all and talked with them. They are getting along fine; they passed the Tariff Bill. They know it was a lot of hooey but they went right on and passed it just the same. The Tariff Bill is going to be great for everybody who don't buy anything or don't eat anything. Now it is bound to do you good if you don't buy or eat and that is the only one it is going to be any good for.

Old Uncle Joe Grundy was born on Monday, started lobbying on Tuesday, went to the Senate on Wednesday and said he would vote against the Tariff on Thursday, but he voted for it on Friday and he is going to retire from the Senate next Saturday, and that is the last of Uncle Joe Grundy until it comes time to pass another Tariff Bill and then he will be right back in the Senate again.

I see where my old friend, Charlie Dawes, landed back. The old Ambassador wouldn't wear the knee breeches over in England. He landed yesterday. They couldn't get knee breeches on Charlie. Charlie says, "It would take the King's own guard to get any breeches on a Dawes."

He has gone out to Chicago; they want him on this gang thing out there—didn't say which side.

Sister Aimee McPherson landed and she had a little trouble with the customs.[11] They claimed she hadn't paid duty on some of her dresses. There was just a little misunderstanding—Mrs. McPherson didn't mean anything—just a little misunderstanding. She thought she was wrapped up in the Lord and they thought she was wrapped up in a Paris gown.

Well, that is about all the news I know tonight. Good night!

Chicago

Well, here we are folks, out in the old city of Chicago. Yes, sir—the great old city of Chicago—broadcasting from a sound-proof studio here. They got this town all wrong. There is no crime or shooting here.

We have got an audience here tonight. We only invited the town's best citizens, just invited the best citizens of the town. We haven't got as big an audience as we thought we would have. We very foolishly barred out the gang leaders and the racketeers, so we are not full-handed here by any means. We are barricaded here in the Wrigley Building, trying our best to keep from mentioning Beechnut.

Now I will try and describe to you what is going on down on the street here. I am standing right by the window. The Bugs Moran gang are holding down the east side of Michigan Boulevard and the Capones are entrenched on the other side.[1] It is lucky for us they can't get in here. Yes, they can. Here they come.

That's too bad, too bad. Just drag him right over there, will you? Just get him out of the way here.

This is Graham McNamee, pinch-hitting for Mr. Rogers.[2] This is McNamee speaking from Station WBBM, describing to you this quiet evening in Chicago. Excuse me, I want to eat a hot dog a minute. The Moran gang, as he told you, are on one side, and the Capones on the other. This is the finals. Boy, what a battle this is going to be! Wait until we open that window and let you hear some of them down there. It is a beautiful night. The stars are marvelous. Boy, you ought to see these stars out here. It is one of the best nights for a battle that I ever saw. I have been coming out here for battles for years, but while they are placing the machine guns, I will give you a little resume of what is going on. A great night. There must be a thousand racketeers. There is not an empty seat—I mean, there is not an empty gun in the place. Boy, what a night this is! This is for the finals. The gang that

E.R. Squibb & Sons Broadcast, June 22, 1930

wins this goes to New York and fights there for the racketeer privilege. Why the coffin rights alone ought to run into a half million dollars here tonight.

We are in the Wrigley Building, and I will give you a little line on some of the notables here. There is Ruth Hanna McCormick, just nominated for the Senate. I am hoping some of them live down there long enough to vote for her. Here is J. Ham Lewis, her opponent, a man with whiskers but a gentleman in spite of being a Democrat.[3] He is a wet, and of course all these boys in the battle are drys, so Ham is pulling for total extermination of both sides.

Here is Samuel Insull.[4] He is wringing his hands. He is afraid they will kill off all the gang leaders and that will destroy, you know, his people that go to the opera. He foolishly built the opera house so you could see the stage instead of the people seeing each other, so he is going to have to rebuild it over again.

Just a minute there. Shut that window down so we can't hear the battle. Here comes Charlie Dawes. Look, he has got on knee breeches. Got the rompers on, Charlie—well! Wait a minute. I will call him to the microphone and have him say a word. Mr. Dawes, come here a minute. Come over here and say something to the folks. Get that pipe out of your mouth. You will get static on this thing here.

"Oh, I say, old chap, this is a ripping battle, this is a ripping battle. This is worth leaving dear old London. I only wish the Senate was in between both sides. Hades and Maria, what time do we have tea?"

Gee, that is mighty nice of you, Mr. Dawes. That is fine. Thank you very much. That is mighty nice, to come here and speak, and to have you come back from London to the old home town folks here and see the boys fighting for the glory of big business. When Mr. Dawes returns to the Court of St. James he is taking back as a house guest Mayor Thompson.[5]

Wait a minute—they are shooting up this way. They are shooting here. Here they come—I am hit—tell them—tell them I died—I died announcing.

This is Floyd Gibbons, pinch-hitting for the late Graham McNamee.[6] When I say Floyd Gibbons talking I mean talking, I don't mean stuttering. It seems great to be back in Chicago and reporting the war here. I have reported wars all over the world, but when I get short of a war to report, I always drop back to Chicago.

The Illiterate Digest took a poll on the situation and here are some of the figures that show you exactly how they did. In the Illiterate Digest, for just ten cents a copy on the newsstands every Thursday, a straw vote was taken and sent out, a questionnaire. There were three alternatives in the vote—dead, wounded or escaped. You could mark any one of them the way you thought it would happen to you. In the Illiterate Digest poll—you can buy it for ten cents a week—it showed 87½ per cent killed, and that up to the time was absolutely within 1 per cent of the prediction. The votes were not coming in as fast as we thought they would on account of a great many being killed on the way to the mailboxes which accounts for the slight discrepancy of 1 per cent. The wounded on the poll showed about 12½ per cent wounded up to the time we went to press, and our statistics exactly bore out that prediction. We only make a mistake of one man. He said he was wounded when really he was only scared and wasn't wounded at all. Now if you add 12½ per cent and 87½ per cent that makes exactly 100 per cent, proving conclusively that there is no use having these gang wars at all if the Illiterate Digest showed you exactly what would happen in advance.

Last Friday, at Hoylake, Bobby Jones of Peachtree Street, Atlanta, Georgia, won the British Open Championship in 291 strokes, which is within a half a stroke of what the Illiterate Digest showed he would do.[7] The discrepancy of the half is explained by the difference in time. They count a half stroke when the ball goes into the hole, turns around and comes back out again. Jones' victory shows that luck triumphs over skill in the long run. It also proves that while the Democrats can't get elected to anything, still they can play golf.

Washington, D.C.—The Illiterate Digest took a poll last fall to determine what Mr. Hoover would think of the Senate by this June. The result of the poll was that he wouldn't think much of it. Present check-up shows he don't think anything of it, but how we made that mistake was the Senate was worse than anybody thought possible, and we hereby apologize for the poll.

I will open the window and let you hear a few of the concluding shots of the battle. This is Floyd Gibbons speaking. Meanwhile, I will turn the microphone back to Mr. Will Rogers who has revived as it is impossible to kill a radio entertainer by shooting him in the head.

Hello, folks. Now, that is just about the idea that most people have of this city of Chicago that we are here in. They really do, you know. And here we are, a nice, little, respectable bunch gathered up here in this Wrigley Building, and the city is as peaceful and quiet. It is so still, it is almost disgusting. I couldn't hardly get anybody to come up here tonight and listen to me talk. Everybody in the city has gone to church, you know. Why, this is just a great, big, overgrown home-loving town, that is all.

Of course, they do have these gangs here, and they do kill each other. Well, that is their privilege. In the old days, no one would have gone to any trouble if the Dalton Brothers started to shoot the James Boys, would they? This is really, all kidding aside, one of the greatest cities in the world. Just think of how this city existed here without collecting any taxes for two years. It existed and kept growing. If other cities could grow as fast as this one, they would hire gangs to come and shoot each other. In fact, I was sent here by Los Angeles to find out how they was getting all this population, and I have orders to sign up any of these boys.

Dawes is going to have a wonderful World Fair here in 1933, one of the greatest that has ever been put on. He is going to have one here that will really knock your eye out because when Charlie Dawes does anything, he does it right.[8] And they are going to spend a lot of money and it is going to be a wonderful thing, and by the time the farmers get relief Chicago is going to be the biggest city in the world.

No, sir, now, folks, you are not going to get me coming out here telling any jokes about these racketeers and gangsters or any of that. I arrived in this city intact, and I am going to try and leave likewise, that is all. They are a fine bunch of boys, and they are just trying to distribute good cheer among everybody, that is all. In fact, I am a kind of racketeer myself. I have been accused of having a racket, and I have come to see what their graft is here, and if theirs is any better than mine. If it is, I may join them, that is all. So before the week is over you are liable to see it Capone & Rogers, Incorporated. It is all right to scatter good humor at the expense of the Senate, for they are harmless, but these boys carry a gun. But you know these gangsters here, they are just big, misunderstood kids, that is all they are.

You know, when you published your census report, that is what knocked this country cuckoo, when Chicago published the census report. That made the whole world get up and take notice, it really did. Just think, you had almost four million people here, three and three-quarter millions, pretty nearly four million people Chicago had here. And you know, of course, you shoot a lot of people here, but you breed a lot too. Your breeding so overshadows your shooting that you have no cause for worry at all. It is only when your marksmanship excels your propagation that you want to start to worry, you know. Not only here in Chicago but all over the country this so-called ''better element'' is trying to do something to combat bootlegging and corruption. Now, I am not an authority and I am not even a member of any Commission, but the only way I know of to stop this whole thing all over the country is for the ''better element'' to stop drinking. Without customers, these boys couldn't exist for a week. Good night.

62

Organization on Unemployment Relief Broadcast

Bacon and Beans
and Limousines

Now don't get scared and start turning off your radios. I'm not advertising or trying to sell you anything. If the mouthwash you are using is not the right kind and it tastes sort of like sheepdip why you'll just have to go right on using it.[1] I can't advise any other kind at all.

And if the cigarettes that you are using, why if they don't lower your Adam's apple, why I don't know of any that will. You will just have to cut out apples, I guess.[2] That's the only thing I know.

Now, Mr. Owen Young asked me to annoy on this program this evening.[3] You all know Mr. Owen D. Young. You know, he's the only sole surviving wealthy Democrat, so naturally when a wealthy Democrat asks me to do anything I have to do it, see?

Well, Mr. Young, he's head of the Young Plan, you know. He's the originator of the Young Financial European Plan. He's head of the Young Men's Temperance Union, and originator of Young's Markets, and Young Kippur. And was the first Democratic child born of white parents in Youngstown, Ohio.

He started the Young Plan in Europe. That was that every nation pay just according to what they could afford to pay, see? And, well, somebody else come along with an older plan than Young's plan, and it was that nobody don't pay anybody anything, and course that's the oldest plan there is. And that's the one they are working under now.[4] That's why we ain't getting anything from Europe.

So when Mr. Young asked me to appear why I said, "Well, I'm kind of particular. Who is going to be the other speaker? Who else is on the bill with me?"

And he said, "Well, how would Mr. Hoover do?"

Well, I slightly heard of him, you know, and I said, "Well, I'll think it over."

President's Organization on Unemployment Relief Broadcast, October 18, 1931

So I looked into Mr. Hoover's record and inquired of everybody, and after I had kind of thrown out about two-thirds of what the Democrats said about him why I figured that I wouldn't have much to lose by appearing with Mr. Hoover, so I'm here this evening appearing on the bill with Mr. Hoover. So now I expect you won't hear any more of "Amos and Andy"; it will just be Hoover and Rogers from now on.

Now we read in the papers every day, and they get us all excited over one or a dozen different problems that's supposed to be before this country.[5] There's not really but one problem before the whole country at this time. It's not the balancing of Mr. Mellon's budget. That's his worry. That ain't ours. And it's not the League of Nations that we read so much about. It's not the silver question. The only problem that confronts this country today is at least 7,000,000 people are out of work. That's our only problem. There is no other one before us at all. It's to see that every man that wants to is able to work, is allowed to find a place to go to work, and also to arrange some way of getting more equal distribution of the wealth in the country.

Now it's Prohibition, we hear a lot about that.[6] Well, that's nothing to compare to your neighbor's children that are hungry. It's food, it ain't drink that we are worried about today. Here a few years ago we were so afraid that the poor people was liable to take a drink that now we've fixed so that they can't even get something to eat.

So here we are in a country with more wheat and more corn and more money in the bank, more cotton, more everything in the world — there's not a product that you can name that we haven't got more of than any other country ever had on the face of the earth — and yet we've got people starving.[7] We'll hold the distinction of being the only nation in the history of the world that ever went to the poor house in an automobile.[8] The potter's fields are lined with granaries full of grain. Now if there ain't something cockeyed in an arrangement like that then this microphone here in front of me is — well, it's a cuspidor, that's all.

Now I think that perhaps they will arrange it — I think some of our big men will perhaps get some way of fixing a different distribution of things. If they don't they are certainly not big men and won't be with us long, that's one thing. Now I say, and have always claimed, that things would pick up in '32.[9] Thirty-two, why '32? Well, because '32 is an election year, see, and the Republicans always see that everything looks good on election year, see? They give us three good years and one bad one — no, three bad ones and one good one. I like to got it wrong. That's the Democrats does the other. They give us three bad years and one good one, but the good one always comes on the year that the voting is, see?[10] Now if they was running this year why they would be all right. But they are one year late. Everything will pick up next year and be fine.

These people that you are asked to aid, why they are not asking for charity, they are naturally asking for a job, but if you can't give them a job why the next best thing you can do is see that they have food and the necessities of life. You know, there's not a one of us has anything that these people that are without it now haven't contributed to what we've got. I don't suppose there is the most unemployed or the hungriest man in America has contributed in some way to the wealth of every millionaire in America. It was the big boys themselves who thought that this financial drunk we were going through was going to last forever. They over — merged and over — capitalized, and over — everything else. That's the fix that we're in now.

Now I think that every town and every city will raise this money. In fact, they can't afford not to. They've got the money because there's as much money in the country as there ever was. Only fewer people have it, but it's there. And I think the towns will all raise it because I've been on a good many charity affairs all over the country and I have yet to see a town or a city ever fail to raise the money when they knew the need was there, and they saw the necessity. Every one of them will come through.

Europe don't like us and they think we're arrogant, and bad manners, and have a million faults, but every one of them, well, they give us credit for being liberal.

Doggone it, people are liberal. Americans — I don't know about America being fundamentally sound and all that after-dinner hooey, but I do know that America is fundamentally liberal.[11] Now I want to thank Mr. Gifford, the head of this unemployment, thank Mr. Young, and I certainly want to thank Mr. Hoover for the privilege of being allowed to appear on the same program with him because I know that this subject is very dear to Mr. Hoover's heart and know that he would rather see the problem of unemployment solved than he would to see all the other problems he has before him combined.[12] And if every town and every city will get out and raise their quota, what they need for this winter, why it will make him a very happy man, and happiness hasn't been a steady diet with our president. He's had a very tough, uphill fight, and this will make him feel very good. He's a very human man. I thank you. Good night.

Good
Gulf
Show

Good Gulf Show

April 30, 1933

ORCHESTRA: [Plays medley of songs]

NARRATOR: Ladies and gentlemen, I guess our next bit of entertainment needs no introduction from me. You all know the Revelers, and in honor of Will Rogers, America's favorite cowboy, they're going to sing an old cowboy number, "The Old Chisholm Trail."[1]

QUARTET: [Revelers sing "The Old Chisholm Trail."]

NARRATOR: And now we come to the feature of our Sunday night Good Gulf Banquet. Ladies and gentlemen, may I present Will Rogers.

ROGERS: We got quite a bunch of notables in here tonight on account of it being free. That's one — that's one thing depression has done, it's made all free entertainment popular. Ah — say this bird Roosevelt he's working all the time and thinking about everything here.[2] You know we got — he found that these New Yorkers here have been hoarding some daylight, and he held 'em up and took an hour away from 'em today, you know. That's all switched around here now.

We've got quite a few — I'm glad the toastmaster didn't introduce me as a humorist, as sometimes. One of them has some humor, and he calls me a humorist — because sitting right down here in front of me with one of the biggest rose buds on his lapel — sits Irvin Cobb.[3] It'd sure trouble me if he'd introduced me as a humorist before Irvin, because Mr. Irvin Cobb I consider our greatest humorist, and when they remove the mantle at some future time, our historians — from Mr. Mark Twain, they won't have to take it very far — just from the Mississippi River right over to Paducah on the Ohio — that's all — over there. I'm sure that Twain would not be jealous of the mantle, but he would of the spats and this rose bud which he has on here.

Well, Mr. Amon Carter of Fort Worth — I don't know how a lot of these guys got in here.[4] Lee Arwell and Amon Carter.[5] Got Mr. Walter Winchell here, who I understand is responsible for really this President's Day, which I'm going to talk on — if I ever get to it here — President's Day.[6] Well, they say Walter originated the idea, and I want to thank him for it. It's a very lovely idea. Mr. Walter Winchell as you all know is maternity prophet of New York. Mrs. Rogers is back here with me, and I hope he predicts nothing in our — along our lines, because his predictions come true. Young married people often go to him to ask him if there's any blessed event in the horizon.

Now, I — boys, you heard that fine band. Wasn't that a lovely band? And I noticed them. That's the only radio band I ever saw that played from music. They had notes, you know, and could play from the notes. Most of them just hear something and then remember it as good as they can. The Revelers, I want to pay my compliments to. I haven't seen 'em since they was way down on the tour in the South. They spent three weeks down there one time, and they gave their services and done some splendid work. That's the greatest quartet in the world — is the Revelers. They not only — not only a quartet, but it's four that sings — that can sing.

Now this is President's Day. We generally recognize anything by a week. We have 'em by weeks. We have Apple Week, and Potato Week, and Don't Murder Your Wife Week, and Smile Week—with everybody going around grinnin' like a possum — for no reason at all—and they have Don't Get Hurt by an Automobile Week. So somebody hit the bright idea, and they says — Winchell says, "Well here, if prunes are worth a week, the president ought to be worth something anyhow."

And so they figured out they couldn't give him a week, but they could — they compromised on a day. The reason we give him a day was — he cuts down on everybody. And they says, "Well, he's been cutting down, so we'll just give him a day instead of a week." So that's how — we're very generous that way. We're wonderful with our presidents. When the sun is shining we cheer 'em, and let it start raining and if they don't furnish them, you know, some umbrellas and goo-losh-es — it's furnished by the government — boy, we give him the boot right then.

The man we're going — I'm going to try to pay a little respect here tonight to on account of being President's Day — we have no precedent in the accomplishments which this man has performed in the last — well, seven weeks is all he's been in there. That bird has done more for us in seven weeks than we've done for ourselves in seven years. We elected him because he was a Democrat, and now we honor him because he is a magician. He's the Houdini of Hyde Park.[7] And maybe this Houdini of Hyde Park can't do everything. He may not get our hands out of all the handcuffs which we have foolishly stuck our mitts out and got 'em into ourselves, but even if he can just get one hand loose — you know what I mean, and leave the handcuff hanging on the other, he will have accomplished a great deal. He's a fast worker. He was nominated — I mean — well, no — I was there when he was nominated — I ought to know about that. But, he was inaugurated at noon in Washington, and they started the inaugural parade down Pennsylvania Avenue, and before it got half way down there, he'd closed every bank in the United States.[8]

Now a Republican woulda never thought of a thing like that. No, no, he'd — he'd of let the depositors close it. And mind you — mind you, Mr. Roosevelt was just two days ahead of the depositors himself. He was there. But that shows you how fast he works. He's ahead of you all the time that way. And he marched on down — drove on down to the White House, and then he says, "I believe I'll call up the boys." So he called up MacDonald and this fellow that come from France—that we can't pronounce his name—and he says, "Come on over here.[9] I want to talk it over with you birds." And — so they've been over here, and they went back smiling but they had nothing signed.

And well, anyhow, then he took the Democrats out of the employment ranks, and he's made postmasters out of all of them. And he's made Christians out of the Republicans — all but Ogden Mills.[10] My friend, Ogden Mills, who made an awfully good speech last night at the Gridiron Dinner in Washington. Ogden is still — he's running around kinda yappin' around, but he's really subsidized by the Democratic party to kind of put up the appearance of a organized minority. That's what.

We have — we have — you'd be surprised at the hordes of

Republicans who are crawling up to this shrine in Washington to pay their respects to this modern messiah, this maverick of the — that once disgraced, the Roosevelt clan.[11] You know, by doing like Gandhi of Europe, and joining the untouchables, the Democrats.[12] You know, only Gandhi was better off, because Gandhi was fairly well robed, but when Roosevelt went into the Democratic party, it didn't even have a loin cloth, at all. Well, now — when he, when he first went in there it looked like — you see, he wasn't going to draw any dividends. Did you notice the first part of Roosevelt's career up to a late year was spent in doing nothing but nominating Al Smith for president?

He'd always nominate Al, be it a breakfast, or a lunch, or a clambake, or a horse race, or even a Democratic party, why Roosevelt would nominate Al. You could wake him up in the middle of the night, I'll bet, and say, "Hey, wake up." And then right away, before he'd ask what you wanted, he'd nominate Al, you know. And he made some fine speeches nominating Al, because he was nominating a very fine man. And — but, of course, the country wasn't ready for democracy, because they wasn't broke yet.

But the minute the country went broke, they put out a yell—a siren call—for the old horse, you know, the old fire horse and wagon, and out it come, but not with Al. The man, our hero himself, was sitting on the seat. And he said to Al — he said, "Al, come on, give me a break this time. Let me have a crack at 'em." And boy, he took a crack at 'em.

You talk about sweeping the country; Roosevelt swept the country like a new toothpaste. He went around — why, say, they rushed up and voted for him just like buying tickets for some new Hollywood sex drama, you know. Oh, he went right over. Even the Roosevelt family, who up to then had only been eighth cousins, looked up an old register and found where there was a long lost brother.

Well, sir, then he — he does everything. He does everything right quick — different from that. Look at the Wickersham.[13] Wickersham worked two years and spent $2 million, and what did he do with his report? Turned in a report and says, "Now I won't be sure. I can't get the absolute truth, but I think there's a little drinking going on around the country."

And Roosevelt says, "I'll do all that in just three words. Just give me three words." He says, "Let 'em drink." That's all. He says,

"Let 'em drink." And he collected $10 million in revenue in the first two weeks, and if he'd had good beer he'd have paid the national debt by now.

Yes, sir, Wickersham — Wickersham turned in all a lot — a lot of figures, and a lot of statistics and things, and Al says, "No, just give me two figures. That's all I want, and I'll show you some results. Just give me three and two. Give me 3 and 2 percent, that's all."[14]

You know, commissions are fine, but they turn in — there's always a lot of data about something that ain't so good. You know what I mean? I mean, it's bad data. They're always — always investigating things that are bad, and the data is bad. Well, what's the use of having a lot of statistics and data on something that you can't do — well, it's kind like garbage: What's the use of collecting it if you ain't got nowhere to put it; you don't know what to do with it. Well, that's the way with commissions.

Now, Mr. Hoover, the most conscientious, fine, hard-working man I expect we've ever had in the presidency — and appointing a commission is not any crime. It's been considered a very fine way of handling anything, but it seems like a presidential commission don't get nothin' done. They don't really earn the breakfast that they give 'em at the White House the day they appoint 'em. That's what they don't do, you know.

And now, speaking of Mr. Hoover, I've got something I think would be of interest to you. I know it certainly was to me. The night before I left — flew back here from Los Angeles — I was talking to Mr. Harry Chandler of the *Los Angeles Times*, and he has — is a great friend of Mr. Hoover's, and Mr. Hoover had visited him at his ranch.[15] And I was very anxious to know the feelings of Mr. Hoover at this time. All of us are, you know. Here's this man come in here and created a sensation which was never — and you often wonder. Well now, I wonder how Mr. Hoover feels going out and this man coming in and doing all this. Is he kinda sittin' up there at Palo Alto and eatin' his heart out, and kinda figurin', "Well, I got a bad break, on this thing"? So everybody — and I asked Mr. Chandler, I said, "Mr. Chandler, that's the way I feel. Now how is it?"

And he told me, "Will, you'd be surprised. The man is absolutely cheerful and feeling fine, and he's in accord with a great many of the things that Mr. Roosevelt is doing." And he says he's just tickled to death that the country is — looks like there's a pick-up around, and he's pleased to death. And I knew — I know I was tickled when I heard that, and I just thought maybe you would all be too, because Mr. Chandler didn't tell it to me for any — didn't think I was going to go blathering around, but I just — but it was interesting to me to know, because—and we all are—because we know he did work hard for us, and we're tickled to death that he's feeling good about it.

You know, those men go about things different ways. Now Mr. — Mr. Hoover didn't get results because he asked Congress to do something. There's where he made a mistake. This fellow, Mr. Roosevelt, he just sends a thing up there every morning. He says, "Here — here's your menu, you guys. Sign it, you know what I mean, right here. Right here it is. What are you going to order?" And he tells them just what they're going to have. That's what he does, you know. Every morning he does that. All of them work different. They know how to work Congress. Now Mr. Roosevelt, he never — he never scolds them. You know, he kids them, that's what he does. He never scolds them, you know. Congress is really just children that's never grown up, that's all they are.

Well anyhow, this — let me look at my watch here. I got to see how much time. Whoa! Well anyhow, Mr. Coolidge handled the thing altogether different. Now there's a man. He handled Congress. He didn't pay no attention to 'em at all. He wouldn't mess with 'em, with Congress at all. He never messed with commissions either. If the fish wasn't bitin' in the Columbia River, and the Abyssinians wasn't practicin' birth control, Hoover never — I mean Mr. Coolidge never messed with them at all. He just let it go along. He knew how to handle the whole thing.

Seems funny me up here telling all this Democratic thing. You know any big company is owned by Republicans, 'cause the Democrats ain't got nothing, you know. And so I asked these people — I said, "How about it here? I'm going to get up and naturally say something complimentary about the Democrats."

So they told me — they says, "Well, it's all right, Will. We'd rather have been saved by a Republican, but we will take a Democrat anyhow." And that's the way it is. We'll be saved. We'll be saved by anybody. You know, I mean that's one good thing about a Republican: He'll just — you know, he wants to get his 6 and 8 percent. He don't care whether it was got through Mussolini, or Hitler, or Sister Aimee, or even the Kingfish, Huey Long, the old

Louisiana porcupine.[16] They'll be saved by him, if necessary, you know.

Now I understand Mr. Roosevelt — somebody told me was listenin' in. Now, Mr. Roosevelt, we've turned everything over to you. We've given you more power than we ever give any man — any man was ever given in the history of the world. We don't know what it's all about. We tried to run the country individually and collectively and along the Democratic line, but, boy, we gummed it so. So you take it and run it if you want to, you know, and deflate, or inflate, or complicate, or, you know, insulate. Do anything, just so you get us a dollar or two every now and again. So you're our lawyer. We're going to turn the whole thing over. Things are moving so fast in this country now that we don't know what it's all about. The whole country's cockeyed anyhow, and we're just appointing you, and you take it. We don't know what it's all about, but God bless you.

Good Gulf Show

August 13, 1933

HALSEY: The Senate by a two-thirds vote, ratifies treaties, amends the Constitution, and overrides the president's vote. A vote of seventy-four senators is more than two-thirds of the Senate. In receiving a greater endorsement than is necessary for such important work, we hope that Mr. Rogers will favor us with a definite announcement of his early return to a coast-to-coast network, regardless of the basis on which he might return.

ANNOUNCER: Thank you, Colonel Halsey.[1] Now folks, we speed west to pick up Will Rogers and Fred Stone and Will Rogers' alarm clock, broadcasting from Hollywood, California.[2]

DUET: [Rogers and Stone sing "We Are Two Dude Ranch Cowboys."]

ROGERS: Fred, that's what the radio wants, is good singing.

STONE: You bet that's what they want. That's why they been tuning in year after year hoping that some day they'd get it.

ROGERS: Well, they got it tonight.

STONE: Bill, you're not taking this singing that we just did serious, are you?

ROGERS: Well, any singin' that I do I'm taking serious. Yes, sir! What are you doing out here anyhow? Did you come out to California to go in the movies?

STONE: No, Bill, I don't want to go in the movies.

ROGERS: No? I never heard of anybody comin' to California that didn't want to go in the movies, you know. Didn't somebody ever

78

The Stone and Rogers families at the latter's Santa Monica ranch home in 1930. Left to right: Carol, Fred, Dorothy, and Allene Stone; Bill, Jr., Jimmy, Betty, Mary, and Will Rogers.

tell you that you looked like somebody that was in the movies? Looked like Durante or somebody?[3]

STONE: No. Bill. Somebody — you see a fellow bought a round-trip ticket out here and he didn't use it, and I came out here to use the ticket.

ROGERS: Come clear out here just to use the other end of a round trip ticket?

STONE: Well, he — he didn't use either end. You see, he just bought it to have a joke on California.

ROGERS: That was a good joke on California. That was a good joke on the railroads too, you know. I thought maybe you come out here with all these governors.[4] There's been a terrible mess of governors out here lately, and — they've been out here on their vacation.

STONE: Vacation? Whose vacation? Their states'? Say, Bill, you helped herd 'em, didn't you?

ROGERS: Did you — did you ever herd a governor?

STONE: Well, no and yes. I herded sheep once in Wyoming. It's just the same thing, ain't it?

ROGERS: Well, yes and no. Herding Democratic governors is just like herding sheep, but herding Republican governors is more like goats.

STONE: That was mighty fine of the Democratic ones to let those goats trail along with them that way. How many of them goats was there in there, Bill?

ROGERS: Well, there was only three. There was California's governor, Nevada's governor, and New Hampshire's.[5] You see, there's only really seven Republican governors in all captivity.

STONE: Well, why do they keep those seven? Shouldn't Democrats have those jobs? Does Post Office Farley know they're still in?[6]

ROGERS: Well, they just keep them kinder as an exhibit, I think. They just use Republicans nowadays mostly in the circuses and zoos. Say, now you're out here, I want to do all that I can to show you around on your little visit. I — if you want to go around and see all the movie people, I can introduce you to all of 'em that I know. I can have you meet everybody but Greta Garbo.[7] Of course, there is no such person as Greta Garbo.

80

STONE: No?

ROGERS: No. Didn't you know that? Why no, there's no Greta Garbo. Marlene Dietrich plays both parts.[8] Why everybody — anybody that knows anything knows that, you know. That's just a trade name, a fake name that they put over. Still there's people comin' out here lookin' for her. Now I'll have you meet Dietrich, you know. Would you like to see a woman with man's britches on?

STONE: No, Bill. If it's all the same to you, I'd rather meet this woman that's had so much — her name in the paper so much, Aimee McPherson.

ROGERS: Now look here, let me have you meet little Janet Gaynor, awful sweet little girl.[9] You know, Janet Gaynor, our little Lillian Harvey, you know, made that wonderful picture, "Congress Dances"[10]

STONE: Aw say, I've been to Washington, and I've seen them congressmen. I never saw one could dance yet.

ROGERS: Well, I mean European Congress, not our Congress.

STONE: Oh, I thought you meant our Congress. All they can do is sit their dances out and just talk.

ROGERS: Now looka here, I'll have you meet Clara Bow. Clara Bow, a real ranch girl. You'd like Clara, you know. She's a real cowgirl. Got callouses on her fingers just from milking.[11]

STONE: I don't like milk. I'm a 3 and 2 percent man. I want to see Aimee.

ROGERS: I'm goin' to have you meet Marie Dressler.[12] Great girl, Marie Dressler.

STONE: Say, I knew Marie Dressler before the Hollywood actor had his first swimming pool. Bill, I want to see Aimee.

ROGERS: Now looka here! Say, I'll show you Blue Boy, best actor in Hollywood.[13] Old Blue Boy. Took a prize at the Iowa State Fair two years. Real star. Old Blue Boy.

STONE: I've been looking at ham actors all my life.

ROGERS: But Old Blue Boy is the biggest ham what am.

STONE: Well, when a hog is the best actor in Hollywood I still want to see Aimee.

ROGERS: Now looka here, I'll have you meet our mayor.[14] You remember our ex-mayor that wouldn't touch the champagne to his lips and drink a toast to France? I'll have you meet him.

STONE: What's the matter with him? Couldn't he trust himself with it that close to his lips?

ROGERS: Peggy Joyce just landed here.[15] Do you want to meet Peggy?

STONE: I don't want to marry. Say, Bill, if you can fix it with Aimee I might do business with you.

ROGERS: Now looka here. All right, tonight's Sunday night. I'll tell you what I'll do. We'll go down to the tabernacle tonight. I tell you what you'll have to do. If you go down there she baptizes you. You know that, don't you? You got a bathing suit?

STONE: No, I haven't got a bathing suit.

ROGERS: Well, they'll — they'll just have to sprinkle you then, that's all. All you can be is a Methodist. Fred, you know, I was just thinking just now when I heard that music to that song. I — I hung around your shows so much in the early days that I really — you know, you had a wonderful song in one of the shows, an Italian one, where you used to have the hand organ and the monkey. What was that?

STONE: "Good-bye, John."

ROGERS: Yeah, that's it.

STONE: I played that show for three years. That was *The Red Mill*. Victor Herbert's.[16] Victor Herbert's music. I'll sing the verse for you.

SOLO: [Stone sings a verse of "Good-bye, John" with Rogers joining in the chorus.]

ROGERS: Fred! By golly, you know, I — I understand from the radio people and the Gulf people that have this program that three — three weeks from tonight you're going to put on parts of your wonderful shows that you used to have in the old days.

STONE: Yes, we've got 'em all cut down — down in condensed form, you know, and Dorothy and I are going to put them on for the radio audience, and I hope they like them.[17]

ROGERS: Aw sure, they'll like 'em. Gee whiz, that will be a great treat to hear those again, you know. And by the way, for the next two Sunday nights we must be sure to tune in and hear our old friend. Georgie Cohan's going to be on this program for the next two weeks.[18] Georgie Cohan is the greatest genius that the theater has produced in our lifetime. There'll never be another Georgie Cohan during our day. And he was great, you know. Now Fred, I'll tell you what you better do. You'd better tell these people what you're really doin' out here in California.

STONE: Well, Bill, you see, I came out here with a new code for broadcasting over the radio.

ROGERS: Oh, that's what we want to know about, these new codes. What is this?

STONE: Well, we're goin' to cut down on the hours.

ROGERS: How you going to do it?

STONE: Well, we're going to make the announcer quit tellin's his — what his product will do. He will tell who is going to pay for the program, you know, and then you've got to buy the stuff and find out for yourself what it will do.

ROGERS: That's a great idea. That's great. You know, then these mouthwash people can't go on there and tell you that it will cure dandruff.

STONE: No, that's it. You see, Bill, as it is now anything will do everything that the announcer can think of.

ROGERS: Why sure, I tuned in on some coffee the other night— some Chase's National Bank and somebody's coffee—and they told about it curing warts and moles, and liftin' a double chin, and reducin' Kate Smith.[19]

Yes sir, I — that's — that's — what were we going to do from there? I forget what we was gonna do there.

STONE: Well, I'll tell you. You know the comedians over the radio?

ROGERS: Yeah. Say, we got to do something about the comedians. I wanted to forget about them. What's the commode — code for shortening the comedians?

STONE: Well, we're going to cut out his puns.

ROGERS: Oh, yeah.

STONE: And when you cut out a radio comedian's puns, you cut his time down 90 percent.

ROGERS: Say, wait. Now what are you going to do about the crooners? What's the code for the crooners?

STONE: Well, we got a code to discourage the crooner.

ROGERS: You can't discourage a crooner. Crooning is a disease. It's brought on by an asthmatic condition of the thorax. And the minute the crooner sees a microphone he has a relapse.

STONE: Well, our code — our code will discourage him.

ROGERS: How are you going to discourage him?

STONE: We'll shoot him after the first verse.

ROGERS: Well, who's going to shoot him?

STONE: Well, the ex-soldiers. That gives them work and also gives work to the ammunition manufacturers.

ROGERS: Well now, what are you going to do about shortenin' the hours of these chambers of commerce speeches? And mayors' speeches over the radio? What's the code for them?

STONE: Well, we're going to have a microphone and it'll be dead, and they're going to talk into that. They'll talk to themselves.

ROGERS: That's great. What are you going to do with this fellow that tells all these lies on the radio — this Jack Pearl?[20] What you going to about him?

STONE: Well, we'll put him with the political speakers where he belongs.

ROGERS: Well, what are you going to do with this guy that comes on the radio every once in a while and says, "All I know is what I read in the papers," and blathers around about everything that he don't know anything about? What are you going to do to choke him off?

STONE: Well, we're going to let the people do with him the same as they've always done with him, tune him out the minute he starts.

ROGERS: Oh, hey, you run that in on me. Oh, that's what they've been doing with this guy. Say, I don't want to bring up anything unpleasant, but do you remember one summer on Long Island many years ago when you and I got ambitious and tried to put out a little circus and wild west show?

STONE: We didn't get very far with it, did we, Bill?

ROGERS: We got so far with it, we'd like to not get back with it, I remember that! All I can remember of that thing is a little song that we composed after we got the little show back home. Do you remember?

DUET: [Rogers and Stone sing "Travel, Travel Little Star."]

ROGERS: [Alarm clock rings.] Ah, there goes that alarm clock, and we had best verse — hadn't come yet.

STONE: Yeah, Bill, I want to see Aimee.

Good Gulf Show

June 17, 1934

ANNOUNCER: [Norman Brokenshire][1]

ROGERS: [applause]* Much obliged. I didn't want — I sure didn't want you all to be thinking that I wasn't going to be here tonight, you know. I was late last time, but I—but I've — I've been here since the studio opened this morning, today. Opened up, you know. That hurts me very, very much. I — I want to do, you know, because that kind of hit me in a very soft spot, being late and missing anything and all. In all my little career in theatrical, in amusement business, starting back way back in 1901 — that is, if you can — whether you'd call mine amusement or annoyance business — in 1901. I worked my way on a cattle boat from Buenos Aires, South America, over into — I got over into Durban, South Africa, and messed around there and worked on a ranch a little bit, and finally joined a little show called "Texas Jack's Wild West Show," way back in 1901.

From then on up — for that thirty-three years ago, I can truthfully say that I never did miss a show in my life, you know. And so even being late, you know, that kinda gets me. I've got to a lot of shows patched up from games. I've been all messed up. One time I got hit in the lip. That's a bad place for me to get hit, and — but I had plenty of lip, though. Patched up from games and things. Flew in all in planes through the night and everything else to make a show, and very seldom even ever been late and all. So I didn't do it.

---

*The tapes of the broadcasts contained, not unexpectedly, much applause and laughter from Rogers' audience. To save space and to improve the flow of the material, the editor chose to include in the text only those references to audience reaction that had a direct bearing on Rogers' monologue or that would have left his remarks unclear if the reference were omitted.

The whole thing come about — I don't know, it was just dumbness on my part. I hadn't broadcasted in a few weeks, and I come on for this little series. I'm on for five now, and then off, and then on again in the fall. And I don't know what got it in my head that our little program run from five-thirty to six. But that's what it was — see? And I come driving in here—come from the theater over there where I'm playing in Hollywood—come drivin' in here just taking my time, and the manager pounced on me. He says, "Come on in here." Well, I didn't know what he meant. I was pretty near half an hour early, seemed to me like. And he rushed me in here, and I thought there was some earthquake or something he wanted me to announce, or somethin', you know. I shouldn't call it that, but I mean whatever they call 'em out here. And I thought it was that he wanted me to announce. And so I sure want to apologize, and I ain't gonna be late no more. I slept here last night. Boy, I've been layin' here like a dog at a rat hole ever since this thing opened, you know.

Now I wanted to come out here tonight and thank you people. The hall is full here, and I wanted to thank you all for — for coming to see my broadcast. I spoke to the manager, and I found out that they didn't come — Jimmy Durante on the Chases and Sanborn Hour has just finished, and they're all hang-overs from his show. And I says to the manager — I says, "Well, gee, it's nice of them to stay."

He says, "No, the Hall of Fame Hour goes on next, and they're waiting for it."

Now I find out that the people that are here — they're just, you know, they're just kinda killing time between shows, and they're really just using me as an intermission. That's all I am.

Well anyhow — so you listeners who know me, you'll excuse me if I explain to Jimmy's crowd—because this is Jimmy's audience—who I am. Rogers is my name, and I'm the grandfather of Buddy Rogers, and — and my great-great-great grandfather founded Rhode Island—Rogers Williams, and — and I work for the Gulf Oil people, you know, the Gulf Oil, and don't get me mixed up with the Texas Oil.[2] That's Ed Wynn.[3] The Texas Oil and the Gulf Oil are — I mean Texas is on the gulf, and the Gulf is down by Texas, and you're liable to geographically get 'em mixed up.[4] But if you can't tell the difference between the Texas and the Gulf, why Wynn is funnier than I am. So you can always tell the difference that way, you know.

And then Wynn — it isn't supposed to say anything about a competitor's product or anything on the radio, you know. You're breaking a terrible thing. But I know the Gulf people — I know the Texas people and they're all awful nice, and I know Wynn. I've known him for many years, since the *Follies* days. He's all right. And the Gulf people that I work for are very nice, if you're on time. And so, anyway — now Wynn — Wynn — and I want to thank the orchestra that kept them there. I heard some Hollywood music last time.

And Wynn sells Fire Chief gas, you know. There's room — there's room for both competitors, you know. Wynn's outfit sells Fire gas, you know, but there's an awful lot of people that want gas that are not going to a fire. So there must be — there must be a place for us somewhere. You know, in fact — I don't want to knock — I don't want to knock Texas and the gas people and Wynn and them, but, you know, did you ever have a cop run up to you and say, "Hey, what's the idea? Pull over there. Where do you think you're going? To a fire?" Well, that's when you got Wynn's gas in there. See? Now our gas, you can't do — you know what I mean. You're within the law, you see? Because a cop can't catch you.

Jimmy, you got a nice bunch. Thanks. Jimmy Durante's up here, and I want to tell you, you got a nice bunch here. Now here's another thing, and the reason I mention who I'm working for is this reason, because *Variety*, that magazine, it's what — it's what *Time* is to readers, and you know, *Variety* is to listeners. And it knows everything that goes on in the air, you know. *Variety* is better informed than us columnists think we are. And it held some kind of a thing not long ago — I bet Jimmy got one of 'em, too. Any of us that broadcast, we got it. It held a kinda *Literary Digest* vote all over the country, and it found that about half of one percent of the people knew who their favorites were broadcasting for, you know. That was funny, you know. Didn't know who it was for, see?

You see, people have gotten so expert in tuning out — you know what I mean? You know, when the actor finished they can tune out so quick that no announcer can get in. You know what I mean? Well, that's just expert tuning, you know, on the part of a listener. Even "Amos 'n Andy," as wonderful as they are — they give a list of how many people, you know, who worked for who and why and which, see? And "Amos 'n Andy," the daddy of all of us and will be for — when we're old men we'll be listening to "Amos 'n Andy." God bless 'em. And even "Amos 'n Andy," there was people listenin' to them that didn't even have a toothbrush.[5] You know what I mean? Not a one. You know, 'cause they had never waited long enough to hear Bill Hays tell 'em to get one, you know.[6]

All of those — and Cantor, a lot of 'em had gone right from Cantor's broadcast, right across the street to the Atlantic and Pacific Tea Company and got tea, you know what I mean?[7] Went right over there. They didn't know he was messing around for this coffee outfit. And all of those — Ben Bernie — there's been just dozens of them that sit all night drinking Anheuser-Busch listenin' to Ben, you know.[8] Drinkin'. They'd even drink gin and listen to him.

And Winchell. You know, Winchell, because he kept tellin' who all was going to have a baby and all that, everybody was under the impression that he was broadcasting for some maternity outfit——

So you never know, you know? That's the listeners. They tune out so quick on us. Now a lot of folks think — have always thought that I was on here with some mixture of Beech-Nut and Bull Durham. Sort of a goulosh made up of the two. But it ain't. Even Roosevelt — even as great a man as our president, Mr. Roosevelt, when he's broadcast, they thought he was on for the Republican National Committee. So that's what we want to get at. I'm for the Gulf — the Gulf Oil Company.

Now let's see what else — but some of 'em don't do that. The other night Graham McNamee give us an example in that, during the fight. During the fight, you know — right during the fight, he says, "This fight is brought to Prima Carnera by Max Baer and the Goodrich Tire Company."[9] Brought right to 'em, you know what I mean. And he got him down one time. He got him down. He said, "He's down. He's down. They're fighting. They're down. They're down. I'll tell you who's down, who has got the other one down, when you buy a set of tires." By golly, it looked like we was going to have to buy some — buy some tires to find out who was down. But that's all right. I mean those men pay lots of money for that, and it's good to let 'em know who all it was.

But I tell you, speaking of that, with all due — of course, Baer had all this wonderful acclaim and all, but we always joked about the poor Italian having such big feet. We said nothing can be bigger than that Italian's feet. Now you ever see them? They're terrible big, you know. But I tell you, boys, I swear his heart was as big as his feet. You know, it really was. He has a great heart, and he put up a very, very brave, wonderful fight. And the reason — and the reason Max won by a technicality is that there just was not room in the ring to knock him plum down. So he was leaning. And the meeting between Mussolini — everybody's wondered what the meeting between Mussolini and Hitler was.[10] It was to see, you know, since Baer won, you know, — maybe we're wrong about these Jewish people. Better let them come back or something. If they can fight that good, we'd better let them in again, you know.

Now that's about all the news we got. You know, we prayed last Sunday, we all did, that Congress would adjourn. I asked you, I said, "Will you help Mr. Roosevelt?" Well, we come pretty near gettin' it. We thought we was going to get rid of them last night, but the devil was with Congress as usual, so they're still with us this morning. If you can do anything at all, folks, for little Finland — if you meet — if you're driving down the street and a man is hitchhiking and he looks like a foreigner, if he's a Finlander pick him up, will you, because they're the only one that paid us anything.[11] And carry him along—— [12]

And Mr. Cordell Hull.[13] You know we couldn't get any gold out of England or France — we couldn't get any silver. We finally made it silver. Pay in silver; it's only worth half as much or a third as much. They wouldn't pay that. And finally our secretary of state, Mr. Cordell Hull, sent 'em a note last week and says, "For gosh sake, will you just pay in anything. I mean any old clothes, old monocles, spats, dress suits, silk hats, anything, you know. Old worsters, English fox hounds, or anything you got. You know, there's a thing that would be worth something, English fox hounds. They're very good." And they wouldn't even pay us in nothing. So now we're thinking up some other thing to send them, and all. Well, that's fine.

Now I'd like to end the broadcast on a good hearty laugh, if you all will all join. And I've got some news for you, and we'll end it on a good hearty laugh. This is Father's Day. [laughter/applause]

90

Good Gulf Show

June 24, 1934

ANNOUNCER:

ROGERS: [applause] Much obliged. I — you know, I'm not going to be late today. I'm — I've got a room here now at this studio. Yes sir, I'm sleeping right here. I got up one of those poles like these firemen have. The minute I hear this program come on, I slide right down, you know. I ain't going to miss no more of these, you know. I was late one day, you all that don't — might not know it, and you'd be surprised though at the amount of people that wrote me and told me that that was an awful good program up to the time I got here, and — and there's kind of a movement on to have me late again — see if they can't increase the lateness of it.

You know, it's hard to tell just what to — what to talk about over the radio. You know, you folks you talked to and you lectured to and you begged to and you even preached and prayed to to buy something, you know, every minute of the day, you know. There's "Buy a Sledge Hammer Hour," "A Rat Trap Hour," "Husbands Don't Shoot Your Wife Hour," and there's everything. I guess — I bet there ain't no nation in the history of the world that, you know, that — was ever so constantly and perpetually preached to and, you know, and advised. You know what I mean. I mean, and told what to do.

And it's hard — it's awful hard to think up something new to talk to you about. Honest. But I'm going to speak to you about something that hasn't been brought up. I mean in public; it hasn't been brought up in public for years. It's awful hard to find that, but I believe I've found it. I'd love to say a few words for the Republican party.

91

For those of you who are not familiar, you know, familiar — it's
spelled R-E-P-U-B-L-I-C-A-N, as in Republican. Your fathers and
your grandfathers, they'll know. Go home and ask them, and they'll
tell you something about it. The reason I know it's not been spoken
of is that you can't speak of something unless you think of it, you
know. And you can't think of it unless something happens to bring
the name up. I don't know how I ever come — I never will know
how I got to thinking of it. I got to thinking of the Johnstown flood
and the Galveston tidal wave and the Chicago fire, and, I don't
know, my thought just naturally drifted to the Republicans.
[laughter] No, now wait a minute. Not that they were responsible
for the above events. I don't say they were responsible, but there
has been people that has always been suspicious of them.[1]

And now, where has the party gone? Where has the Republican
party gone? You know, such extermination has — is really unparalleled in history.[2] It's never been recorded. History does record
that — you know, history says from readin' about 'em — I read
all the papers, and history says that they was a rather kindly people and — and were good to their young and — never war-like.
They never was war-like at all. In fact, they'd step aside and egg
the Democrats on till the Democrats would start a war. See? And
then when it come time to pay 'em for it, why the Republicans
would come in and say the Democrats started it, you know.

And they was a thrifty race, too, you know, and they controlled
most of the money. But they had a certain foresight, you know,
and they'd take over the reins of government about the time that
things were going good. See? That's when they'd come in. Then
when they saw that pestilence and famine was about to overtake
the land, they'd slip it back to the Democrats. The Democrats —
now we get to the Democrats.

Now the Democrats were a kind of a semi-heathen tribe. They were
what you'd call a nomad race, and they could live on little because
they'd never had anything else. But they don't live on little when
they get in office; don't forget that. Their greatest trait — the
greatest thing to recommend the Democrats is optimism and humor,
you know. You've got to be optimist to be a Democrat, and you've
got to be a humorist to stay one. Well, anyway, well, the Democrats,
they had a certain native shrewdness, you know. That they figured
out that the only way to get the money away from the Republicans
was to put on a bounty, or as the Latins call it, a tax on 'em. You

see a bounty or tax is the thing you pay if you have anything, and if you don't have anything you don't pay it, naturally. Well, the Democrats knowing the Republicans had it and knowing that they didn't, they put it on. See?

The theory was that while the Republicans are smart enough to make money, the Democrats are smart enough to get in office every two or three times a century and take it away from 'em, you know. Sure, they get in there every once in a while. It's a long time in-between drinks, but they get in there and lick the Republicans for what they've got.

And do these Republicans howl when this bounty comes due. Boy, they howl like an old sea bear that lost her cub, you know.[3] And the Democrats, they're heartless. If they can get their hands in a Republican's pocket to get it out, is just like trying to pull a badger out of a hole, you know. Now the — so the whole thing is just a revolving wheel, our politics is. One party gets in, and through a full stomach and a swelled head, it oversteps themselves and out they go. And then the other one gets in, and that's all there is to it. Well, that's the way it should be, I guess, for there'd be no living with one of 'em if they didn't know there was another one in existence, you know. So I guess that's why we've got to have two of 'em to keep the other one kind of scared or something.

Now the Republicans admit that they're rich and that they're the smarter ones and can make money faster, so it's a good thing the old Democrats come along and level 'em off every once in a while. If they are so smart, why let 'em go out and make some more because they're going to have to pretty soon.

So they tell me that quite a few places around over the country there's a scattering of Republican camp fires. You know, they're kind of — they're coming out of the caves and hidden valleys, directors' — you — directors' meetings and coupon-clipping rooms, and — and they're sharpening up their campaign speeches to try and get back into the old teepees and post offices. They'll get a few. They'll get a few back on the congressional swindle sheet at the coming election this fall. Yeah, the Republicans is going to win back quite a few seats, but it won't do much good. Because when they get to Washington, why Roosevelt will invite 'em up to the White House for dinner, and he'll talk a lot of homely chat with 'em and show how human he is — and somethin' they haven't been used to in their party, and — and I bet you everyone of 'em will go right out of there and right up — right up to the Capitol and vote for his policies quicker than the Democrats will.

So that about concludes the bedside story of the two great political parties which we work night and day to support. To show that we get along better without 'em, since Congress adjourned last Monday — Congress adjourned, and business has jumped up like it's been shot. Honest, the whole thing, it just went up like that. Market, everything — everything went up. Everybody's feeling better. If they had of adjourned before they'd a met, I expect we'd have been the most prosperous nation in the world.

Now this morning we read a lot of war news about this Paraguayan and Bolivian war down there.[4] I want — along with all this tragedy, there's some kind of humor about that. I've been down in that country many, many years ago. Worked down on ranches. And then I flew over it since then. It's an uninhabited country in between these two nations. And the men — you know, and it's terrible, just swamps and awful country. And the men that's been lost in there has been lost trying to live in the country. You know, the two armies. They've tried — they've died trying to win it back for their side, you know what I mean. Not from war. They've just died trying to stay in there while the war was on. I think that's funny. There's very little humor in war, but that struck me, I guess. And I think if one side would just say to the other, well, surrender. You know, and say, "Well, we lost the war, and you can have the country. But one of the articles of surrender is that you have to live in."

I bet the other side would refuse to be the winner. I bet you they would. They'd say, "No, we'll keep on fighting till you win it."

I didn't get here in time to hear my good friend, Jimmy Durante, that was on ahead of me. I imagine he had something about Mr. Dillinger's birthday.[5] I didn't know it. It was Friday, and I didn't know it, and I didn't know — pretty near all the police knew where to send things. They all sent — and I don't know what Jimmy — I wouldn't known anything about it. I read it in *Who's Who*.

You know the *Literary Digest* has been running another one of those votin' things. There's millions of people in this country now, you know — there's millions of 'em that don't even go to the polls any more. They just wait till the *Digest* starts something and just vote on it. They think that's the main one, you know. They don't know the other one is the one, you know.

94

Well, the Digest has been running one asking if you are pleased with Mr. Roosevelt's first year in office. Now I was reading it, and Keene, New Hampshire, — a town in New Hampshire named Keene, New Hampshire, — 130 votes was in favor of what he had done during the past year and 129 was not. That was pretty close — one vote, see? Well, that showed that Mr. Roosevelt had fed 130 in the town. And 129 in the town were afraid they were going to have to pay for the other 130 being fed. So that was that vote now.

I mustn't forget the program — this program because it comes to you from the Gulf Oil. The making of Gulf Oil, it's an old Indian secret. You know, it's an old Indian secret they got from my Cherokee ancestors down in Oklahoma. It's been handed down from Pocahontas clear on down through to Charlie Curtis, and I got it from Charlie Curtis. It's an old — an old Indian remedy. Gulf Oil is made from roots and herbs and may possibly have, I don't know, it may possibly have a little oil in it. I don't know. [Alarm clock rings.]

Oh Lord, I had a lot of other things here. Hey, wait a minute. Well, good-bye. So long.

Good Gulf Show

July 8, 1934

ANNOUNCER:

ROGERS: You notice the time wasn't taken up by the usual amount of applause. There ain't nobody here to applaud. You know, an awful lot of our letters that we get from people, they seem to kind of resent the audience that is present. They say, "We want to hear. We don't want to hear them laugh and applaud."

Now the question arises: Is it better to broadcast with or without an audience? Of course, I'm speaking now from the comedian's angle, not the singer or the band's or public speaker or anything, but the comedian's. What is the public's reaction to a comedian with or without an audience? Do they want to sit quietly at home and listen to what we have to say and figure out for yourself whether it's funny, or amusing, or mildly entertaining, or boring, or whatever it is? Or do you folks want to take your cue from an invisible audience that you don't see — take your cue from them — them, you know, when to laugh? In other words, do you need a prompter to tell you?

Now from the comedian's standpoint, we like the audience.[1] It helps us, you know, and gives us a little encouragement, and Lord knows, we need it. But does it bore you? That's what we want to know. For you're the one that has to do the listening, and you should have it served to you like you want it, whether you want it raw, medium, or well done, or whatever you want. You see, any comedian has dozens of tricks and mannerisms and facial antics that we can get a laugh on from an audience that can see 'em, but it's naturally lost to you. And about half the time you wonder what the laugh is all about. You say, "Am I dumb? Did I miss

96

somethin'?'' Well, maybe you did, but it was because you just couldn't see it, that was all. We was maybe turning a somersault, or wiggling our ears, or thumbing our nose, or putting our big toe in our mouth, or doing some other marvelously clever trick which we use in a pinch.

And then, too, most comedians are — well, they're — they're just funny to look at, you know. They have some odd defect of the face or just plain homely. Unfortunately, I'm about the only one that's not. Penner or Wynn, Pearl, Benny, and Cantor, in fact any of them that you can mention — well, you have to laugh when you just look at 'em.[2] They're just odd looking. While with me you would say, "Who is that distinguished looking man walking toward the microphone?" While they command immediate laughter by simply doing nothing, I command a kind of a hushed attention, rather an awe, you know. Immediately you say, "There's a man with a message." While their's is an infectious laugh or smile, mine is — mine is of learning, of culture, of quiet dignity — you would say, "And there is a Brain Trust."[3]

Now here's another secret about the studio audience: It's people that particularly like you. You know what I mean. It's like — it's our audience, and sometimes they'll be quite a few in there who are not our own kinfolk, and they have to laugh, you know. They're generally what we call "over-good." They laugh at the serious parts for fear they won't be invited again. Then, too, it's not fair to a theater to be giving a free show in competition to them. If an audience is going to be used, a charge should be made and every cent of the proceeds go to an out-of-work actors' charity, or some equally good cause. I would suggest that one.

But you all argue it out, and then you let me know. See? Wait a minute. Don't let me know. Send the letter — don't send me any letters. I don't answer mail anyhow. Even if it's good mail, I don't even answer it. A night letter to Mrs. Rogers when I'm flying in some distant country is about the extent of my correspondence anyhow. But you write to these folks that's puttin' on this racket. It's — it's Gulf Oil Company, and — I guess it's in care of the National or is this the Colum——? No, no. This is the National. Here's an NBC right in front of me. NBC—No Body Cares—and those are mighty good letters. Nothin' anybody says over the radio today is remembered tomorrow, and it's just as well. No Body Cares. In fact, whatever you say tonight, you can come back on tomorrow night and deny it in case anybody does remember it, but they don't. But it's the greatest thing in the world, and it's the greatest invention of our lifetime. And it's the only thing that I ever knew of — the radio is the only thing ever invented that didn't knock anybody out of any work.

Now you write to your nearest National Broadcasting Company in New York City, in care of the Gulf Oil Company, and let us know if you want your applesauce straight or an audience, see? If you[4] want it straight or with an audience for a chaser. Remember, it's easier on us with a bunch of yes-folks. In fact, I wouldn't mind hearing a little laugh right now. But remember, you are the ones that bought your agony boxes that you're listenin' to, and your word is Roosevelt with us. So write your nearest congressman. In fact, come to think of it, print it. Don't write it. You got all summer to argue it out.

I'll be with you in — about next October for a mess of about fifteen of these intellectual barbecues. Having finished two pictures and a stage play and finally having caught a calf that I been ropin' at between times all summer, I feel that I'm about ready to settle down and do a little steady work. So I'm taking my young with me, and we're going to go clear around the world. I'm headin' for Siberia by way of Honolulu, Japan, Manchuria, and then across the Trans-Siberian Railroad. That's 6,000 miles, the longest railroad in the world. They say there's some planes flying — maybe take a plane and fly clear across there — into Moscow and Leningrad. And then I'm going to find Finland. If Finland can go to the trouble of paying us, I certainly can go to take time out and try to find where they are. If they're as honest as I think they are, I'm not going to book any further than there. I'm just going to stay there and run around with Nurmi.[5] Do you know who Nurmi is? Well, ask your sporting writer. No, on second thought, maybe you'd better not ask him either. He might not know.

Well, then I'm going to Garboland. I'm going to Garboland, and Norway, and Minneapolis, and Denmark, and Germany, weather permitting. The Rogers Commission to Russia is composed of old man Rogers and two hongry-looking sons. Mrs. Rogers accompanies us. She goes with us till the travelin' gets rough and we run out of luxuries, and then we lose her. I think that's going to be the Imperial Hotel in Tokyo will be her last stand. Siberia, and those wolves, and those whiskers, and those long names don't appeal to her. I've got a daughter, too, but she's working. In fact, that's

Will Rogers on the air probably for the Gulf Oil Company between 1933 and 1935. Note the bare lecture, clear evidence of the spontaneity of Rogers' broadcasts.

how we're all able to make this trip, on account of her being workin'.

If I run into Mr. Roosevelt over around Honolulu, maybe I can get him to go on with me. Say, wouldn't he be a great guy to travel around with? He'd be wonderful, you know — just stop every once in a while and let him catch a fish, and everything would be all right. He'd be in good humor and go on. If I can get him to travel with me all through Russia, he'll come back with more ideas than General Hugh Johnson and Rex Tugwell combined.[6]

This is a — it's a secret mission, and when I get back the Senate will investigate me to see if they can find out why I went. It's a commission to end friendly relations between nations. All the others have been good-will tours, and they have been so successful that no two nations are speaking to each other, you know. So mine — I'm calling it a "bad-will" tour. If we've got a friend anywhere, I'm going to see that he don't stay that way long. I'm going to impart facts to him and let him know just what we are. See?

This war with Japan that a lot of our statesmen had already arranged for us this past year, that seems to have kinda fallen down.[7] I think I can get over there and hurry that on. Not a bit of reason why these two nations shouldn't be fightin' right now. It's kind of an off year, and most everybody's layin' off. They have no reason to fight, so that's the best time to have a war. In fact, that's the only time they do have it. If I get over there, I think I can kind of scare that up. My commission will be ready to report to the radio audience in October.

Next October I'll be back here and ready to talk to you. My report will be just as long and just as uninteresting as the Wickersham report was. The reason I'm going to travel so much in Russia and go all over Russia, down the Black Sea and all around, see those big experimental farms that the farmers are supposed to be working on over there, and all that — the reason I'm — you know, Russia today — is they're supposed to have the greatest experiment — to be trying the greatest experiment in the world—outside of us—so that's why I'm going over there.

Now remember, write to the Gulf Oil Company. Remember, write to them, in care of the Democratic National Committee or the National Broadcasting, either one, and let us know, you know, whether you want to hear a lot of laughs and applause or want to hear — anything you want. You're the boss. Anyway you want your radio and all. And good-bye and good luck to you. I hope you all have a fine summer, and I'm going to see you next——[Alarm clock rings.] Oh, here — wait a minute. I wasn't through here yet. I'm going to see you — I'm going to see you next — next fall when I get back with a lot of news. Good-bye and good luck.

Good Gulf Show

March 31, 1935

ANNOUNCER: [Harry Von Zell][1]

ROGERS: [applause] Much, much obliged. Excuse me for keeping my
hat on, but I'm gettin' just a little gray and I don't want it to show
over the radio. Just one or two hairs in there that got mixed in.
Well sir, I've been off the air here — I've been off, I believe, it's
been about seven weeks. I went off purposely to see if I couldn't
give the country a chance to pick up a little. And I've been off seven
weeks, and — and it don't take much lookin' to see that it ain't
done much since I've been gone. So I decided to come back on
again and see if can't get it started up again.

The whole — not only has the whole world — the whole civilized
world — has degenerated in the last seven weeks, but well, not
only the whole civilized world, but the Democratic party, too.
That's quite an admission.

Now what all has gone on in all that time. Well, while I had my
head turned and wasn't on the radio, Hitler broke out on me. I
thought I had him covered. Hitler broke out on me and tore up the
Versailles Treaty.[2] It wasn't a good treaty, but it was the only one
they had. And he tore it up. They was a year making it, and he
tore it up in about a minute. And they had been about a year messin'
it all — fixing it all up, all these nations. We got in on the signing
of it. We got nothin' out of the treaty, outside of the pen that we
signed with, was all that we got. But all the other nations—— How
it come to take 'em so long to sign it up was they was dividin' up
the islands — in the possessions—Germany's possessions—the
islands, and the colonies, and all around. And we didn't get any.
We said, "Well, we went in for nothing." And they all agreed that

102

that was a good idea, and we got out with it — in good shape. No, not in good shape. But, we got out with it anyhow.

So that was that. And then — now — last week England — England sent a delegation over to talk with Mr. Hitler, and see if they couldn't get some other understanding with him, and they thought — but England didn't get to say a word. Hitler talked all day, and — and it wasn't in English, and England didn't know any more when they went home than they did when they got there. So they didn't get much sense out of that. And now — what they was tryin' to do was to see if they couldn't get him in to make some other arrangements about — to see if they wouldn't do something about the treaty. So now they went on, and another man named Mr. Eden from England has gone on to talk to Russia.[3] They're going to talk to Russia. None of the nations — and France is going to talk to Russia. No nation don't like Russia, and they don't like communism and all that, but they would use them in case a war come around.

That's one good thing about European nations: They can't hate you so bad they wouldn't use you. Well, they're up there and they've told Russia, says, "Now, you're communistic, and you believe in dividing up everything." And they said, "Ordinarily, we don't. We don't believe in it. But it looks like we're going to have a war over here and we would like to split it with you boys." So they're — so they're going to let Russia in on a good thing case it shows up.

Well, that's that. Well now, they'll be coming over here pretty soon. You see, they're rushing around now, signing up. Just like a baseball team. You know. All of Europe — they don't know who's going to be partners in the next one, so everybody's rushin' around to get some new signatures on the thing, you know. I bet Dillinger didn't have as much trouble signing up his gang as some of them over there do. They're rushin' around — says, "Who'll help out!" And they'll be coming over here with their propaganda pretty soon. You know, there'll be delegations come and say, "We didn't come to persuade you or anything, but in case civilization is attacked, why, where do you boys stand?"

Well, we better tell 'em, "Well, — if civilization hasn't done any more than it has since the last war, why we're agin it. So we'll just stay with the side that's against civilization. We tried it the other way last time." Well, they will. They'll be messin' around over here.

103

Now that's over. That happened over in Europe while I had my head turned and wasn't on the radio and payin' much attention. And what else happened? Oh, darn it if Mr. Hoover don't deliver a message while I'm gone! Now — Hoover — yeah, I turn around and he breaks — Hoover and Hitler broke out on us.

Well, Mr. Hoover, well you start out in California — I have the greatest regard in the world for him and he's a good personal friend of mine, and I used to ask him, says, "Mr. Hoover, do you think Stanford is going to beat Northwestern in this game this fall?" He lives right there. And my boy goes to Stanford and we have a great interest there and everything, and says, "Do you think——"⁴

And he'd say, "I'm not in politics, and I can't be quoted." He never — he never said a word, and all at once I have my head turned and he broke out on me.

It didn't bother me as much as it did the Republicans. It seemed to upset his own party more than it did the Democrats, because there is a certain bunch in the Democrat — in the Republican party that thinks that Mr. Hoover perhaps wouldn't be the logical candidate. They feel that they would be, I imagine. So they think that it kinda embarrassed the party to have him speak at this time. I read the message. It was a little hard to read as most of his are—kind of hard to get into—but I kind of gathered from just reading between the lines that he really wasn't in a hundred percent accord with all that was going on in Washington. That was just a rough idea that I got from it. I don't know. But they forget that Mr. Hoover, being the last candidate is still the nominal leader of the Republican party. They forget that, these other Republicans do, and that he's the one. He had a perfect right to, and now he's got 'em stirred up. He's got 'em all messed up, and the Republicans haven't been so excited in a long time. They're going to have some kind of a convention out around Kansas City.⁵ They're going to meet in there and start some devilment of some kind. I don't just know what it is.

Mussolini — I had no more than turned my head than he jumped down, and he couldn't find nobody to pick on but Ethiopians down in — he's gone down in some country called Abba-Dabba, or somewhere.⁶ He's off down there. Seems that the Allies — that's an old promise the Allies made that guy, too, right along during the Versailles Conference. When they says, "Now, Mussolini, don't you claim nothin', and then if you ever want anything in Africa our heads will be turned.'' So he remembered that. That guy never forgets anything. So he's off down in there.

Astor — we was gittin' along pretty good in Washington, and Astor come along with his yacht, and the president just can't overlook that yacht when it comes messin' by.[7] So he crawled on it. What he does on Astor's yacht, Lord, heaven only knows. He's never caught — a fish on there yet. But he will get on that yacht. He will get on that yacht and go somewhere.

Well, let's see, what other devilment have we had. The states — a lot of you states have had a lot of trouble during the last seven weeks because your legislatures have met. There's nothing will upset a state economic condition like a legislature. It's better to have termites in your house than the legislature. Well, they're in there trying to figure out ways and means of get — of knockin' some money out of you some way.

Well, let's see. Is there anything else you all could think of that — that's happened? Now — but all that's happened. So I come back now, and we're going to see if we can't get the thing sort of straightened up. I think that's about all, I guess. So long. [applause]

You all through? You want any — you want any — I don't know what this thing is. All right. [applause]

I'm supposed to be through. I'm supposed to be through. I'm just talking to you folks. I think — I don't think the radio gang is on there with us now, and we can have a few words here among ourselves. 'Cause radio audiences take these things very seriously. They think you should have everything all prepared and all written out, you know, just what you're going to say and all.

Well sir, I went down — I'll tell you all about it. I went down to Washington. I come back here, and I went down to Washington last week. I go down there every once in a while. The Senate is my particular hobby. And I go down and see them, and go in — drop in the old joke factory there and see what the boys — see what the boys is doin'. So I went in there. I got out of there the day before yesterday; Friday, I think it was. Went down there, and I always drop in to see Mr. Garner.[8] My office is in the vice-president's office. I go in there and leave my hat and everything. And then I work out of there. He's a great fellow, Jack Garner. I tell you he's a fine human fellow. I wish — I just wish that I knew and felt in my own heart that every man down in Washington that had anything to do with our government was as level-headed and had as much common sense as Vice President Garner. Now he isn't shootin' off around, making a lot of speeches around like a lot of these others. But if he did want to speak, I imagine he would tell a few things.

Well, I get in there — I get in there, and then I go up to the gallery. Well, I got up in the gallery to see the boys operate. See? Well, I got up in there and there wasn't much doin'. Pretty quiet; Huey wasn't in there. So I went in there, and I'm sittin' in there and Harrison from Mississippi, another dear old friend of mine.[9] Pat come in, and he's speaking some Mississippian, and he comes over and shakes hands. I've known him for many years. And he's one of the big leaders in there now. So Pat come over and chatted with me, and he excused himself and said, "I got to go down on the floor and put in a bill." He says, "I'm going to put in a new NRA bill."[10]

I says, "My Lord, are you going to start that thing again?" You know. I said, "You'd better change the name of it. You know what I mean, because there's been a lot of trouble over the NRA." And I said, "Pal, if I was going to put in a new bill, I believe I'd pick out three other letters and put it in under an assumed name."

But anyhow, he went down there. When he went away, why then in comes Senator Capper.[11] Senator Capper, a dear old friend of mine, a Republican from Kansas—a Republican but a gentleman. A rare combination! Well, Senator Capper he comes up, and me and Capper we was sittin' there talking, you know, farming and everything. He's always doing something for the farmer out there. He's got a lot of farm journals — mostly writes editorials for 'em, but he's a mighty good old man and has the farmers' interest at heart. And he was telling me about the dust storms. That's another thing that come up since I was off the air, that dust storm. Poor farmer spent a lifetime fixin' his farm and everything, goes down and looks down at it, and it's up above him. But they're going to fix that. The administration is sending Mr. Tugwell out now to see about, stop that wind out there.

Well anyhow, I got to — there ain't no sense to what I'm doin'. I got to get back up there. I'm sittin' up in there with Capper. Capper says, "Will, would you like to have lunch with me?"

Well, I said yes. It was the best offer I'd had up to then. And I said, "Yes, I'll go."

He said, "All right, we'll get the vice president."

And I said, "Well, if you get him that will make it worthwhile."
You've got to be careful who you go out with down there. So we
went down, and he dug up two or three others and went down,
and we went on, and we had five or six, and we all went down
in the Senate dining room and have lunch. And Nye was there.
You know, Nye that runs all this ammunition thing.[12]

And I don't think I'm betraying any confidence when I tell you
that Mr. Nye tells me that out of this ammunition thing they're going to have — introduce a new bill to take the profits out of war.
And he assured me that they was gettin' it ready and that they was
going to have it ready in a few days. And, so he said that's what
they was going to do. They're gonna put in a bill where in case
there is a war that nobody will be allowed to make any — any profit from it. And I think that's a great idea, and I know everybody
does. I think it would be still a better idea and would keep us out
of a lot of war if they put in the bill in there that not only couldn't
we make any out of our own war, but we couldn't make any out
of anybody's war. If we knew we couldn't sell anything to any other
nation while they was at war, we'd never get in it. That's just a
little idea of mine. That ain't in the bill. Too much sense to that
to ever get in the bill. I know that.

Well anyhow, Nye is there. He's there. While we're sittin' there
talkin' by comes Mr. Barney Baruch.[13] Mr. Barney Baruch. And
he's made a very fine witness over there, by the way. And he come
by and spoke to us. He didn't eat with us, but he went on. But Nye
told me he'd made a fine witness. He helped them out a lot, and
very patriotic—a fine man. I think he's done a lot of things as head
of the War Industries Board and all.

Well, while we was sittin' there — he had just got away when Huey
bobbed over. Oh yes, old Huey got in. He come in with a gang,
and he left his table and come over there and sit down with us
and—now get this—and the minute — the vice president, he'd gone
out in the meantime. He'd finished. He had to go somewhere. He
had to go take a nap as a matter of fact. He's awful nice. He won't
sleep in the Senate. Now this Nye—now get this—there's Senator
Nye, Senator Capper, the Republican from Kansas, and myself, and
then Shipstead, the Farmer-Laborite, you know, the only one in
there that don't owe any allegiance to either company.[14] He's —
you know, — well, he was there with us.

And then by golly, Huey come over, and we get Huey started,

which wasn't any effort whatever. We get Huey started, and——
[off microphone] Are you in there? This guy says I'm blatherin'
about enough here. I got to get to this. Wait a minute. If we run
over on "Amos 'n Andy's" hour, I got to get to this.

Well anyhow, Huey got started, and then come Borah.[15] Now get
this combination. See? Now there's Borah, Nye, Capper, Shipstead,
and Huey and me all sittin' there, and Borah says, "My goodness,
it's wonderful nobody's got a camera here, you know, being seen
in company like that." That was a hot combination, you know.
That Borah, there's another man I got great regard for. Now there's
a guy I'd love to see the Republicans nominate. They'd get
somewhere. Senator Borah. Yes, sir, Borah, he's all right.

Well, we're all there. So I get to asking Huey — I says, "What you
doin', Huey?"

And he says, "I'm writing a book."

I said, "Oh, Lord, don't write a book. You can't sell a book. I tried
that."

He says, "Yeah, you was darn fool enough to charge for it. I'm going to give mine away." He's always got a answer, you know.

Well anyhow, I said, "Now Huey——" Then we got him started
on his plan.[16] By golly, and he sits there and wrote. He didn't eat
at all. He just sit there. He'll stop eating if he can get you to listen,
you know. And he wrote out all these things on there. And I come
to find out — and Borah, he was askin' him questions, and Nye
was asking him, Shipstead and we all, and we find out he says.
I says, "How much you got to have, Huey, before you divide up?"
You know. I'd always been agin him and everything.

And he says, "Well, I don't make 'em divide up till they get over
a million."

I says, "My Lord, you don't lose anybody." Well, gee, we all joined him after that.

And so then he got to showing what he was going to do, and he
wrote all over the back of this program. And he says, "Will, you
know what — you know my plan, Will." He says, "You've read
my book."

And I said, "Yes." I hadn't read it, but I told him I read it.

Well, we sit there, and we had a great lunch. Capper paid for it.

The Republican pays, as usual. And everything that the Democrats is doin' now the Republicans pay for it. And so we had quite——

Somebody — everybody asks me, says, "Will, how long is this going to go on, all this spending all this money and everything going like this?"

I says, "Well, it will go on just as long as the Republicans has got any money. That's all I know about it."

Well, we had this lunch there and anyhow, and had a — oh, oh, here we go off. Gee, I wanted to tell you a lot more. But so long. I'll see you next Sunday. I'm going out to California. Good-bye and good luck.

Good Gulf Show

April 7, 1935

ANNOUNCER:

ROGERS: How are you? How you coming, anyhow? Well, here we are. We're right back out in California, the old orange juice belt, the old sunshine state. Of course, it didn't show up today. We ain't had — we ain't had any sunshine today. It rained instead.

But I've been riding today. Been riding way off around up in the hills, back in the Santa Monica mountains — riding up in there. Run on to a kind of peculiar thing. I was prowling around up on the trails back in the hills there, and I saw about — well, I think I saw about four deer — about four deer, but about five Republicans showed up. Now that's an omen that don't look so good. Now, in the old days I'd ride through there — a few months ago I could have rode through those hills, and I wouldn't see them at all. I'd see more deer. But these Republicans are coming out of the brush now, and you'd be surprised at the amount of them that's showin' up, you know.

And they — they — you know, in the old days they would — they — in the old days they wouldn't cuss Roosevelt. I mean they would — they wouldn't cuss directly at him. They would kind of like billiards—they would bank off of Tugwell to Moley, you know.[1] They would shoot at poor little Tugwell and then go off to Moley, then off of the Brain Trust, then down to Roosevelt. You know, maybe three-cushioning. You know what I mean. Now, oh boy, they got all the nerve in the world. They're going direct now. You know what I mean. They're just shooting direct at him without any three-cushioning.

Big excitement out here is whether the movies will move. Well,

110

I don't know whether the movies will move or not. I know I've made some that never did move. The movies — all us people in the movies is watching our state legislature. Well, I guess every — I guess everybody in every state is watching the state legislature. Legislatures, they kind of like animals in the zoo. You can't do anything about 'em, only just stand and watch them anyhow. But — but man is still the main animal among them. You put a bunch of legislatures — you know, you take them and put a bunch of them together, and they can think of more funny things to do than — than a bunch of monkeys in a zoo. See? So man is still preeminent.

Well, we cuss the lawmakers. We do — no matter what it is; whether it's state or national legislature, we cuss 'em, you know, but — but I notice we're always perfectly willin' to share in any of the sums of money that they might distribute. You know what I mean. We cuss 'em for distributing it, but we're always there when it's handed out. We say it's wrong and unsound, but we don't refuse to take it. No, we'll grab it every time. We say our government is nutty. That's what we all say about it. That seems to be the general opinion — that the whole — that the way the government is run now is all nutty and that it's throwing away money. But anytime any is thrown our way, why we've never dodged it.

The general contention is that nobody is spending any money but the government. Well, I guess that's right. The government is spending all the money. Well, an awful lots of businesses are doing better than they have for the last three or four years. Newspapers, especially, they've done fine; automobiles, lots of things — and newspapers, especially. Their advertising has leaped, and subscriptions have gone up. And then Amon Carter down in Fort Worth was telling me everything's going along fine with all the newspapers.

Yet all the editorials — you know what I mean. They're all against Roosevelt. They all say he's a dud. They say that this thing can't go on, that the government is spending all the money. Yet, they're doing better than they have in years on the government money. It shows absolute honesty on the part of the press, you know. It shows that they — yes, sure, shows that the editorial policy of the press — it shows that the editorial policy, you know — they're not against — you know, they're in favor. I'll say they're not in favor of the man who's bringing the business into their advertising for 'em, you know. So they're honest in it.

Well, anyhow, well, you know, I figured out — it's a peculiar state of affairs that exists, and everybody that is doing better than they was three or four years ago—are making more money—got it in for the president. But they don't seem to realize they're doing better on the money that he's spending. You see what I mean? They're doing better on his money. Now we all know that the government is spending all this money and that's not a good state of affairs to exist. The country's in bad shape when there ain't nobody spending any money but the government. But now, what you going to do about it?

Course, one remedy would be for the people that have money to — for them to start spending it instead of the government, but that seems just about as unpopular as the Roosevelt idea. In fact, it's worse. Well, you know, if we sit down and passed a bill tomorrow, and said the government can't keep on spending this money — but for government to exist somebody had got to spend money, so from this day on — from this day and date, we the governments are going to stop spending money, and made it compulsory that the people do the spending. Boy, what a howl would go up from that, you know. They couldn't make that law stick. People would say, "No, we saved it, and we have worked, and we've made it, and we got the right to do as we please with it." So that little idea is out. The people ain't going to spend. That's out.

So what other idea have we got? We got to keep on working with ideas. Well, if the government is throwing this money away, the only thing I see for the ones that are throwing — for the ones that they are throwing it to—outside of those that are absolutely needy of it — in need of it, you know—well, the only thing I see is have them refuse it. You know what I mean. If you don't believe in what Roosevelt is doing with this money, why refuse it if it comes. Just say, "No, it's government money, and it's tainted. And I don't believe in the government — and I don't believe in the government spending all this money, and hence I don't take any part of it."

You say — no, you have paid this out—— Now, for instance, take me, for instance. I'd say, "No, we — the government paid this out for the people to eat, and here they are coming to see my pictures with it. I don't agree with that at all." You know. Now, you can imagine me saying that! You know what I mean. If I was that way, it would be the way to look at it. You know, I ought to refuse to accept the money. It's government money. I don't believe in the government spending this money, so I'm not going to take it. Here's a man that maybe wants to pay his loan at the bank. Well, maybe the RFC loaned him the money.[2] You know, they're doing that a lot. And they get the money from the government, and they go to pay the bank. And the bank says, "I don't believe in it." The banks — naturally, all the banks say, "I don't believe in the government spending all this money." But when the man comes to pay his loan with the government money, they don't say, "No, I can't take it; I'll just carry you myself." Boy, what a laugh that would be.

Now, of course it's going to cost the taxpayers a lot of money to loan this fellow the money to pay off his loan to the bank. You know, it's going to do that, but nevertheless — they kick on that, but they don't refuse to take it. They ought to say, "Well, no, I ain't going to take it. I made the loan. It was me that made it, and I should be the one to stand by it." You haven't heard that. At least I haven't.

Well, anyhow — anyhow, there's not a person in America that received a dollar, no matter where it come from — you know, that received a single dollar, no matter where it come from that hasn't grabbed it, you know — without asking any questions. It might have been paid out for relief for a starving child, but if it reached us we was the starving child. And it didn't make any difference.

So the only thing I see for the fellow that don't believe in all this spending is to not participate in receiving any of it. I can't very well legitimately criticize a fellow for spending money if I receive some of it without any criticism in the receipt of it, you know. If I don't believe it's so, I'll at least make a little attempt to say that it ain't right when I grab off some of it. So this $5 billion that they're starting in to spend, we all know that that's too much money; it's too much money to take out and throw away, or give away, or whatever they do with it. We know that. We all know that, but until we refuse to take some of it—when it comes our way—we ain't got much right to holler.

Now that brings us down to taxes. You know what I mean, that brings us down to taxes. Boy, when you bring us down to taxes, you're going to hear a howl like a pet coon. You know, brings us down there. This money coming from all the government is throwing away — well, it just sort of looks like it — where's it coming from? Everybody says, "Where's the money coming from we're spending?" Well, I don't know, but just offhand, I'd say it's coming from those that got it, you know. Now I don't know. That may be just a rough idea of mine. I don't know, but I kinda believe that's where it's coming from.

There's one good thing about the American form of government. The fellow that's got nothing, he don't pay nothing. You know. And, too, lots of times the fellow — he has got something, but — and he ain't got any money to pay, you know. He's got something but he ain't got any — nothing to pay with — to pay his taxes with, but he can at least let 'em have the property back and get an even break anyhow, you know. But the big yell comes nowadays from the taxpayers, the big taxpayers. I bet you when the Pilgrims landed at Plymouth Rock and they had the whole of the American continent, you know, for themselves — you know, just them and them Pilgrims there, who landed up there, and all they had to do to get an extra hundred and sixty acres was shoot another Indian, you know. Well, I bet you anything they kicked on the price of ammunition. I bet they said, "What's this country coming to!" You know, what I mean — like we're doing now. "What's this country coming to! We have to spend a nickel for powder." Of course, they got the lead back after they dissected the Indian, but——[laughter]

I don't know, ain't it funny? No matter what we pay—I don't care whether we pay high taxes, low taxes, medium taxes, or no tax, anything—the yell is always the same, a hundred percent. They just yell a hundred percent. Of course, we know our government is costing us more than it's worth, but do you know — but do you know of any other cheaper government that's running around? Do you? I mean, if you do, they'll sell you a ticket there anytime.

Now you can try Russia. I was over there. Yeah, you can try Russia. There's no income tax in Russia, but there's no income. Now Hitler — Hitler ain't got no sales tax — you know what I mean — but he ain't selling anything. Well, that's fine. Mussolini, you don't have to pay a poll tax to vote in Italy, you know, but nobody votes. Well now, so — now the whole question is, "How can we make such a holler on what the government wants to collect back from us?" The thing is, you know — it looks like we can't have everything like we want to, you know. But the whole question is — is the government — how much of this money which we are asked to pay back to them in taxes have they paid us? You know what I mean. We must have got quite a little divvy of it some way or other — indirectly. Admitting, as everybody does, that the government is the only one spending money, and if they're the only ones spending anything, then anything we're gettin' must come from them. It looks like an endless chain to me, only when it reaches our link, well, we don't want to cut any back into the kitty.

I don't know what it's all about. This is just to kill time up here until something else comes on. I don't know. I don't know anymore about this thing than an economist does, and God knows, he don't know anything. Everything nowadays is just to make talk.

But next week I'm going to present to you my scheme, you know. You see, every man nowadays has got a scheme to bring us out of the wilderness, you know. Well, not so much to bring us out of the wilderness as to bring himself out, you know. I've been studying the Townsend Plan, and the Long Plan, and the Coughlin Plan, and the Roosevelt Plan.[3] Hoover, he broke out with a plan here the other day. And I'll work it — maybe I'll do it next week. I don't know if I get around to it. I'm working on what's called the Rogers Plan — you know what I mean. Yes, sir, the Rogers Plan. Just about three more welch rabbits every night, and I'll be ready for the Rogers Plan. I'm going to have it in shape, you know.

Anyhow, don't do anything. Don't sign up with any of these other plans. Don't you boys sign up, because I believe I've got a better offer for you anyhow. And don't be too critical of the present plan, you know, of the Roosevelt Plan. It's working, you know. For as long as we're all living on the loot, why we can't holler about it. See? But remember now, about next week I'm going to give you the — I'm going to give you the Rogers Plan. I'm just working on a few planks of it there now, and I ain't got it quite in shape. But I don't care what they offer you, I'll do better.

Oh say, wait a minute. Can you tell me the time? I got to tell you about the movies. This is what I started to tell you about the movies. The legislation — well, if they put certain taxes on us, they — we were going to leave. One gentleman, Mr. Sam Goldwyn, this morning, said we're going to England.[4] We ain't goin'. I'll tell you, I bet you we don't go nowhere. I bet you — I bet you that we don't go east of Vermont Avenue.

The movies — we're in an industry that kind of depends on the good will of the people. And they overlooked the biggest thing in all this moving: You can't get much good will by dodging taxes, you know. Because I don't care where you go, they'll bring you in there. They'll say, "You boys don't pay anything." But those guys that said you don't pay nothing, they ain't there next year. They're washed up and gone home. That ain't going to go.

115

But I don't know where we're going to go. If we go to New Jersey, I can see, here's a scene from New Jersey—you know, you folks on the radio maybe can't see this like my audience here—here's Miss Greta — here's an actress playing a scene in front of the camera in New Jersey, "I love you. [smack] Damn those mosquitoes!" [laughter] I love you!

Now say, we go down South. They're talking a good deal about us going down in North and South Carolina somewhere. Well, there's a wonderful state. I've been down there a lot. They're great old states and all, but naturally the influence of the people would have an effect on you. Now if we go down in North or South Carolina, I can just see Greta Garbo coming before the screen. You know what I mean. After mixing with all those North and South Carolinians, and I love that dialect and all. And Greta Garbo says, "Yeah, ah sho do love you, doggone. Ah sho do love you." Yes, sir. "Yas, ah sho do love you." I tank I go home. I ain't going to mess around here no longer. [Alarm rings.]

Oh here, wait; I ain't through. I got a lot more to say. Good-bye. Next Sunday night look for the Rogers Plan. Good night.

Good Gulf Show

April 14, 1935

ANNOUNCER:

ROGERS: [applause] Much obliged. I — I've been reading all day—
and I guess you all have, too—in the papers about all these bright
young college boys and girls marching, you know marching to keep
from going to war. It's a good joke on them. We ain't got no war.
They — they — you know, it's kinda like a fellow on a hunger
strike, you know, when there ain't nothin' to eat no how. A fellow
marching to keep from going to war here in this country nowadays
is sorta like — you know, well war is kinda like meat, you know.
You can't have it because you can't afford it. My cow men friends
will shoot me for that. I didn't mean that.

Well, anyhow, the nations that want war — if there is any of them
want it, which I doubt very much. They can't get it, you know.
You can't go out and get a war like you used to could — just on
a minute's notice, you know. Wars are gettin' kind of hard to arrange. You got to book them way ahead. These students learning
— you know, these students learning to march in the peace parade,
that will give them just about the training we give our soldiers in
a regular war, you know. They'll just about be ready for it then.

Well, tonight, I was going to unfold to you at least an inkling of
the Rogers Plan tonight, but getting up a plan — say, there's more
work to it than I thought there was. I tell you, a fellow's got to be
crazier than I — than I — than you think, you know. You got to
be sure plum nutty to think up a plan in a week, you know. These
old boys that have got plans, they've been working on 'em for a
long time.

I've been gettin' a lot of mail and advice this week, and the col-

117

lege professors have been wanting to help me. You'd be surprised at the amount of them that Roosevelt has let out. They're out of work, and they're just dying to get in with some other plan now. And they want — then the big moneyed interests I been hearing from them. They've been trying to find out what I've got to offer them in their plan. Seems like they claim that Roosevelt left them out entirely, and they want to get in with me, I think. They — they claim the Republicans have included them in their plan, you know, Mr. Hoover's plan, and Odgen Mills' plan, Wadsworth, all those various plans, but that they're afraid while they'll be in the plan that they won't be in the votes.[1] There won't be enough votes in that plan to get much, so I don't know — I haven't done anything about it.

You see, all these people with plans have written books. All of 'em. Huey's got a book, and all of them's got a book — and everybody — Mr. Hoover's got a book. Roosevelt wrote two or three books. Well, I got all these books, but I never did read none of them. But to find out what their plan is, I got to read 'em, so I got to read 'em this week. So that comes under the heading of work. So next week — next week I ought to be — I ought to be ready to start in — you know, really gettin' right down into the meat of the Rogers Plan.

Say, I got to do a little — to do a little — a little thanking here tonight. Eddie Cantor last Sunday night, they tell me, paid me a very lovely compliment. Radio is so young that it hasn't reached the point where you can say anything about anyone or anything but the thing you're supposed to advertise. To mention a competitor is like a politician saying something complimentary of his opponent. It just isn't done, that's all. So thank you, Eddie, very much. It was very nice of you. And I don't know what it is you're peddling. What is it Cantor's selling now? I mean, what is it? What's Cantor selling? Huh?

VOICE: Pebeco.

ROGERS: Pebeco Toothpaste. Fine. Eddie, all our audience knew what it was, Pebeco Toothpaste. Well, buy some of it. He's a very nice boy. Buy some of it. I know I will, and in return, Eddie, Good Gulf Gasoline has got no superior. Not only has no superior, but it has no equal. Not only has no equal, but I will go further. Well, how much further can you go! Well, I'll go quite a bit further. You can look back in your mirror above your windshield, and everything behind you, you can bet, is not burning Good Gulf. Now that's about as far as I can go for the money I'm getting! Hot dog! How's that for an ad!

Well now, anyhow, another little announcement. On last Sabbath evening, I referred to the Pilgrims — our Pilgrims landing on Plymouth Rock. Well, boy, you ought to wait 'til I heard from New England. I split New England just wide open. It seems there's a town up there called Provincetown, and they have adopted a slogan which says, "Don't be misled by history or any other unreliable source. Here's the place where the Pilgrims landed. This is by unanimous vote of the Chamber of Commerce of Provincetown. Provincetown has been made the official landing place of the Pilgrim. Any Pilgrim landing in any other place was not official."

If he landed on Plymouth Rock, well, it just served him right, that's all. It served him right. Nothing but a chicken should be named after 'em, Plymouth Rock. That's for the town people. You country people got that gag. That's for the town folks. Plymouth Rock, not a White Leghorn. All right now. Country folks is smarter than city folks anyhow. You never have to explain a joke to country folks. But who but a chicken, or a seal, or a Pilgrim would land on a rock anyhow?

Now in the first place, I don't think that this argument I have created up there — you know, it's so terribly important. The argument that New England has got to settle in order to pacify the rest of America is, "Why were they allowed to land anywhere?" That's what — that's what we want to know, as the race has never been any comparison between the Pilgrim and an Indian. Now I hope my Cherokee blood is not making me prejudiced. I want to be broadminded, but I am sure that it was only the extreme generosity of the Indians that allowed the Pilgrims to land. Suppose we reversed the case. Do you reckon the Pilgrims would have ever let the Indians land? Yeah, what a chance! What a chance! The Pilgrims wouldn't even allow the Indians to live after the Indians went to the trouble of letting 'em land.

Well anyhow, the Provincetown officials, they sent me a lot of official data, that when the Pilgrims landed they found some corn that the Indians had stored and that the Pilgrims were about starved and that they eat the Indians' corn. And they claim that the corn was stored at Provincetown. You see, the minute the Pilgrims landed they got full of the corn and then they shot the Indians, perhaps because they hadn't stored more corn. I don't know.

Of course — but they'd always pray. That's one thing about a Pilgrim. He would pray, mostly for more Indian corn. You've never in your life seen a picture—I bet anyone of you—have never seen a picture of one of the old Pilgrims praying when he didn't have a gun right by the side of him. That was to see that he got what he was praying for.

Well, now, we got to get on something important. California's been crowing around about having no dust or no storms. But the last day or so it's been mighty cloudy, and it looks just like it did when I was back in the Middle West a week or so ago. It looks like it's going to rain, but it don't. They say that the dust is headed west. California is great to pass laws. The legislature is, and they just liable to pass a law prohibiting the dust to come into this state. We have a legislature that'll do it if you'll just remind them of it. I know.

I've been reading a lot about this dust and been reading a lot in history, and Rob Wagner's script that's got a story about it was good and all these. And that's how every civilization since time began and the whole world has been covered up. It's been this dust. It's a terrible thing to happen to those people that are out there in the Middle West where it is happening. But on the other hand, it's a great tribute to feel that the Lord feels that you have a civilization that is so advanced than the rest of civilization that it is the first place to be buried under. There's something in that, you know what I mean. Just think of our Middle West. I didn't think at first that we was that smart in Oklahoma, in Kansas, in Texas, and western — eastern Colorado, but our Almighty, He must know. Now that it would ever cover up California for the same reason, I've got my doubts. Civilization out here has not reached that point of perfection where — where the Lord sees fit to cover it up. He might see fit to cover it up, but not on account of civilization. It will be to keep somebody from looking at it or something.

My wife and daughter has just returned from a trip down in Egypt, and they went way up the Nile—flew up the Nile—and went in at Luxor and went way down, she told me, hundreds of feet down in underground that had been covered by the dust and storms of centuries and centuries to see old King Tut and Ramses and the old Pharaoh's tomb. That was a great civilization, you see — buried in the blowing sand. See? Any old civilization they've ever dug up — sometime they go down and find two or three layers of civilization. It's all been covered up because they plowed under ground that they shouldn't never plowed under in the first place, you know. And they cut down the trees that should never have been cut down anyhow.

You know, we're always talking about pioneers and what great folks the old pioneers were. Well, I think if we just stopped and looked at history in the face, the pioneer wasn't a thing in the world but a guy that wanted something for nothing. He was a guy that wanted to live off of everything that nature had done. He wanted to cut a tree down that didn't cost him anything, but he never did plant one, you know. He wanted to plow up the land that should have been left to grass. We're just not — I don't know, we're just now learning, you know, that we can rob from nature the same way as we can rob from an individual. All he had was an ax, and a plow, and a gun, and he just went out and lived off nature. But really, he thought it was nature he was living off of, but it was really future generations that he was living off of, you know.

Now Roosevelt, do you remember, here a couple of years ago — do you all remember this? Roosevelt suggested planting millions of trees in all the dry regions. He said every so many miles we'll put a row of trees clear across the country. Well, the Republicans had one of the best laughs they've had since 1928 when they read that. Imagine the government going into the tree-planting business. What a nut an idea. And it was nutty. It was so nutty that it will be about ten or fifteen years before they'll be compelled to do it. That's how nutty it was.

And another one of his ideas when he took the young boys off the roads and off the streets and put them in these CCC Camps and had 'em all planting some little trees.[2] The press had a big laugh. I remember reading it in the papers, you know. They called them "sapling planters." "Look at these young kids. They got 'em all planting saplings." Well, if the sapling planters had started in about the time the Republicans took over the government from Grover Cleveland, we'd today be able to see the sun.[3] [applause]

But now wait a minute. Wait a minute. Wait a minute, you Democrats. It wasn't all Republicans that did this. The old Democrat had an ax, too. You know what I mean. In fact, that's all the Democrat had had for years, is an ax. He ain't had nothing

121

else. He's practically had to live off of an ax. He had nothing else, of course until here lately. He traded his ax for a post office, you know. He got that now. He's living off the post office now.

But I must get back from these political parties and get back to civilization, for there's nothing in common between politics and civilization. There ain't nothing in common between those two at all. If history has shown the Lord does bury each succeeding civilization, and buries them in accordance to the advancement of the people in that neighborhood, I feel proud that I come from that particular Middle West belt. I know — I know that William Allen White of Kansas feels proud, and Amon Carter of Texas feels proud. If a civilization had to be buried as it becomes advanced enough, well, we feel proud that we're the ones to be plowed under first, that's all.[4] In years to come the archeologist — I hope I've got that right. I say archeologist. I hope that word is right. The archeologist will dig and find Claremore, Oklahoma, and people will come there to the ruins and dig down and say, "Here lied a civilization." You know?

Well, then later on they'll unearth the state capitol, you know, and then eventually as Washington is covered up, on account of it's being the least civilized, it will be the last place to be covered up. They will excavate in there and find the old Capitol and decipher some of the old hieroglyphics — you know, what people of those days humorously called laws, you know. And they'll come from the four corners—I'll bet they'll come from all over the whole country—four corners of the earth to see what queer race lived there, you know. And they'll find places called banks where the money changers were, you know, men who in those ancient days lived by interest alone. Oh, there ain't no telling to what all they won't—— [Alarm rings.] Ah, wait a minute here. There ain't no telling. Shoot, I just got started telling you what all they was going to dig up in Washington. Well, good-bye and good luck to you.

Good Gulf Show

April 21, 1935

ANNOUNCER:

ROGERS: [applause] Thank you very much. Today is — today's Plan Day. I'm sort of giving an inkling of the Rogers Plan to agonize the world. But you know the Townsend Plan and various others of a similar nature went down in Congress with a tremendous majority, so it looks like a kind of a bad day for plans. I think Townsend was conscientious, well-meaning, humanitarian old gentleman.

I believe if he had lowered his sights and called for maybe $50 instead of 200 a month, and took out the clause where they had to spend it. Old people, you know, are naturally kind of conservative — and saving, and they'd of hated to spend money every week if they really didn't need to. Our government is the only people that just loves to spend without being compelled to, at all. But the government — but the government is the only people that don't have to worry where it's coming from.

One bad thing about the Townsend Plan was that it built up false hopes in the minds of all old and worthy people. You know, you got 'em to expecting something which it didn't look like they'd be able to receive. Now Friday, Congress did pass a bill to give — to give $15, and the state is to match that, and make — and they give 15, and that would make $30. Well, the Senate — it's got to go before the Senate yet. I think the Senate should raise that at least 5 or 10 more and then the state, and that would give them $40 — or maybe 40 or $50. See? That's just my idea. I don't know whether it will be carried out or not.

We — you know, we're the last civilized nation—if you can call it that—to do anything for old people. All we do is just let 'em — we just watch 'em get older, is all we do. We give them enough — but we should give them enough so that it will get them out of poor farms and let them live where they want to. Lots of wise guys can kid about this old fellow Townsend and call him a nut, but he's got a lot to do with getting the old folks any pension at all, I think.

He throwed such a scare into Congress that — that they might have to pay $200, that they finally settled with him for 15. So, maybe the old gentleman — maybe if he'd asked for 500 — why, maybe he would have got 50. I don't know.

Well, anyhow, as I say, it was a bad week for plans. Even Huey, who is the king of the planners — he had tough week going this last week, too — with his "Share the Wealth." Secretary Ickes and Relief Commissioner Hopkins, who handles more money than any man in the world, they said, "No, Huey, you're not a-goin' to share any of our wealth, you know."[1] Well, that wealth Huey was kinda figurin' on sharin' for a while.

You know, the national problem is in this country today is not who shall be relieved and whose money shall relieve him, but who shall be the one that plays Santa Claus—and actually hands out the presents, you know. That's the main problem today, it's who hands out the presents. Huey says he should wear the whiskers. And Ickes and Mr. Hopkins, they say no — says, "We've got sleigh bells ourselves."

Governor Talmadge down in Georgia, he had a plan.[2] It hit a rut and knocked him right out of the bread line last week. It's been a bad week on plans all around. I'm not going to get discouraged, though. In fact, these other failures — well, they've really given me confidence, you know — more hope that my plan will be a success.

My plan, to state it in a nutshell, and — in fact, that's where all plans come from — and the nuts should never be cracked. But here is my plan in a nutshell. My plan is a plan to end all plans. It's to do away with all plans. That's what it is. This country has been planned to death, the same as we were sloganed to death during the war. Had we never had a slogan, we would be at peace with the world today. But every time anybody thought of a new slogan, why we dived deeper and deeper into the war. We saved democracy, and we ended all wars. There just wasn't anything we wasn't able to do with a slogan.

And we're performing the same miracle with plans. There ain't but one place that a plan is any good and that it would really work and that's on paper — on paper, a plan. But the minute you get it off the sheet of paper and get it out in the air, and it blows away, that's all.

Now, Mr. Roosevelt, he dragged more he-schoolmarms — yes, he did — he dragged more he-schoolmarms out of little red schoolhouses, and they had more plans than they had shirts. He could ask for a new plan, and they could drag a fresh one out quicker than they could fresh pair of socks.

Republican presidents, they never — that's one thing about Republican presidents. They never went in much for plans. They always — they only had one plan. It says, "Now, boys, my head is turned; just get it while you can." Somebody come along, and they used that. It was a plan to plow under part of the cotton. We did, and other nations like Brazil found out where we plowed it under, and they come and dug it up, and now they've got more cotton than we have. Somebody had a plan to teach hogs birth control — and now it's a habit with them. Now you can go out and find a deer quicker than you can a hog now.

Somebody had a plan to plow under every third acre of wheat, and the wind came along and blew out the other two acres. It was all a fine plan — a fine plan well carried out. We wanted to raise commodity prices, and Mr. Wallace, naturally, he wanted to give the farmer a profit, the same as the manufacturer.[3] Now we find there's more people eating than there is raising. You see, that's why you can never get the thing straight with the farmers. You know, because there naturally is more eating than there is raising. And it's a good thing, too. The guys that eat are going to commence hollerin', you know. So that's what they're kicking on now. They're kicking.

So plans just don't work. If they're milk and honey to you, they are poison ivy to somebody else, you know. NRA, that was a fine plan. It was based on the theory that everybody that had could help those that hadn't. That was all the NRA ever was. But the minute we found out that while it might be helping other men, it certainly wasn't helping us. And it blew up. If it wasn't helping us so much, why it wasn't so hot.

125

NRA was started with a lot of parades and ended in almost a revolution.

Father Coughlin's got a plan. Father Coughlin, I know him; he's a well-meaning man. He'd like to help his fellow man to better his conditions. But whether his plan will work or not is another question. But even if your plan don't work, it's no — there ain't any discredits, you know. Our own Saviour had a plan — in fact, ten of 'em. He left them to us, and he knew they'd help us, and we know they'll help us. He said, "Love thy neighbor as thyself," but I bet there ain't two people in your block that's speaking to each other.

We know there should be no war. We know that old people maybe they should get $200 a month or maybe more. We know that everybody should "share the wealth." We know that all these things — we know 'em all in our heart, but I don't know, we just ain't going to do 'em, that's all. Now, Huey's plan to "share the wealth," it's a marvelous idea. Huey's a smart guy, don't overlook that. And in our own downright conscience tells us that there's no reason why, well, anybody should have more than you. There ain't nothing wrong with the plan, only this one little defect: Nobody ain't going to share it with you, that's all.

I know a lot of tremendously rich people that should share their wealth with me, but they just don't see it that way. And I know folks that ain't got as much as I have that think I ought to share it with them. Well, I just can't hardly see it their way either, you know. That is, even if I can see it that way, I'm not doing it.

Well, we take the case of Huey. Suppose Huey was asked to divide his publicity with the other ninety-five senators. Now what a fine thing. Say, Huey, we just want you to split this publicity with them, see? Well, that would be just like getting J. P. Morgan to split what he had with a Navajo or something, you know.[4] Morgan would say, "Well, why should I split with the Navajoes? I got nothing in common with the Navajoes."

Well, that's what Huey would say, "Why should I split with the other ninety-five senators. I've got nothing in common with them."

Now everybody got a plan. Congress got a plan; their plan is to pass all resolutions that have an appropriation connected with it. Anything that carries an appropriation Congress will pass it, see? They'll vote it, but they don't vote where the money is coming from. That's what Congress plan is, to keep it secret where the money is coming from. That's one of their plans.

Mr. Hoover's got a plan. I don't know exactly what it is, but it's got something to do with moving east next fall — a year from this next fall. I think that's kinda roughly it. Ogden Mills, he's secretary of the treasury, a very able man — he's got a plan. His is to see that Mr. Hoover don't move east; he says he's got more money than Hoover and is naturally more able to move himself. Teddy Roosevelt, Jr., he's got a plan.[5] His is that there should be a Roosevelt in the White House but not this one. Mrs. Roosevelt, she got a plan — plenty of 'em.[6] She plans — she plans to do bigger and more things during the next administration. Now the Republicans, they got a plan. Their plan is to do nothing and then Roosevelt can't either. Do nothing and then Roosevelt can't either. The Democrats have got a plan — well, they got millions of them. Couldn't hardly mention all of theirs, but theirs — but the Democrats' plan is — next year is election year, see? Hold the post office, boys; they shall not pass. That's all.

Now, big business — we're always hearing about big business, see? Big business has got a plan. Theirs is — they talked to Mr. Roosevelt, "Quit trying to reform us, and give us a chance to recover." That's what business says. "Quit trying to reform us and give us a chance to recover."

Roosevelt says, "Can't you reform and recover, too?" Well, that looks like it's kind of hard there.

But big business answer is, "No, we can't do anything with a cop on every corner watching everything we do. Give us a chance; then, honest, when we're able we'll reform." And then, besides, they asked Mr. Roosevelt, "We never — Mr. Roosevelt, we never know what you're going to do next."

Roosevelt says, "Neither do I!"

Business says to Roosevelt, "Look how England has recovered, for they're being let alone. Their business is being let alone, and nobody is bothering 'em."

Roosevelt says, "Yes, you pay as big an income tax as England does, then we'll recover, too."

So it just seems, you know, all these plans, but none of 'em pleases everybody, you know. So my plan, which is still in the nutshell, is when a senator or congressman—or even a man of great ability — we must quit joking about those boys, because they're good guys. The reason a congressman or senator is all right, everytime we ever let one out, a worse one gets in — that's all I know.

But anyhow, here's my plan. I got to get back. When a senator, or a congressman, or anybody else—a man or woman—comes to Washington with a plan, is send 'em to Russia. Yes, sir, send 'em to Russia with the plan. That's the home of plans, you know. That's the home. Russia, they eat and sleep and drink plans in Russia. That's why there's starvation there, because you just can't digest a plan. It don't eat right. Everything in Russia is run by plans; everything here is run by accident.

Now my plans is — my plan is "Don't Plan." Whatever you do, don't do it perfectly; live haphazard. You know, just kind of go through life haphazardly. Well, even more than we are now. There's nothing in the world as common as an idea, and there's nothing in the world as hard to carry out as an idea. So let's — let's all just kind of call a moratorium on plans. If the Republicans would forget their main plan, which is to get into the White House, and the Democrats would forget their main plan to stay in there, and if the others — all these various third parties, would just look at their history which shows that none of them ever did get in there, why we'd all recover overnight — if they'd forget about the White House.

So if you hear a man expounding a plan over your radio, run, don't walk, to the nearest dial and tune him right into the ground, folks. The plan — and the plan will go right back into the nutshell where it belongs.

Well, I beat my clock tonight. I'm all right. I'm finished; that was it. Say, here — that's the first time I ever beat the old alarm clock. But here's something I bet you heard all day, all day today.

[Rogers sings "In Your Easter Bonnet."]

I heard that on the radio. It's pretty. It's my favorite tune. With it being Easter and so many marvelous ceremonies, I've heard that on — [continues to sing] So long.

Good Gulf Show

April 28, 1935

ANNOUNCER:

ROGERS: [applause] Thank you very much. We're here an hour earlier today. It seems kind of funny to be — with everybody advised to spend and the government spending everything, and then — it seems sort of funny for somebody to save a little daylight nowadays. Put a little bit of it on the budget or something.

Do you remember my act on the radio last Sunday night? Well, even if you don't remember it, don't — I mean, it don't matter very much. Fact, I'd about forgot it myself. But as well as I can remember it, I introduced a plan. It was a plan — it was a plan to end all plans. That's what it was.

Well, it looked like it had the very — the very opposite effect. This last week has been one of the biggest plan weeks I've known of. It's the biggest plan week the country has suffered in years — this last one. In fact, I think they could have named it "Plan Week." Now one of the big things that President Roosevelt made his original hit with was when he said, "If I'm wrong, I'll be the first to admit it." So when I say we should end all plans, it looks like I'm wrong and I'm the first to admit it.

So it looks like we've got to have plans, and I've really got to get busy on one. I won't give it to you today, but I'm gonna dig one up. If you want a plan, brother, I can sure give you one now. I presented facts and figures to show you that plans didn't work. Now, I did that last Sunday, see? Do you think that discouraged the planners? Not on your life. It just seemed to encourage them — looks like.

129

Right on top of my advice to not plan — well, there came a plan from Secretary Morgenthau, who's secretary of the treasury.[1] His father used to be ambassador to Turkey, a fine old gentleman and a good friend of mine.[2] But this Morgenthau, the young fellow, a very able man, — he come out with a plan to put a bigger and better tax on these big estates — these tremendous estates. An inheritance tax it is. An inheritance tax — that is, a man who died.

And on an estate of say $10 million, why the government will takes about 90 percent of it, and then giving the off-spring 10 — after Mr. Morgenthau gets through with it. And then on estates of a 100 million, 200 million, a billion, and like that, well, the government just takes all of that and notifies the heirs — says, "Your father died a pauper here today." And he died a pauper here today, and he's being buried by the — let see what it is, the MEBA — that is, the Millionaires' Emergency Burial Association. It's a kind of a branch of the RFC.

Now mind you, mind you — I'm not telling all this — I don't hold any great grief for a man that dies and leaves a million — millions and hundreds of millions and billions. I don't mean that. But I don't believe Mr. Morgenthau's plan will work, because he gives figures in there that shows what this new inheritance tax would bring in every year. He says in 1936 we get so much, in 1938 — oh, right along. He give these figures to show what it will bring in every year — that is, as long as the Democrats stay in.

He seems to know — he seems to know just who's going to die each year. And how much they're going to leave. Now, brother, that's planning, ain't it, when you can figure out that! Now suppose, for instance, he's got scheduled to die J. P. Morgan. He's got him scheduled to die on a certain year. And you can bet, if they can arrange it, they'll have him die while the Democrats are in — so they can get the benefit of that estate anyhow, see?

Now, according to plans, J. P. Morgan — he's got to die in order for Mr. Morgenthau to reach his quota for that year. Now while I think Mr. Morgan is a nice man, I never met him but once. That was the time when he was on trial in Washington and he had the midget on his knee.[3] I met him there — but he was a very nice fellow, very able, nice fellow — and I don't hear from him but very seldom. I thing his patriotism might compare with some of the rest of us, but whether he'd be patriotic enough to want to die on this year's schedule or not — just to make Morgenthau's budget balance — I mean that's asking a good deal of a man to just die right off just so I can balance my budget. He might be rather unreasonable and not want to do it. I say, old men is contrary — you know what I mean. And rich old men is awful contrary. They've had their own way so long. You can't——

So in order for Mr. Morgenthau's plan to work out, I — well, I say for it to work out a hundred percent, he's got to bump these wealthy guys off, or something. Well, now, the government's doing everything else, you know, but there is a humane society.

You know, there was another — there was another big plan developed during the week. Did you read about Aimee McPherson meeting Gandhi in India? Yes, Sister Aimee met — she had a date with the Mahatma over there, you know. Yes, she had a date with him. It's what the French call a rendezvous. I'd like to have had the talking-movie rights to the conversation between Mahatma and Aimee. I'd love to heard what they said. I think Mahatma wanted her to stay in India and help him with the untouchables, and Aimee says, "Brother Mahatma, you ought to come to Hollywood, you know, and try and get near Garbo and meet some of our unapproachables."

Well, speaking of plans, I will say this for old Huey. He didn't break out with any — he didn't hatch any new plans during the week. He's just settin' on the same eggs he was.

Now a little later on I want to tell you — a little later on — to be exact, I think it's seven o'clock our time out here, and I guess that makes about four hours difference, eleven hours in the East. You know what time it is. But tonight later on, the president of our United States is going to be on the air. He hasn't spoken to us since last September. He's spoke to a lot of people, but not us, I mean. He must have something important to say, because he just don't go shooting off every time he sees a microphone like some of these other candidates do. They can't pass a microphone without yowling in it.

And I don't know what he's going to talk about. Maybe he'll talk about Mae West.[4] Everybody else is. In fact, I bet he'd rather talk about Mae then some of the things — some of the things that he'll feel obliged to talk on tonight. You can explain Mae's husbands easier than they could the NRA, I'll bet. You know, speaking of Mae, I'll bet there's nothing that would embarrass a successful person, you know, any more than having some old husbands show up on you at the wrong time. Just when she thought she had him in Brooklyn, he showed up.

The president is liable to talk about catching fish off Astor's yacht. He's been down there. But I bet he don't talk on that, for he never did catch anything on that old tub. There's fish in the ocean, but that yacht gets theirs out of the fish market. They used to have photographers — you remember, they used to have photographers — that did nothing but just follow our presidents around just to take the pictures of 'em when they fished, you know. Remember that? Even Mr. Coolidge used to drag in a little inoffensive little perch now and again. Poor little fish — he'd drag him in just for the Sunday supplement. And Mr. Hoover threw out and hooked some old mudcat for a hungry land sometimes. But there's been three photographers starved to death during Roosevelt's administration waitin' for this Astor's yacht to approach even a crawdad. They ought to put skis on that Astor yacht and go fur hunting. [laughter/applause] Much obliged. You remember your history, don't you! You remember how some of our big estates were founded.

He might talk about the bonus. The president might. He's kind of switched over on that. He has a plan of paying it. I never saw so many schemes put forward, you know. They want to pay it—all of them—the soldiers want to receive it, but it's just the way — everybody's got their own way and want to do it. I don't know how they can have so many different schemes when it's — it's paying the same bunch of men and the same bunch of money. Seems to me like they'll have to do with the bonus like we have to do with everything else now to get anybody to take it. They'll have to wrap it in cellophane.

But he may speak on that. And I'll touch lightly on it because I don't want to interfere with anything he would say. Mine is just a — mine is just a little preliminary — introductory remarks to his. Of course, he's liable to touch on some of these new schemes to spend this $5 billion. You know, you can't spend — now there's something you've got to have a plan for. You can't spend $5 billion in the old-fashioned way. I'll bet you couldn't put a strong man in the treasury warehouse full of $100 bills and give him a scoop shovel, and he couldn't shovel out that much money in the rest of his life, you know.

We used to — we couldn't spell a billion dollars much less to realize

132

it and count it or anything. But we now — now we're a nation we learn awful fast, and we won't be long now till we'll be aworkin' on the word trillion — that follows — billion and then trillion. You'll read in the papers, "Congress has just been asked to appropriate $2 trillion to relieve the dependents of a race of people called Wall Streeters." The paper will go further on to say, "This is a worthy cause, and no doubt this small appropriation will be made, as these are dependents of the once proud race — the once proud race — and after all, they're wards of the government."

Now they got another plan. They got another plan. They've figured out what's wrong with this country. I'll bet you couldn't guess it in a million years. You couldn't guess this plan they've figured out what's the matter with the country, and they're going to spend a half a billion dollars on it. I'll bet you couldn't figure out what it is. Well, you know what it is? Well, it's the people trying to cross the railroad track without looking both ways.

It's going to fix the grade crossings — that's what that is, you'll say, "Well, the problem is to teach the people to look both ways. Drive up to the track and look up and down and then cross." Yes, well that's exactly what is the matter with us — even when it don't apply to railroad trains. Everybody's — everybody looks one way — in 1928 and '29, you remember? That's when the train hit all of us. There wasn't a soul — there wasn't a soul in the United States that looked both ways then. Now we've gone to the other extreme. We're so scared now that we drive up to the track and we won't do anything. We just stand there. We just stand there and look and look, and we won't cross the track at all. We even won't trust our own eyesight. If a train goes by and it looks like everything is O.K. and we might be able to cross, we won't do it. We're so scared that we think it might turn around and come back and hit us again.

That's what the president is liable to talk on. It's to try to get us to quit standing there looking and shaking and being scared that something's going to happen to us. He'll tell us this is the same track, you know, — this is the same old track and you've been crossing it for years. And all we have to do is just to use some judgment and carry on just as we have been for years. But we won't believe him. He's got to go to work — and now he's got to build a runway over the top of all these railroads — over the top or under the bottom and get that under there. They get that all done — course, I think it's a good plan. Mind you, I'm not against it. I think it's a fine plan, and it will give a lot of people to work and do a lot of things, although I don't think that it will do everything that it's supposed to do.

I don't think it will save all the lives, 'cause I think this grade-crossing thing — you'll just rush right over the grade crossing and right on down and get hit at the first intersection by a bus. That's what you'll do. That's one thing about buses. You know, there's one thing about a bus, they're bigger than trains are now, and death is more certain with a bus. When you get hit with that, there's no lingering illness with that at all. And the buses come so much oftener than the trains do anyhow. A lot of times — a lot of times people have had to wait pretty near a day to get hit by a train, you know, they come so seldom, but buses — there's so many of them, you can get hit pretty near anytime.

I'll bet you never did read, too, of a train ever hitting a car with just one person in it — just the driver, just one lone passenger. They just wait — they just wait till the car gets loaded, and then they hit everybody, and—— [alarm rings] Oh, here, wait a minute. I'm not through here. Now, next Sunday I'm going to try and dig you up — if you want plans, brother, I've got one. Good night. Thank you.

Good Gulf Show

May 5, 1935

ANNOUNCER:

ROGERS: I tell you, I'm in no — I'm in no condition to address the country today. After opening a thousand letters and not a dime among 'em, I — I'm just on the verge of becoming a bolshevik. It's just things like that — you know, that makes a man a Russian.

When Jim Farley, the postmaster general, started this thing to show that he could sell more stamps than any postmaster since Will Hays — and then the silver interest — they were behind it in order to push the sale of dimes. Farley with his stamps and Key Pittman of Nevada up here with his silver, and — they started the whole thing.[1]

Of course, it's nothing but Huey's old Share-the-Wealth Plan. That's what it is. It was a plan put in to, kind of, stop Huey — only Huey was going to do it in dollars and these boys with dimes. These fellows wanted to get everybody in America a dime, and Huey wanted to get 'em a dollar. Just the difference in philanthropy of the two people.

Maybe the reason I'm kind of prejudiced against it is I haven't received any dimes. But maybe the reason I haven't received any is that I haven't sent out one yet. I was kind of like big business is in this country now. I was waiting to see if this thing works without me investing anything first.

Did you ever see — did you ever see or hear of anything in your life as nutty as that thing was, you know? And my Lord, it was worse in Hollywood than anywhere. Everybody — imagine now, everybody was to spend a dime and everybody was to receive $1,600. I tell you when a country falls for a thing like that, it just

135

makes you doubly sure that our school system is a failure. [Rogers leaves air for sixteen seconds.] We like to gamble. We really do. We like to take a chance. We take 'em every day in a car rushing to save a minute with nothing to do when we get the minute saved.

But our whole Depression was brought on by gambling — not alone in the stock market but in expanding and borrowing and going in debt, all just to make some money quick. But you know, looking it up you'll find that we come by our gambling instinct honestly. Just to show that, in 16 — I believe it was 1612, the state of Virginia financed — they financed the first lottery in this country. They financed the government with a lottery. They didn't have any way to raise any money, and nobody could think of a sales tax in those days, and nobody even thought of a gasoline tax. Up to then they'd never needed any tax money for there wasn't any politicians. But in 1612 some wise guy decided that he would like to live off of the other Virginians. And instead of living off of the forest, he says, "I'll just live off of those boys." So they called him a politician. And they had to get him some tax money. So politics started — it really started on these shores, as I say, in 1612. And in 325 years—the short space of 325 years—it has grown in leaps and bounds until it's now become America's leading racket.

Lotteries has played — it really has played a great part in our whole history of our country. Now if I remember right — I know it's just a hundred years — in 1712 Philadelphia put on a big lottery — a giant lottery. It tells a lot about it in those early things there. Now notice the dates: Virginia in 1612, Philadelphia in 1712. It just took Philadelphia exactly a hundred years to get the news that Virginia had put one on — and that the thing worked. Now the old Quakers in Philadelphia, they might have been mighty moral people, but when you dangled a nice fat prize in front of them they reached down between the leaves of the old prayer book and come back with enough to purchase a few shares in this lottery.

In 17 — I think it was 1750 — if I remember my dates, in 1750—stop me if I'm wrong—Yale University needed some money. Now get this. Yale needed some money and a new stadium, and so they put on a lottery. Now, not only was it history but it was a success, and they built a lot of new buildings in Yale — at Yale. In 1772 — if I remember — I remember the date because it was twenty-two years later. In 1772, just twenty-two years later, Harvard heard what Yale had done — you see, in those days Harvard was only twenty-two years behind Yale, and — of course, they gradually lost ground from then on. Harvard needed some new buildings and some football players, and they pulled a lottery. They drew the buildings, but they never drew any players. And they never held any more lotteries. They become so disgusted, they took up the English language instead of the American language, and today it's the only — it's the only college that's carried on in a foreign tongue.

Now, here's something I bet you you didn't know. I bet you didn't know this. I bet you you didn't know the Revolutionary War was largely financed by lotteries. They sold tickets on that, you know. They made it a sporting event instead of a war. George Washington — history shows that George Washington always had number one lottery ticket in every lottery. George had number one — and one time he won. That's when he bought Mount Vernon. Yes, sir, they made a sweepstakes out of the Revolutionary War. They sold England some tickets — but not the right ones. They didn't win anything.

Well, that was then. And then the reason I can remember this date because it was just a hundred years later. Seems that all of these lotteries run in hundreds. In 1812, coming on down — in 1812 there was a great wave of unemployment through the country. Couldn't blame that on the Republican party anyhow. That was in 1812, and they financed the money for public works by lotteries. They did that by lotteries. Got public works in 1812 by lottery. Now they do it by magic.

Lotteries in our history come clear on down to Louisiana. You all remember when Louisiana — the Louisiana Lottery. It was doing great till they drew Huey Long and then they stopped it. Every time a church wants to raise money, they put on a raffle. A raffle, that's just kind of the Ford of lotteries. [laughter] Much obliged. I thought that was a pretty good little gag, too.

Now wait a minute. Millions — millions of dollars were spent yesterday on the Kentucky Derby, and there's just hundreds, and hundreds and hundreds of millions that goes out of this country every year to foreign lotteries. Now here's my plan. Now mind you, this is not the real Rogers Plan that I've been talking about. This is a temporary plan till I can get my mind on a better one — which may be next Sunday or may possibly be later. I propose — I'm proposing a giant lottery. The more gianter the better. Let the government, you know, build a big one. It's to be put on by the government. Still there's a lot of kick about the government going into

137

business, so we may have to let the United States Chamber of Commerce put it on. Or, maybe the American Federation of Labor, or the Elks, or the Legion.

But my plan is to let each organization sell all the tickets they can, you know, for the lottery. The government sells, the U. S. Chamber sells, the Federation, the Elks, the Legion — every organization, women's clubs, everything. Then the one selling the most is automatically the best organization — business organization, and then we don't have this argument over who's the best. If the U. S. Chamber wins, they will have proved it instead of just admitting it like they are now.

In most lotteries, I imagine they take out about 20 or 25 percent for the charity that they're doing it for. You know. But in my plan — my plan — the RLTEPUICTOABO Plan, that's the Rogers Lottery Temporary — Until I Can Think of a Better Plan. Remember the initials now, RLTEPUICTOABO Plan—Rogers Lottery Temporary Emergency Plan Until I Can Think of a Better One.

I take 50 percent of the whole fund. It goes to relief. Ten percent goes to expenses. See what I mean? And commissions to the people that sell the tickets. Now the 40 percent goes to the winners. You say, "Yeah, but will they invest this money when they know they're going to get only 40 percent of it back?" Certainly they will, because the winners — the losers wasn't going to get anything, and the winners ought to be tickled to get that much back. They don't know whether they're going to win or not anyhow.

All of this money is to go to pay for all relief. Now, mine, it does away with all this relief money they're spending. This replaces all relief and all things of a charitable nature.

But this is the big thing in my plan. How are you going to make the rich fellow — the old conservative rich fellow — buy any tickets? Well, make — every man has got to buy and spend 5 percent of his salary or his earnings has got to go — or he's got to spend of his gross income 5 percent. If he makes a hundred thousand a year, he's got to buy $5,000 worth of tickets. If he makes a million, he's got to buy $50,000 worth of tickets. Now, he's got to give half of those tickets to a fund, and this fund is to provide tickets for all people that can't afford to buy any. See?

That's for the poor people — for the poor people, women and children and all, charity patients in a hospital — every man, woman, and child in this country must have a ticket. In that way we keep this a democratic country. You see, according to my plan, you make — you make the moneyed interest pay for the less fortunate. It's the only plan that a rich man won't kick on because he's still holding a couple of thousand of tickets of his own. See what I mean? After he give up half of them — you can always get money out of a rich guy if you can show him where there's a chance that he's liable to bring something home with him, you know. Then, too, he feels like he's provided thousands of tickets for the ones, you know, that maybe couldn't afford a ticket.

The whole thing is a sort of glorified Wall Street, only you don't need as much money and you have more chance to win. That was the idea. Now here's another new angle to my plan. Don't make the lottery on a horse race. I propose that the real big lottery — that the real big lottery be made on our national election — on a presidential election, which is about, you know, it's about to die out on account of interest anyway, you know. I don't know, we're just losing interest in it. Our two national parties have got to a point where there's no difference in them anyhow. You can't tell a Democrat from — whatever one will promise, the other will see him and then raise him. Then if there's a third party it adds up what the other two have promised and it'll promise as much as both of them combined, and the general public, I don't know, they've just lost all interest and don't care nothing about it.

Everybody that — in my plan now everybody that has hopes for running for president on any and all tickets his name is in there. See, it's all in there like it is with these horses — in the Grand National or the Kentucky Derby or any of these sweepstakes. Their names are all in there. And a couple of weeks before election — or a month — you draw out these names, and there'll be hundreds of tickets on each candidate. There won't be just one winner. There'll be lots of winners and lots of tickets on each candidate. And thousands of cash prizes. Some tremendous prizes, you know.

So in the draw you make it Mr. Hoover, Mr. Vandenberg, or Franklin Delano Roosevelt, Teddy Roosevelt, or Eleanor Roosevelt, or Buzzy Roosevelt, or Sister Roosevelt, or Father Coughlin, Upton Sinclair, Townsend, Huey, the governor of Kansas, Ogden Mills — maybe Clark Gable.[2] Now when the drawing is over, then those that have drawn tickets on these various candidates, see, now get this — well, then they get out and start working for them, don't you see? They start working for them. So that way, you would get the interest in the election which you haven't got now. Not because

139

they want him for president, but because they want to collect on these tickets, don't you see?

In that way, we can make our elections a big event. We can make — we can make the American election as big a thing as the Grand National in England, you know — and just as important to the world as that is, or maybe we can make it as big as the Kentucky Derby or the Santa Anita handicap. We would make everybody election conscious, you know. We'd even sell tickets all over the world and get some of this money back over there, instead of us sending it over there, you know, because those people are great gamblers. Any — Europeans are bigger gamblers than us, and they'll likely go where the biggest lottery is.

Now we can't have the biggest army and the biggest navy and all that, but we can have the biggest lottery. And I believe if you take — if you take this plan — if you adopt the Rogers RLTEPUIC-TOABO and put that in — and put that in — and put on the biggest lottery that has ever been, I believe we're going to get our debts back. That's what I think. Because if they send a dollar over and we nick sixty cents out of it, we're going to make some money out of it, aren't we?

Well, that's what I got. I'll rush over — I've got to rush before this fellow's going to blow this horn. I've looked the whole plan over, and I can't find a flaw in it myself because I haven't showed it to anybody else. I haven't told anybody else about it. The poor would be for it and the rich would be for it and the candidates would be for it, and—— Well, here's the main thing it would do: It would give a national election the thing they lack now, which — you know, which is dignity, and prestige, you know. That's what it would give them. [Bell rings.] Thank you very much.

Good Gulf Show

May 12, 1935

ANNOUNCER:

ROGERS: [applause] Thanks, mothers. Get this. This is Mother's Day. It's Mother's Day. Of course it's pretty late in the evening now to remind you of it. If you didn't know it before, there's not much you can do about it now, unless you — well, you might possibly — you might possibly shame you into going or phoning to a florist. They're keeping open this evening just to accommodate late consciences.

Mothers, it's a beautiful thought. I was just in here in another studio listening to a friend of mine, Rabbi Magnin, a very popular Jewish rabbi out here.[1] He's delivering a beautiful thing over Mother's Day, and I felt ashamed to come in with my little words, you know. I mean well, but I ain't got the words. But Mother's Day, it's a beautiful thought, but it's somebody with a hurtin' conscience that thought of the idea. It was someone who had neglected their mother for years, and then they figured out I got to do something about Momma, you know. And then they said, "We'll give Momma a day." And knowing Momma that was easy, they figured, "Well, we'll give her a day, and it will be all right with Momma." Give her a day, and then in return why Mother gives you the other 364. See?

I think that was awful liberal of whoever thought of the idea of giving her one out of the 365. That was tremendously liberal. They could have had — you know, we have Apple Week, and Don't Beat Your Wife Week, and Safety Week, and everything. They could have given Mother a week, but that would have been giving Mother a little the best of it, so they says, "We'll give Mother a day." Of

141

course, I doubt even then if the thing had have gone through if it hadn't been for the florists. They grabbed it and started putting the idea over, you know. These florists, they did that.

Of course, florists, they got mothers, too. Florists have, but they've got more flowers than they've got mothers, and — and they've got a great organization, the florists have. It's nothing unusual any day for me to get a telegram saying, "Congressman Jasbo just died. We have a special spray of beautiful lillies holding until we hear from you." Maybe I didn't no more than know Congressman Jasbo, but it just shows you — [Rogers speaks away from microphone.] I just dropped — it just shows you — I have a habit of playing with a few money while I'm talking — and it just shows you that these florists are on the job every minute.

The florists, they've just practically corralled this Mother's Day business. They — they have led us to believe that no matter how we have treated our mothers during the past year that a little bouquet of hyacinths or verbenas will square it, you know, not only with mother but with our conscience, too, when as a matter of fact you don't have to be squared with your mother. She knows you better than you know yourself.

A mother is the only thing that is so constituted that they possess eternal love under any and all circumstances. No matter how you treat them, you still have their love. I was telling that to my wife today, and I was telling her a little thought that I wanted to use in there, and I said, "You know, Betty," I says, "a mother and a dog is the only two things that has eternal love. No matter how you treat 'em." And my wife made me set the dog out. Said it — well, it didn't sound very good and it might sound disrespectful to a mother, but I certainly didn't mean it that way. But it's the only thing that really is. You know what I mean.

So the poor old dog he'll have to go. I can't use it on account of — my wife made me leave the dog out, but he still loves you just the same, just as much as a mother did. But this being — maybe some day, we'll have Dog Day, too, or something, and I can use that on the dog. I really do. I hate to leave the dog out, but my wife runs this outfit. Well, anyhow, they both — they both certainly — no matter what you do to them, they all love you. And now, Mother, you know, no matter if the children don't write to her, that don't ever make any difference. It don't. It don't. It don't. Her faith is just as long as her memory, you know.

142

Mothers are naturally glad to have this day dedicated to 'em, you know, and they're glad that we pay them this homage and rememberance, but it hasn't increased their love one bit, I don't think. It's made no changes in her. She can see through this Mother's Day thing, you know. She knows that we were almost forced by law to do something about her. And there's no conceit — there's no conceit in a mother. She's not taking it conceitedly at all, and there's much wisdom in her, you know, and she knows how it comes about.

But to get back to this flower business, there's nothing in the world more beautiful than flowers. The florists and the horticulturists, they've done great things to nurse these flowers along until they're beautiful beyond — well, anything we could possibly think of. And every home that can possibly afford 'em should have flowers all you can. But on the other hand, there's an awful lot of need and want in the country, and I got a plan. I've got another plan. My plan is not to eliminate flowers. I'm strong for flowers, but they've just got one drawback. You can't eat 'em. And I imagine an awful lot of mothers today would not have rebelled if you'd sent 'em a ham. Yeah, a cut of beef or a whole lamb or something.

What I'm getting at is suppose the growers — the meat growers, had been on the job and linked Mother's Day up with their organization like the florists have, you know. If they'd done that, instead of receiving a bunch of hollyhocks, she'd receive a cluster of pork chops, you know. So my plan is to give mothers — is to give mothers more than one day. Pardon my generosity toward mothers. It may be unfounded, but I would just give mothers at least twelve days a year. I'd say, for instance — I'd say the first day of every month is going to be Mother's Day. You'd have to have initials for it, because you have to have initials to get anything by now. The initials would be the RM — RMISWD — WD — RMISWD, Remember Mothers in a Substantial Way Day. That's what it would be called. Remember Mothers — the initials RMISWD, Remember Mothers in a Substantial Way Day.

January the first we'd start off and that would be Mother's Forgotten Christmas Present Day. All sons and daughters who had forgot to send anything Christmas, they'd have a week more to remember it in. Incidentally, could send her some presents that they got that they didn't care for, too. Then February the first would be Gloves and Mittens and Overshoes Day. She'd have worn out the old ones chopping wood to cook for you. Then one day would be Mother's

143

Dress Day. Mother hadn't had a new dress since father went to jail for it. And then they could have that. And one day would be Mother's Transportation Day. That is, those that could afford it could give their mother a car or something. The modern mother, she don't want lilacs or a corsage of pansies or something, but give her a Model T Ford — or you could give her anything — give her a car — Chevy or a Ford, or anything, or a Chrysler. And those who couldn't afford it could give her a bicycle. A modern mother could ride it. You know that I mean it. Shorts and a bicycle would be a great thing for her, you know. She's right there, you know. She'd take that in preference to a little spray of Johnny jump-ups or trumpet vines or something.

Then one — then one of the twelve mother's days would be — would be called — let's see — PMRD — oh, Pay Mother's Rent Day. That would be one day. That wouldn't be bad one. Pay Mother's Rent Day. It looks like a big idea. I don't know of any project that has any bigger field to draw from, you know, 'cause practically everyone has a mother, if I can get all of them in there. So watch the Rogers' Twelve Mother's Day a Year Plan—the RTMDYP—Rogers' Twelve Mother's Day a Year Plan.

Father had a day, but you can't find anybody who remembers when it was. It's been so confused with April the first. This has been one of the biggest years mothers has had. It's been a great year for mothers. The Dio — Don — triplets — quin — well, there's a mess of 'em.[2] I don't know how many there is. Up in Canada. That's kind — you know, they've — you know, that's been a great boost for motherhood. It's put motherhood on a mass production basis. And then there's an awful lot of twins out in Hollywood. Pretty near everybody in Hollywood's been having twins and triplets and all, and it's made the mother of only one chick practically discouraged. That's about all I know about the mother business.

Since my lecture last Sunday night on the evils of putting your trust in getting wealthy by waiting for somebody to send you some dimes, I've received thousands of letters — over a thousand — that's correct, over a thousand letters and three dimes. I got three dimes. So I seem to been the only one that made any money out of this craze. Am thirty cents in the clear up to now. I'm not knocking the plan as much as I was last week.

You know, last week I told you about the Rogers Giant Lottery Plan. Well, that's received endorsement beyond any expectations that

I possibly could think of. You know, there's bills in Congress now to carry on and legalize lotteries, and I received a wire this week from a congressman friend of mine who wants a copy of my plan to read in the *Congressional Record*. Now, I feel pretty good about that; that's the highest praise that a humorist can have is to get yourself into the *Congressional Record*. Just — just think, my name will be right in there along side of Huey Long's and all those other big humorists.

You see, ordinarily you got to work your way up as a humorist and first get into Congress. Then you work on up into the Senate, and then if your stuff is funny enough it goes into the *Congressional Record*. But for an outsider to get in there as a humorist without having served his apprenticeship in either the House or the Senate, why that's — mind you, I'm not bragging, but by golly I feel pretty big about it.

Did I ever tell you—I don't know whether I did—did I ever tell you about the first time I had any of my — I ever had any stuff in that daily? Well, I'd written some fool thing, and it pertained to the bill that they was arguing, or that they was kidding about rather, at the time in Congress. It's in the Senate, rather. So some senator read my little article, and anything that a senator reads goes into the *Record*. And as it was during his speech, it naturally went in. So another senator rose and said, you know as they always do if you ever seen 'em, "Does the gentleman yield?" They always say that. They call each other gentlemen in there. But the tone — the tone that they put on the word, it would be more appropriate — you know, the way they can say gentleman — you know what I mean. It would sound right if they come right out and said, "Does the coyote from Maine yield?" You know what I mean. That's about the way it sounds, you know.

He says gentleman, but it kind of sounds like coyote, you know. And then the man says, "I yield," for if he don't, the other guy will keep on talking anyhow.

So the coyote from Maine says, "I yield to the polecat from Oregon." You know, he don't say polecat, but I mean he says gentleman in such a way that it's almost like polecat. Well, anyhow, that's the way they do. They're very polite in there.

Well, anyhow, but I must get back to my story. When this senator read my offering, the other senator said, after all the yielding was all over, the other senator said, "I object. I object to the remarks of a professional joke maker being put into the *Congressional Record.*'' You know, meaning me. See? Taking a dig at me, see? They didn't want any outside fellow contributing. Well, he had me wrong. Compared to them, I'm an amateur, and the things about my jokes is they don't hurt anybody. You can take 'em or leave 'em. You know what I mean. You know, you say, well they're funny, or they're terrible, or they're good, or whatever it is, but they don't do any harm. You can just pass them by. But with Congress, every time they make a joke it's a law. You know. And everytime they make a law it's a joke.

So, since then I've had my lawyer — I've got a lawyer there in Washington to protect my interests. And every time they put any of my stuff into that *Congressional Record* I'm going to sue 'em. I'll sue 'em, and here's the grounds I'll sue 'em on: For putting in — for putting my material where it won't be read.

But listen, no kidding, they're a likable bunch of guys. And say, do you take the *Congressional Record?* If you don't, you do so. Have them send you a copy all the time. Write them. They'll send you one. There's some mighty good stuff in there sometimes. Pretty near all the articles in this month's issue is by Huey, but they got some good writers in there, but a lot of 'em are lazy and they won't contribute. You see, they get paid whether they contribute anything — whether they say anything or not. See? And you know the way our congressional business is being carried on nowadays, being a senator — a congressman is not much. It just really consists in receiving telegrams. That's about all it is.

They just get up and see how many telegrams they got. And these poor fellows — you know they are. I've got great sympathy for our lawmakers. They're just deviled to death. ''Do this or we'll defeat you.'' Another telegram says, ''If you don't do this, we'll defeat you.'' And the poor fellows, you know, the legislatures, their lives are just made unhappy. I come to the conclusion that they have a pretty tough time. Well, while maybe they get paid good — we'll admit that. They're paid well, but considering their worry they earn it. You take thousands and millions of our worthy people are on relief now. They're the ones that everybody naturally sympathizes with. But they have one thing that they can be proud of. Maybe, though, through no fault of their own, they're on relief or something. But they have one consolation over a congressman or a senator; they can receive a letter and open it without being called a horse thief or a demagogue or a man that's going to poison the well, whether it's awful to drink just to get elected or something. That's what happens — the poor old lawmaker receives every time he opens his mail.

That's a good deal for me to say about them. But I feel that they are having a tough time. And the rich man, nobody's living in more fear than he is today. He's afraid Roosevelt is going to sneak up on him in the night and sandbag him and take all he's saved. And the ordinary well-to-do man, the medium class, he thinks he's carrying the whole load. And last, Mr. Roosevelt, his troubles — he's got a lot of troubles besides reelection. He's got more worries than all the other ones. It just looks like a time when everybody thinks that somebody else is oppressing him, you know. We are living in an age, you know, when everybody's got it in for us or oppressing us in some way. If the rich are worried then the senators are worried, and the congressman's worried, and the president is worried, and the middle class is worried, and it just looks like when you add it all up, why, nobody seems to have got the best of it anyhow.

So everything's about equal. And if all of them would just quit laying it on to the others for causing the ills and admit — well, maybe I had something to do with it myself, you know. Maybe, my troubles are not all somebody else's. And when it's all said and done, you know, maybe none of 'em — maybe all of 'em ain't as bad off — as bad off as we think we are.

But we have — we have got a complex now where we're just fearing everything. Any class — one class is a — is in a rage against another, and another one against another, and that's the way we're going through it. And none of us will admit that maybe we was — maybe we was in the wrong. [Alarm rings.]

Wait a minute, here. Ain't got through. Good night. Thanks. I'll finish this thing next Sunday night, my oration on this. A big plan for fathers next Sunday night. Good night.

Good Gulf Show

May 19, 1935

ANNOUNCER:

ROGERS: [applause] Much obliged. I first want to tell the radio audience where I'm at. I'm broadcasting from Sacramento, California; that's our capital out here, a beautiful state capital located in the civilized end of the state. Thought you all ought to do better up here on that than that. [laughter/applause] That was put in purely — I said that purely for your benefit.

It's one of the old cities founded during the gold rush days, Sacramento was. They used to use gold for money at one time in this country, but now it's the only thing you can't use for money. You can — you can print some money or you can issue some bonds and pay the bankers interest on 'em, but — you can use pretty near anything for money in this country with the exception of gold now. They keep that. They keep what gold we've got in the — it's in the warehouse for ballast, I reckon. I don't know what they're usin' it for. They will let you draw out a little bit every once in a while for your teeth or something.

We've got quite a distinguished audience up here — out here today. The governor was coming. It's 4:30 up here in this place now. It's 4:30 in the afternoon out here — in Hiram Johnson's time.[1] Hiram Johnson, senator, he runs this state just as much as Huey Long runs Louisiana, only Hiram don't say anything about it—but runs it better. Well, it's 4:30 out here now, and we got quite an audience here. The governor — I met him at breakfast over there. Said he was coming, but he had to go out of here and crown some queen. Said he crowned the same queen twelve years in a row out here, and he's gone out there. That's Governor Merriam.[2] The folks

148

all back East know him as Governor Merriam — and he won from
Sinclair. He's one of the few Republicans to escape the '32
massacre. Like everybody that was elected in 1932 that had to hold
office during this — well, I'd call it the TYFOH time, Tough Years
for Office Holders.

You got to have initials for everything now, so that's what this
period is, the TYFOH, Tough Years for Office Holders. Well, people that were elected in 1932, they're not right sure yet whether
they was the winners or not. They kind of think that maybe the
fellow they defeated was really the winner. But anyhow, this fellow
— he's got a terrible job. He's got to raise about 200 million extra
dollars out here, and there's nobody in the state that wants to help
him out on it in any way.

He's got a legislature here. In fact, we got quite a few of them here
in the hall this afternoon. We've got quite a few of the legislature
— always an undesirable element pretty near anywhere you go.
We're up here — we're up here with a movie company, and the
legislature, as I say — they're here, and people can't hardly tell
which is which.[3] We're up here making a comedy to try and put
over on the people, and they're up here working on one to try to
put it all on the same people. Their comedy is going to have a little drama in it. For anytime — anytime you — anytime you stick
a couple of hundred million dollars on a state in taxes, why you're
getting into tragedy then. That's what you're doing. See?

They're — they're going to have — hang around — they're going
to put a good deal of it, I think — a good deal of this tax they're
going to put on the movies, you know. So I guess I'm about the
only one that will speak to any of them, you know. I've been up
here working on this movie, and I met quite a few of them and
talked. You know, they're going to put this big tax on there.
They've got some kind of income tax, three times bigger than
anywhere else. But the joke on us movies, they won't hook us so
bad because we don't have to pay on what we're advertised that
we get. We only have to pay on what we get. So this legislature
that's in here this afternoon — when they collect that tax they're
going to get a terrible jolt, you know. None of these press agents'
salaries ain't going to go, you know.

I believe I'm about the only movie actor that hasn't been kicking
and hollerin' about going somewhere else. But they ain't going
nowhere. None of the movies ain't going any further east than East

Hollywood, none of them. But — well, anyhow — so they're in here, and I'm glad to welcome them around here. If I can offer them any advice while I'm here — they've asked Mr. Cobb and I to come over and speak at the legislature, and we're trying to think up something foolish enough now that they might adopt.

Well, anyhow — then — let's see, what else we got about the legislature. There's an awful lot — there's an awful lot of lobbyists up here, too. I stayed over here at a hotel, where I believe I'm the only one in there that ain't a lobbyist. You know — you know, there's an awful bunch of them. In Washington they had — they had to put a code in just for lobbyists. There's so many of them now in Washington that they have a code there for 'em, and according to the code you're not allowed to accost or go near a senator while he's speaking on the floor. You've got to wait until he sits down, you know.

You know in this movie thing, another thing — they don't realize that us movie folks — our careers don't last very long, you know. Naturally, we're just in as long as our looks. Now take me. I'm going twice a week now for a facial. And I'm liable to have to stretch that out into three times, you know. But they're doing pretty good, the legislatures. The other day they repealed a law up here where — where everybody that's married — you know, when you was married you had to give three days' notice. You used to have to in this state, to give the intention of marrying. Well, they did away with that now. That was longer than most of the marriages in California was lasting. So they did away with that. So now you don't have to file any intention of marrying at all. In fact, you don't have to give your right name according to this new law. You just pay a small amusement tax is all.

Then they passed one here the other day — they passed one here — the legislature — to give the Indians the liquor. Well, I don't mean you actually give 'em the liquor but allow them to get it if they can. They're allowed to buy it. One old California cowpuncher from over here in Mono County, he put that over. He put that in there — the bill through. He told them we ought to give the Indians something back — their land or the liquor, so they compromised on giving 'em the liquor. We kept the land and give 'em the liquor.

There's nothing wrong about the morals of the bill for the poor Indian hasn't got enough to buy any anyhow, but it did raise the Indian's social standing up to the white man's. He is equal with us

150

now. The Indian can get out and get drunk according to law now, where he couldn't do it before. The Indian used to be the ward of the government, but now we all are. Everybody's an Indian.

This legislature up here will have to be gettin' through in about another week because the money runs out, and they just get paid for — what is it? About another week, isn't it? About another week, they said — and then they money runs out and they don't — they pay them so many days, and they messed around this time and ain't done nothing. They're gonna have to stop, and they don't know what they're going to do. They've got this limit on the pay, there ain't anything that will dampen a man's public spirit any more than to cut off his salary, you know. He just kind of loses his taste for doing something for his fellow man after that.

A lot of state capitals, or state legislatures, have tried burning down the capitol to get 'em out, but this way California's got is the best way. You just stop the pay, that's the quickest way to get 'em out. But they're liable — they're liable to raise some kind of fund, for the government has given money for all kinds of relief, and Roosevelt hates to see any place close down. And I wouldn't be surprised if he don't keep this thing going right on through, you know — just like he does — just like he does with his three C camps. He wants to do that to keep the boys off the street. He's liable to give 'em money out here just to keep you senators off the same place. It would have a name, too. It'd be called the SSRF, State Senators' Reconstruction Fund.

We've been out here on a boat where we're making this speech — I mean, making our movie, rather, in here. So I — so I just come in — I just come in from out there. Oh, say, I want to compliment my old friend, the state of Texas, down there. They drew the first prize — they drew the first prize in this lottery — this lottery — this relief lottery.[4] They pulled down the grand prize, $29 million — Texas did. Texas got $29 million. New York got next prize of 24 million. Pennsylvania got third with 23 million. This is one of the biggest lotteries that was ever pulled off anywhere. It beat — it beat the Grand National or the Irish Sweepstakes. Pennsylvania got 23 million, and they was all Republicans. You know, I think that speaks awful well for the Democrats. It just shows they're human after all. They're 'ot going to let even a Republican starve. Now I'll tell you—— [laughter]

California, we didn't get so much. You legislatures know that. We didn't do so good. We only got about 14 million, or something like that. I don't want to criticize, but I think Mr. Hoover criticized a little too early, you know. I think he knocked us out of 10 or 15 million there. We'd have got a little more if it hadn't been for him. You can't knock the man that's paying you, you know that.

I've got here today what we call — artists have all the time a guest artist. Mr. Cobb and I — Irvin Cobb and I are here working on a picture together. We're up here taking scenes on the river. We're working on the Sacramento River. And we could have worked on the Los Angeles River, but they'd have had to haul the water too far.

I hope some of these relief agencies — I hope some of these relief agencies are going — they're talking about it — Mr. McAdoo, our senator, is, and he's going to get them to see if he can't get them to irrigate this Los Angeles River.[5] But we're up here now work-ing on this. We was going to take this — it's supposed to be a scene laid on the Ohio River near Paducah, Kentucky, Mr. Cobb's home. We couldn't do it there because he couldn't go back.

And in the story — in the story, which is from a very popular book called *Steamboat Round the Bend*, we play steamboat captains, he and I, and we have a race. Cobb is the captain of the *Pride of Paducah*, and I'm the admiral of the *Claremore Queen*. If this news of *Claremore* gets back to Claremore that they had a big steam-wheeler named after 'em, it'll be a surprise to them. Mr. Cobb is the author also of our most popular picture *Judge Priest*, the best I ever got mixed up in.[6] He's getting another *Judge Priest*-type of story ready for us. We have Mr. Jack Ford directing us up here — the same man that directed Mr. — that directed *Judge Priest*.[7]

Cobb's been on a riverboat before, and he's kind of our technical director, too. He's familiar with it. I was never on one of those things before, and he tells us how to act and not to walk off when the thing has left the shore and tied up. And now I take great pleasure in introducing my very good friend and one of America's greatest humorists, writers, and all-round human beings, Irvin Cobb! Hello, Irv. [applause]

COBB: Thank you, Bill. Thank you, ladies and gentlemen. As I under-stand it, a guest artist, so-called, is supposed to stand up here and let the real performer riddle him with questions, and I think Bill has got a few little queries he wants to put to me this afternoon. He has a morbid desire to smoke me out on my private life.

ROGERS: Well, how do you like — you're out here, Irvin, and how do you like Hollywood?

COBB: Well, Bill, asking a man how he likes Hollywood is like asking a man with a wen on his nose how he likes having a wen on his nose. You in time get used to a wen on your nose, but you never really care for it.

ROGERS: What is a wen? I don't — we don't use 'em in Oklahoma. What's that?

COBB: Plural of wind.

ROGERS: Is it a wart?

COBB: Yes, it's a wart. If it grows on your neck you fasten your collar button on it in Oklahoma.

ROGERS: Say, I didn't know what it was. Honest, I didn't. Do you like the movie business, Irvin?

COBB: I didn't know it was a business. I thought it was a racket.

ROGERS: As long as you stay in it, the more you realize it is. That's right. What would your advice be to men of your age and looks? Would it be to come to Hollywood? I mean, would you——

COBB: If there is one that answers to that description, it's a rotten thing to say about both of us. I really didn't come. I don't want any competition.

ROGERS: Do you — I've noticed on the set — for the few days we've been working up here — do you make up for pictures? Do you make up — do you use makeup or anything?

COBB: Will, I — I carry a cigar, and if I've been to a banquet the night before I generally have a good cigar.

ROGERS: Do you find down in Hollywood — you've been there quite a while. I see you a lot. Do you find the night life down there with the movies kind of gets you or anything?

COBB: I haven't been up late enough yet to see.

ROGERS: What's your favorite night spot down there in Hollywood? What is it?

COBB: A good American-plan, two-dollar-a-day hotel.

ROGERS: What do you do to keep your weight down like it is?

COBB: I don't keep my weight down. It's my weight that's keeping me down.

ROGERS: You do — you are looking a little thinner, I believe. Have you ever seen Greta Garbo? You've been out there messin' around a good deal. Have you ever seen her?

COBB: No. I think she comes under the head of Aryan myths. I never saw her. I think Garbo must be like Santa Claus. Everybody talks about it; nobody ever sees one. But I'm living in the house she used to live in. She left me a legacy. I found a Swedish hot water bottle after she left.

ROGERS: He is at that — that's no kidding — he bought the place — he bought this place.

COBB: People who haven't heard the news drive in looking for Greta, and they see me sitting there. And one old lady from the Middle West said, "Oh Lord, how that girl's changed," and drove right out.

ROGERS: He sure does. She had a great place. He bought that, and he lives down in there. Did you ever see Mae West?

COBB: Yes, years ago, but I don't want to brag about that because apparently everybody — everybody who used to know Mae claims they're married to her.

ROGERS: You ain't liable to show up in this thing as one of her old husbands or anything are you? You're liable to, you know.

COBB: Oh no, they're no novelty. They'll be having choruses of them in New York in a couple of weeks.

ROGERS: Do you feel yourself kind of going Hollywood in any way, you know? We all kinda do. It kind of gets us down there. Do you feel yourself doing that?

COBB: Well, I find that I'm talking to myself, and worse than that I'm answering back. And I've been cutting out paper dolls at odd times——

ROGERS: Saying your own "yeses"?

COBB: Yes. I'm living in Yes Man's Land, which is worse than No Man's Land was during the war. I haven't worn slacks yet.

ROGERS: Do you find——

COBB: I'm still sticking to my first wife. I guess I haven't gone Hollywood.

ROGERS: Do you find that this censorship that Will Hays has got in on us now is — does it kind of interfere with you? Sort of cramp your emotions in any way?

COBB: Well, I notice as a result of Will Hays' campaign, they no longer talking about putting a tax on raw film.

ROGERS: Raw film! [laughs] Say, now listen — who's — who's — who's your favorite male actor?

COBB: Well now, Will, that's an embarrassing thing to ask me. With my affection for you, as a tribute to you, I ought to say my favorite actor is that sterling, finished performer—maybe he don't know it yet, but he's a finished performer—Will Rogers! But since I must be honest before this great audience, I'll admit that my favorite is — Stepin Fetchit.[8]

ROGERS: [Bell rings.] Aw here, wait a minute. I wanted to ask you about the women, but you're all out. Well, good-bye, and thank you, Irvin, very, very much.

155

Good Gulf Show

May 26, 1935

ANNOUNCER:

ROGERS: [applause] Thank you. Well, back here in Los Angeles with you all. I just — I was up — I was up in Sacramento last week, and — up at the capital — California capital. They asked me — they wanted me to address the legislature, but I — we finished the scenes we were taking in our picture up there, Irvin Cobb and I, and I rushed back. I didn't get to do it. But it wouldn't have done much — there's nothing much you could do about a legislature. I mean it wouldn't have done much good to address them. It's almost hopeless, and just about all you can do is just pay 'em and then hope for the best.

Funny joke on this, though. They run out of money Wednesday, and they're working for noth — they're not getting anything now, so they're getting just about what they're worth.

Well, now, let me see. This is the — let me see — this is those — those children — what's the name? They're the Dones — Dones — Don — Dionne. You pronounce it like — like neon, Dionne, that bunch of babies up in Canada, whatever the name is. This is Rogers' Plan Day, and the first big plan I have here — I've read in the paper today about the mother of the Dionne quadruplets — quintriplets — anyhow, there's quite a covey of them. Well, the mother went over to see 'em Saturday, and the nurse wouldn't let her in. You see, the nurse works for the government — the Dionne quintuplets — and the Dionnes are one of Canada's biggest products, and — in fact, the premier of Canada is running for reelection this year, and his platform is "The quintuplets were bred and born during my administration."

So the nurse — now you know how these head nurses are. There's nothing outside of a motor cop with more authority than a head nurse, you know. Well, she told the mother—you read it in the paper—"Don't you come up those stairs," you know. And the poor mother couldn't go in and see if they was her five or some other five, you know — that they substituted.

Well, that's what I call pretty tough when a mother can't see her own babies. If she's only got one baby, why it's tough, but when she's got five babies — why it's five times as tough. Well now, here's my plan. If I was this mother, I'd go off and raise five more, but I'd have it understood with the government beforehand, "Now listen, Canada, these are mine. I'm going to get me some more."

Well, the bonus had been the big thing the past week.[1] They'd just as well pay it. It's going to cost more to talk about it than it is to pay it. It's one of those things. I — I don't think some of them want it settled. They run home and get elected on it, and then they get back and hope nothing will be done about it, because they want to go home and be elected on it again. It would be a good joke on some of these politicians if it was settled, wouldn't it? They wouldn't have any platform to stand on — no more than a soap-box orator.

Mr. Roosevelt made a mighty good speech. It was a Hoover speech but delivered with the Roosevelt personality. Shows you that Mr. Roosevelt can put over pretty near any material, no matter how poor it — no, but it was. It brought out — they had some awfully good points. He put over some very good points. You see, there is — there's a lot to be said on both sides, and there's an awful lot more that is said by those that are not telling the truth on either side. That's the trouble.

You see, the thing has reached such a point that everybody's touchy about arguing about the bonus, you know. You know, it's almost like arguing over religion now. This bill, I think, was lost because of 'em insisting on the wrong bill — that printing that money was the line in there that killed this bill, I think. There's an awful lot of folks that are for the soldiers, but then they just ain't so crazy about the printing press.

Now, some say that the printing-press money ain't so bad. Of course, all I know is just what little I read in the papers, written by — all I know is just what little I read in the papers written by Arthur Brisbane, my good friend. Now Arthur, he makes out an awful good case for the old printing press. He says it knocks the bankers out of their 3 percent, and if all the bankers were against it, why he must be kind of bordering on the truth. When you see — when you see all the bankers in one huddle, and then you go over and get in an opposition huddle by yourself, you can't be all wrong. You know what I mean. If they're all going one way, there is something wrong with it.

Of course, that's another thing—don't ever argue about—is this inflation and deflation thing. There's two different schools of thought in this country on the value of money. People who have money are against the printing press, you know. They're against printing any more money. And people that haven't got any are in favor of it, you see? That's the two schools. Both — both of them, mind you, are equally honest. It's awful hard to recon — reconcile two views like that. The only way I see for folks to ever view the money question alike is for everybody not to have any. Then they'll all look at it the same way; or go the other way and let everybody have some, and then they'll all look at it the same way. But if nobody's got any, the old printing press will look pretty good. You know what I mean. But if everybody's got some, in the ash can goes the printing press.

Some economists, you know — there is economists that tell us, you know — there's a lot of 'em that tell us it wouldn't do to print any money. But no economist knows what it would do, for he's never seen it tried in this country. It was tried during the Civil War, but there ain't any economist that's ever figured out a way to live for that long, you know. He ain't been living since then, so he don't know really what happened.

Now you can take the same dose of medicine will kill one guy, and on the other hand another bird will take the same dose and get up and do the rhumba afterwards. So nobody knows just what it will do. But to be perfectly frank with you, there's quite a few problems that — well, to be honest with you, I don't hardly know anything about this. I kind of hate to admit it, but I don't. There's quite a few problems that's agitating the country that I'm not really a hundred percent decided on myself.

I would never make an economist in the world. An economist is a man that can tell you anything about — he'll tell you what can happen under any given conditions, and his guess is liable to be just as good as anybody else's, too. They say about this money problem — they say — and I get all my money information from Jesse

Jones, head of Reconstruction Finance.[2] He says that the trouble with inflation is you can't get it stopped. You know, you get it started and you can't get it stopped. Well, now, why not put a bill in there with a proviso in it that the minute you print these first bills—like they going to pay the soldiers' bonus—the minute you print those, you burn up the printing press. That'll stop you. I imagine it would. I don't know how you'd print any more if you didn't have any more press.

Now maybe a little shot of printing money would be just what this country needs. They say there's nothing that will make a guy pull his dough out of a bank and start buying something with it as quick as to know that his dollar is going to go down in value, you know. That's what they say. Well, when money's going down you want to have it in something besides a bank. So a little scare — a little scare might have been just what was needed to kind of get things started, 'cause the banks is certainly mildewed with money. Of course, as I say, it's kind of a rough idea that I had — that I don't know anything about.

But I must get back to the bonus. As I said before, I believe that if they had tried the other bill where they didn't say where the money was coming from it would have passed, for every appropriation bill that we have seen passed during the past couple of years it — it didn't state where the money was coming from, and we don't know yet where it's coming from. We don't know. We don't know. So where this bill made its mistake was even in suggesting where it come from, you know. The bill should have stated, "This money to pay this bonus is coming from the same place as all the other money is coming from." Well, it would have passed in a minute, for when you're getting money from an unknown source it don't make much difference to you where it's coming from — you know, because you don't know. And we don't know yet.

Now, I've got a bonus bill — you mustn't never criticize anything nowadays unless you've got a plan. I've got a bonus bill or plan. After all, a bill is nothing but a plan and a plan is nothing but a bill, and both of them is nothing but a pipe dream anyhow — a pipe dream on paper.

My bonus bill, first — it would take — it wouldn't take near as much money to pay my bonus. In the first place, I wouldn't pay any of the soldiers, only the ones that needed it. See? And it wouldn't take near as much. You've got to prove that you needed it. See? When the man proved that he needed it, lots of them wouldn't want it — you know, wouldn't need it. That's right. There's lots of them, as I say. So pay the ones that really need it. Pay it right over to them. Now, how would you get the money? Now, here's my plan. You go back over the income taxes of, say, from 1915 to about 1920, or '19 or '20, covering all the years of the war, you know, and it states in your income tax where your money was made from. It states where you got the money. See? Well, levy a tax against all increased incomes derived directly from the war. They say they're going to tax war profits out of existence in the next war. Well, all you do is make it retroactive. Make it apply to the last war. They're always making some bill out that way, course a lot of those haven't got the money now but then lots of them might have. See? And you might get a lot of money out of it at that.

Anyhow, that's a new idea, and course that's about as far as I can take it. From now on I'm just turning it over to Huey. You see, I can think of a lot of ways and plans, but I'm in no official position to do anything, you know. I can't do anything about 'em, but I kind of work with Huey. He's my inside man in there, and I make the balls and let him throw 'em. See? But I really believe this scheme ought to get somewhere.

McAdoo, and Mr. Barney Baruch, La Follette, Borah, and a lot of the prominent men in there, all of those fellows have been hollering about, "Take the profits out of the next war."[3] My scheme is, "Why not take it out of the last one, too." Of course I guess the Supreme Court would figure out some way where you couldn't do it. Four of them would say you could anyhow. [laughter/applause] Thank you. You all are close readers there.

So I don't care which scheme I propose, I'm not alone in it. Any scheme that I propose, I've always got either four or five of the Supreme Court with me on anything that I suggest. You know, speaking about this taking profits out of war, they're always talking about it, but they never have passed a bill. Did you notice that? They've been talking about it ever since the last war, but there never has been a bill passed to take the profits out, so now is the time. And make it retroactive — retroactive — I said that again because I like to use that word. I just learned it. Retroactive. It means that you can go back and get something that you forgot to get at the time. In other words — in other words, they can turn around and go back and run over you after missing you the first time. That's what you call — that's what you call retroactive.

They say you can't — they say you — now, you read in the papers everyday that you can't get a bonus plan through that Roosevelt won't veto. Well, now, he can't veto this one that I'm proposing here. In the last war — it's the last war that you're trying to pay the boys from. That's the war that you owe them the money from. Well, go back to the last war and get the money. You got the proof and the papers right there before you. See what a man's average income was before the war started. Then see what his increase, you know, what it went up to during the war. Then put the tax on it.

You know that's a pretty good scheme. I'm beginning to believe in it myself, you know what I mean! That's — that's a good — that's too good for Huey. You know what I mean. I'm going to turn that over to Joe Robinson or Pat Harrison, you know — somebody that can do something with it. Huey don't get that idea. Huey, that's out. You ain't going to get that. That's too good for you.

So get in behind the Rogers Plan. The Rogers Plan, that's what it is. Don't wire your congressman. Now be sure; don't wire your congressman. See? Don't wire him. That's another one of my plans is to see if there's not some sort of a sanitarium that they can arrange just to house people who wire their congressmen. You know what I mean. It — if there's a more useless vocation in this country ever invented, I don't know what it is, unless it's bridge or people who write chain letters. That may be it. It's not often that I propose a plan where I'd have the backing of Congress and the Senate 100 percent, but I believe on this Don't Write Your Congressman Idea, I'd have their backing. That's the Rogers Plan for Chronic Wire Senders. People who send useless wires, you know, — I was about to say, people who send useless wires to useless congressmen, but I wouldn't say a thing like that. That's kind of raw, and I wouldn't do a thing like that. I wouldn't say that.

So on either one of these Rogers plans don't wire your congressman, you know. Don't wire him; even if he could read, don't wire him, you know. Amon Carter, a friend of mine down in Texas, is going to be — he'll be the charter member—— [Bell rings.] Wait a minute; I ain't through. He'll be the charter member of this Don't Send a Wire to Your Congressman thing. I wasn't near through with all my plans. Well, so long. I'll see what'll happen next week, and I'll have some more. Good-bye.

Good Gulf Show

June 2, 1935

ANNOUNCER:

ROGERS: [applause] Much obliged. Thank you very, very much. First place, we all feel pretty bad out here in California, especially in Hollywood. We're pretty broke up. Greta Garbo left us last night. Greta left us to go home. It was a tremendous personal loss to me. Only consolation I have is that Mae West is still with us. Greta — Greta left us last night. She says, "I tank I go home." When she gets over there in Sweden and sees those salaries, I tank Greta will come back.

Well, wasn't that fine — wasn't it fine about 'em finding that kidnapped boy.[1] That was great. And you know, I believe those government men will get those fellows. They got that department — that's one department that's operating mighty efficient now, and the government is always looking for some new way to spend money, they ought to put more men in that department. Ain't that right now?

I had quite a fine visit today with one of Mr. Roosevelt's cabinet. Mr. Roper, secretary of the commerce, did me the honor of paying a little visit out to my ho-gan a while ago.[2] I just got rid of him just now. You know, these old Roosevelt cabinet boys, they not so particular where they go now. They'll go pretty near anybody'll talk to 'em. I don't know just where he was when this Supreme Court blow fell, but — and I had just too much tact to ask him.[3]

But a funny thing, while we was sitting there — we was sitting there and I'd been reading the morning papers, and in the rotogravure section on there there was a picture of the Supreme Court, and it was laying there — right there in the Sunday morn-

162

ing paper, and he didn't say anything. He just looked at it, and he started — just kind of frothing at the mouth. That's all. See? I had the good sense to kind of kick the paper out of his sight, you know, so he couldn't see it. I'm awful tactful that way.

Well, out our way here I've been noticing Mr. Hoover's health has been picking up a whole lot. Doctors couldn't do him much good up to now, and the weather hadn't done him much. That Supreme Court certainly cured him. He's feeling awful good now. I'm going up to hear him — I'm going up to hear him in a week or so at Stanford University. He's delivering the consolation talk to the graduates up there. One of — one of our progeny is unfortunate enough as to be thrown out of employment up there in June. I tell you, college has been a wonderful thing during this Depression to get the young folks — to help the young folks to get together and play, and run, and jump. Of course I think the CCC — you know, the CCC, they've answered the same purpose better than the colleges. They — they give them a pick and shovel instead of a golf stick or tennis racket. And it gets the same results at the end, you know. And then in a CCC camp, you don't have to hear some professor, you know, lecture on the advantages of Russia.

But I'm anxious — but I'm anxious to hear what even a smart man like Mr. Hoover can tell a young man nowadays, you know. I want to know what he's going to tell 'em. Of course — of course, Mr. Hoover will kind of sub — sub — subtly — how do you say "subtly?" I mean, you know, kind of in a nice way, kind of in an underground way. Mr. Hoover, I think he'll kind of hint to them to get out and join the young Republicans. But even that won't save a young man nowadays. The only salvation — the only salvation I can see for the young is to increase the college term to an additional four years. That's another one of my plans. Give 'em four more years in college, and it will save parents an awful lot of worry, too. Just think of taking a son or a daughter Maggie off your hands for another four years. You'll say, "Well, what could they learn in another four years?" Well, there must be some little something about making a living that they haven't learned yet, and they could kind of work on that for the next four years.

Oh, and say, before I forget it, this week the Women's Federation of Clubs is meeting in Detroit, and I wrote a thing the other day about an Indian, a Cherokee Indian lady from my home who is running, and she's the first vice president of the club.[4] But there's some objection to her because she's an Indian, you know. She should

163

be rightfully be made president of all the federated clubs. Well, when Frank Hawks and I were playing our charity tour a few years ago around, the women's clubs handled it, and they did it awfully efficiently, you know, and they raised a lot of money.[5] Everything was — there was nothing charged off for anything, and the women's clubs did it. And this particular woman did it in Oklahoma, for in one week we got a hundred and fifty thousand dollars for the drought sufferers — more than any other state we played in.

And this lady, as I said, is wonderful. And, of course, I hate to see her kicked out because she's an Indian, because she's a wonderful woman. And so, any of you women who are going to Detroit next week don't you vote my Indian out, or I'll be on you from now on, I'm telling you. Say, listen, don't get our intolerance reaching as far down as the Indian, 'cause you monkey around with her and I — I'm Cherokee, too, so's she — and I — we'll just get together and run you all out of this country and take it back over again.

Say now, listen here, we got to get busy and get talking. There's been an awful lot of things happened this week. I thought the bonus week was a big week, but Lord me, the people mixed up in the war — the ones mixed up in the war, they wasn't nothing in numbers compared to the ones that's been mixed up in the NRA and the farm mortgage relief and a dozen other of these things that was thrown out. The Supreme Court, they've been the talk of the town this week. You know, they hadn't agreed on anything unanimously in over some eighty years. That is the term those gentlemen have been in there. Even I've kidded them so much that I think they all got together and said, "Boys, we got to agree on something."

Well, anyhow, they knew that folks was kidding about it, them always disagreeing five to four. That's the way they've always been split. And they got together and they said, "Ain't there something in the world that we could possibly agree on?" Well, they met and they sit and they talked, and then they pondered. You see, a young man he just thinks, but an old man when he's sitting and thinking, why he's supposed to be pondering with him.

Well, those nine, very fine old gentlemen—old lawyers, you know—they pondered, and they finally thought of something. They thought of something. They come to the conclusion that the NRA was 100 percent in disfavor with them, so they all agreed. So the poor old NRA — there's one thing the poor old NRA it did — you know what I mean — it did one thing for history. It brought the Supreme Court to a unanimous decision anyway. And it's the only thing in our time that's ever done that.

Now what was the effect? All the big strong Republican papers — you know what I mean, the old conservative Republican papers, why, the day that they passed that you'd have thought that the Armistice Day had been declared, you know. Big business, they threw confetti, cut salaries, and did everything. They just had a big time, you know. And all hollered, "At last we're back to the Constitution." And we was all just tickled to death, but it's been so long since we seen the old Constitution that we kinda forgot what it looked like, you know. But we naturally, we thought that it would take care of us in any and all emergencies, you know.

Now lots of folks holler for the old Constitution, that is just the way she was in the old days. But, you know, if you ever think back a bit we've changed. We've been messing with it so much that it don't look the same one, anyhow. We first got an amendment where nobody was allowed to drink. Now that was just as fine a thing as was ever thought up, but nobody wanted to be told that they couldn't drink, you know. We a nation — we don't want anybody to tell us anything. Even if it's good for us we don't want to hear it, you know. So then we decided that that amendment should be rubbed out, you know, and then we put it back again. We first got it out, and then we got it back in again.

Then the next one — then the woman wanted to vote. Up to then they'd run everything, done everything but vote. So the old Constitution — we give the Constitution another rap in the jaw with that. Women promised us that if they had the vote they'd clean up politics. They did; they got in and cleaned up more than the men did. Now we're not quite sure if we didn't make as big a mistake as we did with the Prohibition Amendment. They admit themselves—the women do—they will admit — you talk to them about it — they'll admit that about all they have added to the whole voting and political thing is just more votes, or more bookkeeping and other facts.

But it wasn't — it ain't the women's fault that things haven't been made — politics is bigger than any race and it's bigger than any sex. You could keep politics clean if you could figure out some way where your government never hired anybody. You know what

I mean? Politics would be great if there was nobody ever hired. But the minute one job shows up, politics shows up just ahead of it. You know what I mean. It's there when the job gets there. So politics is going to be with us from now on, even — even if we give the children the vote. It ain't going to clean politics up, you know.

But I know — you ask what's all this — what's all this got to do with the Supreme Court? Well, I'm getting around to that. I'm working my way around here. Mr. Roosevelt come in office, and he saw—or he thought he saw—that there was a great many social injustices. You know, he says a lot of things that ain't right. There was a lot of things that wasn't hardly split up so that everyone had an even break. So he told Congress some of his ideas. Well, you know how Congress is. They'll vote for anything if the thing they vote for will turn around and vote for them. Politics ain't nothing but reciprocity, you know. But where Roosevelt made his mistake was in making these changes without reading the Constitution. See?

Now get this. That's where Roosevelt was wrong by not reading the Constitution. Not only didn't he not read it, but even the Supreme Court, they didn't get around to reading it for two years. Then just by accident one of them happened to pick up this — pick it up, and it was just an accident this thing come about. He was kind of reading up on some case over in Brooklyn, New York. Remember that? A case in Brooklyn, New York, where some folks was a-sellin' some sick chickens, you know. It all come about over a chicken. Now get this. It all come about — this ain't my joke. This is theirs, see?

It all come about over selling some sick chickens. Roosevelt, in his legal ignorance, had said that you couldn't sell a sick chicken. That is, the NRA didn't allow you to, that you had to have a veterinary certificate saying that the old hens or the roosters was feeling ready for the pot. Well, that didn't — now offhand, now that don't seem such an oppressive law, as the Republican papers have made it out. That didn't seem so oppressive, does it? You know what I mean. That don't seem such a terrible law. From a hygenic standpoint it was a good law. And from a humane standpoint, because nobody wants to hurt an ill chicken. But you know — you know, you don't want to bump off some old Shanghai rooster when he ain't feelin' well. He may have the croup or something, you know?

Now enters the Supreme Court. Now get this. Now enters the Supreme Court with an old moth-eaten copy of the Constitution in its hand, and there is a clause in there that says — interstate commerce. Now get this, interstate commerce. In other words, they trace the ancestry of one of these sick pullets back to a fine old state — of New Jersey. See? He'd been brought over the line into Brooklyn. New Jersey, the home of Dwight Morrow, bless his heart — the most humane rich man that ever lived.

Now, the Supreme Court says that on account of this old sick fryer crossing the state line that that dissolves itself into what is legally termed interstate commerce. And that they federal government— that's Roosevelt and his accomplices—had no right to say that a fellow in Brooklyn should not eat a sick chicken; that maybe Brooklyn likes its chickens just a little bit under normal, you know. [laughter] Now wait a minute. Now wait a minute.

I know that perhaps there's a lot of you people here that are saying to yourselves, "What is all this nut stuff that Will is talking about? What is it? It's not funny, and what's it all about anyhow?" Well, I distinctly want you to understand that this is not any of Rogers' comedy. This comedy, if any, it belongs to the president and the Supreme Court and the U. S. Constitution — all this mess. The chicken was just the cause, you see. The whole thing of doing away the NRA, and the doing away with the New Deal, and the making of Roosevelt as just another president, see? He's just another president — now — was all done over a crate of chickens. Now that's what the whole decision was.

Roosevelt met his downfall over this old Shanghai, see? A crate of chickens that had been sold in Brooklyn. We fought England over a mess of tea, which nobody over here ever drinks anyhow. And now the whole social structure of the North American continent is changed by Brooklyn buying a sick chicken. Poor old Hugh Johnson's once proud Blue Eagle, you know — his proud old Blue Eagle — Eagle's neck was wrung by a lowly dominique broiler, you know. [laughter]

Now — now wait a minute, you guys. He didn't even have the distinction of being a Rhode Island Red, you know what I mean — or one of the feathered beasts whose ancient ancestors dates back to Plymouth Rock. Plymouth Rock, the cradle of New England hardheadedness, I'll hear from that. It wasn't even a buff Cochin. You know what I mean. It was just, perhaps, one of those hill roosters. Have to figure that out for yourself. [laughter] That will be enough of that. It was just one of those that upset — upset the whole New Deal — maybe changed the history of the United States. And there's such a rare possibility that it may reach such a — it may reach such a calamitous — well, maybe disastrous result to the country. Not that it would merely bring on a war, but it might go further — it might elect a Republican.

I tell you — I tell you — [over applause] I tell you, good people it's a serious thing—— [Alarm rings.] Aw, wait a minute; I only got started here. Aw, left me right when we was about to elect a Republican. I'm sorry. Well, good-bye now. So long.

Good Gulf Show

June 9, 1935

ANNOUNCER:

ROGERS: [applause] Thank you very much. Much obliged. Feel kind of nervous today 'cause my old friend, Fred Stone, is out in front, and I want to do a good show for him, see? He's out here — he's got a great job out here in the movies now playing Katharine Hepburn's pappy, you know.[1] Boy, I'd like to get in one of those things with Katie. I wouldn't care where I played. I'd just like to get in there. I never did see it. I'd like to get a crack at that Mae West, too.

Well, I got some good news for you all today. I mean tonight. Maybe where you're listening to it maybe it's dark. Out here it's just in the middle of the afternoon. Some — something's the matter with this California weather. It's unusual. The sun's shining today. Yup, quite a blow to all of us that live out here. You know, when a country gets so big that it's not the same time all over the country, it's too big. It is. A country shouldn't be so big but where it's different times all over the place.

We ought to split this country up, anyhow. Let the Republicans have the East, you know. You see? Let the Republicans have all the East — with Wall Street, and then let 'em run it just like they want to, you know. And then the Democrats they take the West. Take Roosevelt, too. Take him for a while, if he makes good. If he don't we'll let him out, see? We'll just take him on trial. See? And we call it Roose-west, see? Of course we'd have to put some initials to it to make him feel at home, you know. We couldn't just call it that. We'd have to have a lot of initials or something. He wouldn't know what to do without a lot of initials to juggle with.

He could come out here in these broad spaces where he could try pretty near any plan he wanted, you know. And things are so far apart you couldn't tell whether it's working or not. Then the beauty about him, if he was out here and the Democrats were all out here there'd be no Supreme Court to worry anybody, 'cause nobody on that court ever was west of the Mississippi River, anyhow. No Frank Kent or Mark Sullivan to bother him, and no *New York Herald* or *Chicago Tribune* to make life miserable for him.[2] They're just — they've got about the same standing out here—those papers have— as the *Police Gazette*.

If a person wants to be a Republican, why let him go east, and if he wants to be a Democrat, why come west. And if he's not so hot about either party, why let him — let him — let him go down to Huey-siana. He can go down there with Huey and share the cotton, and share the mule, and share the corn pone, and the pot likker, and chittlins, and everything, you know. And let Huey have the dissatisfied from both sides.

Then take the Army and Navy. Let either the East or the West have the Army or Navy, you know. Let one have the Army and the other one the Navy. See? Then they never could fight. There wouldn't be any fight because the Army wouldn't have a boat and the Navy wouldn't have a horse or a Ford. That way you'd keep 'em from fightin'.

The same — the thing sounds — it's got some possibilities at that, you know. I know a lot of you will say, "We must preserve the Union," you know. You've heard that. "We must preserve the Union." Well, we — say, the Union is over preserved right now. It's pretty near pickled.

When Roosevelt comes west to take over the management of the Democrats, he's got to leave those professors back there. We're not going to let him bring any professors out here. He's got to come out on his own. And that Astor yacht, too — that thing, too — it don't fit in with Jeffersonian principles. A yacht is purely a Republican tool. If he wants to fish — he's always wanting to, trying to fish off that yacht. If he wants to fish, we'll give him a can of worms and let him go to Hoover Dam. Can you imagine a Democratic president sittin' in there fishin' in Hoover Dam?

I don't know who the Republicans would have to run their country. I guess they'd run it with — I guess they'd run it with — like they do all their business, with a board of directors, I suppose. A Republican don't feel good unless he's on a board of directors.

Course they'd have all the money. The Republicans would have all the money, but the Democrats would have all the fun. We'd have a lot of fun out here. All the rich — all the rich Republicans — all the rich Republicans, and they'd naturally go back East to be among people of their own standing.

Then, if the country split that would naturally do away with the national debt. That's what Russia did, you know, when it went under another government. We'd split up and that would do away with the debt, see? Both sides would start in owing nothing. And the Republicans would perhaps continue the same way, but the Democrats it wouldn't take them long to dig up a deficit. And then the Democrats could take whatever they're using for money, and they could inflate or do anything they wanted to with it. And the Republicans, who say we should never have gone off the gold — well, if they had their own country they could go back on it, if they want to.

I can't picture — personally, I can't picture a more ideal existence all around. The only trouble would be neither one would be happy because they wouldn't have nobody to lay anything on to, you know what I mean. They wouldn't have any other side to lay it on to. So I doubt if the plan — if the plan will ever get very far, because this is not a time for common sense.

But I started in to tell you all the good news for you that I'm off the air during the heat spell. I was the first one of these broadcasting termites — a broadcaster, he's just like a termite; he gets in your house, and you can't get him out every Sunday. Well, I was the first one to discover that an audience needed rest, and I've split all my broadcasting up, kind of, in doses. So I'm just going to let you find out your own way of settling the affairs of the world during the hot spell. I won't be able to advise you for about two or three months.

A man that talks on the radio to an audience in warm weather kind of affects his mind and the audience's, too. Heat and reason don't go together, anyhow, you know. There's going to be a lot of spouting from the radio. I'm just warning you what you're going to get this summer. There's going to be a lot of spouting from the radio and from the speakers' platforms all this summer. There'll be more perspiration than common sense flowing, and the whole political thing has come now to a pretty direct division point. I mean there's been a direct split in the parties.

171

Roosevelt thinks that while the Supreme Court was perfectly justified in what they did, he feels that the law should in some way allow certain injustices to be remedied. He thinks there should be a law saying how long you can work a man and the lowest sum that you can pay him. And the Court says you can't do that. Well, that's a pretty big question, but there's no way of the underdog getting any assistance by law — why, things won't look any too rosy for the underdog.

Of course, the other sides say, "We got where we are as a great nation by this set of laws that we're living under, so why change them! Let the Constitution alone." And that's mighty good logic, too, I want to tell you. But here's something they forget. They can rightfully — you or I can rightfully say we got where we are by these laws, but there's a lot of folks that haven't got anywhere under 'em, you know. And the prospects ain't any too bright for 'em to get any further. So they might not be averse to some small change in the Constitution. They might say, "Yes, give us what you've got, and we'll say it's a perfect Constitution, too." See?

So it all gets back to just how good has the Constitution been to you? That's all it is. How good has it been to you. And nobody can answer that question but yourself. I would say that to the big majority, almost a unanimous majority over a long course of years, it's been a mighty fine old document, and any person will think mighty serious before he'll vote for any change in the Constitution. [applause] That's right, go ahead and applaud because I think that's darn good. [applause] That's fine, but that's as I say for every person to decide for themselves. You know how you — you know whether you've done better or not. You don't need — you know better than any politician can come along and tell you. Even a doctor can't tell you what to do in a case like that. He don't know what you've ever done.

I think the thing's got to be put to a straight-out vote. And let it be put up to a vote and see what happens. Both sides want the country to be prosperous. It's not a — it's not a political thing. Both sides want the country to be prosperous. It's just a difference of opinion in arriving at it. It's what they disagree on. Both sides, I think, are equally patriotic. Neither has a corner on patriotism, and neither has a corner on brains. It's just — what should we do to recover?

Now the Republicans say that Roosevelt's schemes are all to reform

172

somebody. Well, there's a good deal of truth in that. He wants to reform somebody. Let them recover first, and then they'll reform. They say, "If he'll let us get a little ahead, why we'll reform." See? And Roosevelt wants to know why they can't reform first, see? Now — now, that's the whole thing in a nutshell. Well, I mean it was in a nutshell up to the time I just uttered it.

Now, here's another way — here's another way of putting it. Roosevelt wants recovery to start at the bottom. See what I mean? In other words, by a system — by a system of high taxes, he wants business to help the little fellow to get started and get some work, and then pay business back by buying things when he's at work. Business says, "Let everybody alone. Let business alone, and quit monkeying with us, and quit trying schemes, and we'll get everything going for you, and if we prosper, naturally the worker will prosper." That's exactly what business says, and they're justified from their angle in saying that.

One wants recovery to start from the bottom, and the other wants it to start from the top. I don't know which is right. I've never heard of anybody suggesting that they might start it in the middle, so I hereby make that suggestion. To start recovery halfway between the two, because it's the middle class that does everything anyhow. But I don't know anything about it, and that's why I'm resigning tonight and turning the whole situation over to Father Coughlin and Huey Long.

During this hot weather I don't want the blame of settling anything wrong, see? You know what I mean? Anyhow, I know things are going to get better in spite of both sides. Then when things do get better, then you'll hear the yell that will go up. Now watch this, see? The Democrats will swear that recovery was due to them. Now the Republicans, on account of this late decision of of the NRA, they'll say it was due to them throwing — the Supreme Court throwing out the NRA. So they're both going to get in. Nobody wanted to claim the credit for the country blowing up, but wait until it starts picking up and they'll both be on it then. See?

I don't think either one of them knows what it's all about, to be honest with you. Both sides are doing nothing but just looking towards the next election. That's all they're doing, anyhow. You don't — you don't hear anybody talking any more about, "I wonder when these folks are going back to work. What are they going to do about things picking up?" All you hear now is, "Do you think

Roosevelt will be reelected?'' and, "Who will the Republicans run?'' Shows you what their minds are on. Their minds are on their own business. That's all it's on now.

Well, they don't have to give a thought to that. If sentiment at that time is strong enough against Roosevelt—now get this—if sentiment at that time is strong enough against Roosevelt, why the Republicans can nominate Shirley Temple and win with her.[3] You know what I mean. In this country — in this country people don't vote for; they vote against. You know that. You all know that. They don't vote for; they vote against. The votes was against Hoover. They were against Mr. Hoover. It doesn't matter who was running. Not taking anything away from Mr. Roosevelt, but the vote was against Mr. Hoover. And this year it will either be for or against Mr. Roosevelt. The other fellow won't cut any figure no matter who it is running. The whole thing will depend on conditions. If things have picked up and are continuing to pick up right up to, say, election time, why the Republicans can go ahead and hold that convention, but it will be just for exhibition purposes only. And they can charge admission and take the money and send the candidate they nominate on a four-year tour of the world or something, you know.

On the other hand—get this—on the other hand, if things are bad by next summer and fall, Roosevelt will get the blame without the Republicans or any opposition having a single — gettin' up and making any single speech. They won't have to do an ounce of denouncing at all. Nobody don't have to make speeches to bring these things about. They ain't, if the votes go against Roosevelt. And the Republicans then, in that case — the Republicans can nominate the night watchman of the convention and win with him. Don't matter who it is, you know.

So all this talking and all this spouting, and all the hard feelings and all the perspiration that's going to be smeared about all this summer will just be a total loss. Conditions win elections and not speeches, and these denouncing orators should remember that every time they cuss the president they lose friends. They may get some applause from a partisan audience, but we still think it's the highest office in the whole world. And we always think, and we have justification in that to thinking, that it's always held by the highest type of men, regardless of which party they belong to. So any denouncing, no matter which side he's on, he loses more votes than he gains.

Now — oh yeah, got to get — on this — on the new NRA. Rather, this SNRA that's it, Synthetic National Recovery Act. We've added an S to it. It's a good idea. It's a splendid idea. It don't make a fellow — it's to be kind of fair to the workers, you know, but it's got no power, and the man they're trying to reach with it is the one you can't reach by persuasion, you know, or you can't shame him into it. He's been shamed by better men than you. But as I say, it's too hot to argue over all this stuff, you know. And the Gulf Oil Company's got a fine program. It's going to keep going on at this same hour all summer. Frank Tours is one of the finest legitimate orchestra conductors in America.[4] He's one of the few — he can read music. I don't know how he can tell jokes or not, but he's really a musician, you know. That's rather a novelty in orchestra-leading nowadays. I know Frank, and Fred knows him here — a wonderful leader. Him and his orchestra, and then Jimmy Melton, that wonderful tenor, you know, and one of the finest voices in America, he'll be on the program.[5] And the world-famous Revelers Quartet, Mrs. Allie Miles, Lew Lehr, Henry Neely — a great show, so tune in and get 'em.[6]

I want to thank you all for how nice you've been to me during all of this little course of blatherin' around. A lot of you — I didn't get as many letters saying you were taking this serious, you know, as we did. Now don't get all heated up in arguing and get mad over these problems all summer, you know. As I told you a while ago, conditions and not oratory is going to settle this next election. Everybody is trying to save the country, only they're trying to do it in different ways, and it's too big — the country is too big for all of them put together to spoil, anyhow. See?

So, good-bye and I'll see you this fall. Thank you very much.

APPENDIX

Will Rogers made fifty-three weekly broadcasts for Gulf Oil Corporation from 1933 to 1935. Although post-broadcast transcripts exist of each of the programs, sound recordings—and, thus, verifiable records—are available for only the sixteen included in this volume. The following is a complete list of all of Rogers' radio programs for Gulf. Transcripts of each are on file at the Will Rogers Memorial, Claremore, Oklahoma. Asterisks (*) denote broadcasts reproduced in this volume.

*April 30, 1933
May 7, 1933
May 14, 1933
May 21, 1933
May 28, 1933
June 4, 1933
June 11, 1933
*August 13, 1933
October 29, 1933
November 5, 1933
November 12, 1933
November 19, 1933
November 26, 1933
January 7, 1934
January 14, 1934
January 21, 1934
January 28, 1934
February 4, 1934
February 11, 1934
February 18, 1934
February 25, 1934
March 4, 1934
June 10, 1934
*June 17, 1934
*June 24, 1934
July 1, 1934
*July 8, 1934

September 16, 1934
September 30, 1934
October 7, 1934
October 14, 1934
October 21, 1934
October 28, 1934
November 4, 1934
November 11, 1934
December 23, 1934
December 30, 1934
January 6, 1935
January 13, 1935
January 20, 1935
January 27, 1935
February 3, 1935
*March 31, 1935
*April 7, 1935
*April 14, 1935
*April 21, 1935
*April 28, 1935
*May 5, 1935
*May 12, 1935
*May 19, 1935
*May 26, 1935
*June 2, 1935
*June 9, 1935

NOTES

ARMS CONFERENCE (April 6, 1930)

[1]Florenz "Flo" Ziegfeld, Jr., American theatrical producer, best-known for the *Ziegfeld Follies*. First produced in 1907, these elaborately staged musical revues featured a bevy of beautiful chorus girls and many of the leading stage performers of the day. Rogers appeared with the *Follies* from 1916 to 1925. Before that, he starred in Ziegfeld's *Midnight Frolic*, a late-night, nightclub revue.

[2]Rogers began his stage career in Saint Louis in 1905 with a vaudeville act that highlighted his roping skills.

CHARLES LINDBERGH (April 13, 1930)

[1]Plutarco Elías Calles, president of Mexico from 1924 to 1928; "strongarm" leader of Mexico during much of the 1920s and 1930s.

Charles Augustus Lindbergh, American aviator who made the first solo, nonstop transatlantic flight, from New York City to Paris, May 20-21, 1927. An international hero and a booster of aviation, Lindbergh made a much-heralded good-will flight to Mexico City from Washington, D. C., in December of 1927. Rogers, who also was touring Mexico, witnessed Lindbergh's arrival in the Mexican capital.

[2]Two Germans, Captain Hermann Koehl and Baron Gunther von Huenefeld, and an Irishman, Commandant James Fitzmaurice, completed the first east-to-west transatlantic flight on April 13, 1928.

[3]Dwight Whitney Morrow, American lawyer, banker, diplomat, and Republican political figure; United States ambassador to Mexico from 1927 to 1930; United States senator from New Jersey from 1930 until his death in 1931. Morrow's daughter, Anne Spencer Morrow, married Charles Lindbergh in May of 1929.

[4]Elizabeth Cutter Morrow, American writer, educator, and charity worker; wife of Dwight W. Morrow.

[5]Grace Anna Goodhue Coolidge, wife of President Calvin Coolidge. An educator and a graduate of Smith College, Mrs. Coolidge enjoyed wide popularity as first lady.

PRESIDENT HOOVER (April 20, 1930)

[1]Herbert Clark Hoover, Republican president of the United States from 1929 to 1933; mining engineer, government administrator, and United States secretary of commerce from 1921 to 1929. Hoover was born of Quaker parents in West Branch, Iowa.

[2]After the death of his parents, Hoover went to live with an uncle in Newberg, Oregon.

[3]Glenn Scobey "Pop" Warner, famous American football figure who coached at Carlisle Institute in Pennsylvania from 1899 to 1903 and 1907 to 1914 and at Stanford University from 1924 to 1932.

[4]Lou Henry Hoover, Iowa-born wife of Herbert Hoover; a geology graduate of Stanford University.

[5]Calvin Coolidge, Republican president of the United States from 1923 to 1929; United States vice president from 1921 to 1923; known popularly as "Silent Cal."

[6]The Hoovers lived in Tientsin, China, during the Boxer Rebellion.

[7]Betty Blake Rogers, wife of Will Rogers. The couple was married at the Blake family home in Rogers, Arkansas, on November 25, 1908.

[8]As federal food administrator during World War I, Hoover was responsible for controlling the production and consumption of food.

VICE-PRESIDENT CURTIS (April 27, 1930)

[1]James Edmond Fechet, American army officer; major general and chief of the Army Air Service from 1927 to 1931. The provisional wing of the Air Service conducted maneuvers on the West Coast in late April of 1930.

[2]William "Billy" Mitchell, American army officer who served as commander of the Army Air Service from 1917 to 1918. Mitchell was court-martialed in 1925 because he had criticized the departments of war and navy for mismanagement of the aviation service. Convicted, Mitchell resigned from the army in 1926.

[3]Clara Bow, American motion-picture actress who symbolized the flapper age and the "Roaring 20s" as the "It" girl of the decade.

[4]Alphonse "Scarface Al" Capone, infamous Chicago gang leader who became a symbol of lawlessness in the 1920s and early 1930s.

[5]Arthur Brisbane, American newspaper writer and editor whose column, "Today," appeared in more than 200 daily and 1,200 weekly newspapers.

[6]Charles Curtis, Republican United States senator from Kansas from 1907 to 1913 and 1915 to 1929; vice president of the United States from 1929 to 1933.

[7]Thomas Riley Marshall, Democratic vice president of the United States from 1913 to 1921.

[8]Thomas Woodrow Wilson, Democratic president of the United States from 1913 to 1921.

[9]John Sharp Williams, Democratic United States senator from Mississippi from 1911 to 1923.

[10]Charles Gates Dawes, Republican vice president of the United States

from 1925 to 1929; ambassador to Great Britain from 1929 to 1932; Chicago industrialist and attorney.

[11]Joseph Ridgway Grundy, American textile manufacturer and banker; president of the Pennsylvania Manufacturers' Association from 1909 to 1930; Republican United States senator from 1929 to 1930.

[12]Curtis' mother, Ellen Papan Curtis, died in 1863. Charles Curtis' ancestry was supposedly one-sixteenth Kansa and one-sixteenth Osage Indian (related tribes).

[13]Vice President Curtis, a widower, became embroiled in a social precedence controversy involving Dolly Curtis Gann, his half-sister and official hostess, and the matrons of Washington society.

[14]Leona Curtis Knight, youngest daughter of Charles Curtis. Mrs. Knight delivered one of the seconding speeches for her father's nomination for the vice presidency in 1928.

[15]Henry Ford, American automotive pioneer and manufacturer; founder and president of Ford Motor Company.

ALFRED E. SMITH (May 4, 1930)

[1]Theodore Roosevelt, Republican president of the United States from 1901 to 1909; immensely popular public figure.

[2]Alfred Emanuel "Al" Smith, Democratic governor of New York from 1919 to 1921 and 1923 to 1929. Smith, an Irish Catholic and anti-prohibitionist, ran unsuccessfully for president in 1928 on the Democratic ticket.

[3]Madison Square Garden in New York City was the scene of the Democratic National Convention of 1924, which lasted a record seventeen days.

[4]Catherine A. Dunn Smith, wife of Al Smith who, like her husband, was a native of New York City and an Irish Catholic.

[5]Joseph Taylor "Joe" Robinson, Democratic United States senator from Arkansas from 1913 until his death in 1937; minority leader of the Senate from 1923 to 1933; vice-presidential running mate of Al Smith in 1928.

[6]Owen D. Young, New York City attorney and corporation executive; chairman of the board of General Electric Company from 1922 to 1939; chairman of an international conference in 1929 that formulated the so-called Young Plan for payment of German reparations.

[7]Andrew William Mellon, United States secretary of the treasury from 1921 to 1932; Pittsburgh financier with interests in mining, manufacturing, and banking.

MOTHER'S DAY (May 11, 1930)

[1]Florence Nightingale, Italian-born English nurse who was the founder of modern nursing. She became a legend for her monumental service during the Crimean War in the 1850s.

[2]Edward Albert, Prince of Wales from 1911 until his succession to the

British throne in 1936; reigned briefly as King Edward VIII; extremely popular as a bachelor prince.

[3]Will and Betty Rogers had three children living in 1930: William Vann, Mary Amelia, and James Blake. A fourth child, Fred Stone, had died in infancy a decade earlier.

[4]Helen Adams Keller, famous American author and lecturer, blind and deaf from the age of two. She lectured throughout the United States, Europe, and Asia, raising funds for the training of the blind and promoting other social causes.

[5]Alice Lee Roosevelt Longworth, daughter of President Theodore Roosevelt, wife of Speaker of the House Nicholas Longworth, and famous Washington hostess.

[6]Ruth Hanna McCormick, Republican United States representative from Illinois from 1929 to 1931; daughter of Ohio financier and politician Marcus Alonzo "Mark" Hanna and widow of publisher and congressman Joseph Medill McCormick.

[7]Nancy Witcher Langhorne Astor, one of the beautiful Langhorne sisters of Virginia; the first woman to sit in the British House of Commons, serving from 1919 to 1945; wife of Lord Waldorf Astor.

[8]Waldorf Astor, second viscount Astor of Hever; multimillionaire British political figure and newspaper publisher.

[9]Helen Wills, California tennis star who won her first of seven United States Open titles in 1923 at the age of seventeen. She also won twelve Wimbledon crowns.

[10]David Lloyd George, British political leader who served as prime minister of Great Britain from 1916 to 1922.

[11]George Bernard Shaw, leading British playwright, novelist, and literary critic. His works include *The Devil's Disciple* (1900) and *Pygmalion* (1912).

H. R. H. THE PRINCE OF WALES (May 18, 1930)

[1]Charles Spencer "Charlie" Chaplin, English-born comedian who starred in several classic American and British films. A near-legendary figure, Chaplin achieved universal fame for his portrayal of the "Little Tramp."

[2]Henry VIII, king of England from 1509 until his death in 1547.

[3]Edward VII, king of Great Britain and Ireland from 1901 until his death in 1910.

[4]George V, king of Great Britain and Northern Ireland from 1910 until his death in 1936.

[5]Victoria, queen of Great Britain and Ireland from 1837 and empress of India from 1876 until her death in 1901.

[6]Harry Lauder, popular Scottish singer and songwriter who was knighted in 1919 for entertaining troops during World War I.

[7]Gerald Frederic Trotter, groom-in-waiting to the Prince of Wales from 1921 to 1936. Trotter held an honorary title of brigadier general.

[8]Emily Price Post, American author and syndicated newspaper columnist who became famous as an arbiter of good manners; author of the bestseller *Etiquette* (1922).

[9]George Lane, American-born rancher in Alberta, Canada, and a friend

of the Prince of Wales. He earlier had purchased a ranch for Edward that adjoined his own Bar U.

DWIGHT MORROW (May 25, 1930)

[1]John William Davis, American attorney and political figure; Democratic United States representative from West Virginia from 1911 to 1913; ambassador to Great Britain from 1918 to 1921; unsuccessful candidate for president in 1924.

[2]Nicholas Murray Butler, American educator and Republican leader; president of Columbia University from 1902 to 1945; recipient of the Nobel Prize for Peace in 1931.

HENRY FORD (June 1, 1930)

[1]Benito Mussolini, founder and leader of the Italian Fascist movement; dictator of Italy from 1922 to 1943.

"Amos 'n Andy," long-running radio serial first broadcast in 1928. It featured two white comedians, Freeman Fisher Gosden and Charles J. Correll, in almost every male role. The escapades of two black taxi drivers and their friends in Harlem attracted an enormous and faithful listening audience.

[2]Brigham Young, American religious leader who headed the Mormon Church from 1847 until his death in 1877. A polygamist, he was survived by seventeen wives and countless children and grandchildren.

[3]Thomas Alva Edison, American inventor and scientist, famous for such innovations and improvements as the incandescent electric lamp, the phonograph, and the microphone. Edison, who celebrated his eighty-third birthday in 1930, was the honored guest at a Golden Jubilee of Light celebration hosted by Henry Ford at Dearborn, Michigan, in October of 1929.

[4]Clara Bryant Ford, wife of Henry Ford.

[5]Edsel Bryant Ford, only son of Henry and Clara Ford; president of Ford Motor Company from 1919 to 1943.

[6]In the early 1920s Henry Ford launched an anti-Semitic tirade in his weekly newspaper, the *Dearborn Independent*. A series of articles attacking Aaron Sapiro, a Chicago attorney, resulted in a suit against Ford for defamation of character. The automobile manufacturer was forced to issue a formal retraction of his attacks on Jews and to make a personal apology to Sapiro.

PROHIBITION (June 8, 1930)

[1]William Claude "W. C." Fields, renowned American comic actor who performed in vaudeville and the *Ziegfeld Follies*. He also appeared in a host of films, where he usually played swaggering, drunken, down-at-the-heels rascals.

Brandon Tynan, Irish-born American actor and dramatic author. A

Ziegfeld Follies regular, he also wrote such plays as *The Passion Flower* (1909) and *The Melody of Youth* (1915).

[2]George Higgins Moses, Republican United States senator from New Hampshire from 1918 to 1933; president pro tempore of the Senate from 1925 to 1933; prohibitionist and staunch supporter of the Hoover administration.

[3]Albert Einstein, noted German physicist who received a Nobel Prize in 1921 for his work in theoretical physics, notably on the photoelectric effect.

[4]Carol II, king of Rumania from 1930 to 1940. In 1925, after Carol had renounced his right of succession to the throne, he deserted his wife and went to Paris to live in exile with his mistress. In June of 1930 he returned to Rumania and supplanted his nine-year-old son, Michael, as king. Ten years later, pro-German Rumanians forced Carol to abdicate and restored Michael to the throne.

BOSTON (June 15, 1930)

[1]Frank Gilman Allen, Republican governor of Massachusetts from 1929 to 1931; chairman of the board of a Massachusetts leather goods firm from 1929 until his death in 1950.

[2]Ben Lyon, American vaudeville and motion-picture actor, singer, and dancer.

Virginia "Bebe" Daniels, popular American actress who made her film debut in 1908 at the age of seven. Her marriage in 1930 to Lyon, another favorite of Hollywood, generated considerable publicity. The couple remained together for forty years until Bebe's death in 1971.

[3]Ridley McLean, American naval officer; rear admiral in the United States Navy from 1927 until his death in 1933; commander of Battleship Division Three in the naval service.

[4]Coolidge served on the board of directors of New York Life Insurance Company.

[5]Patrick Jay "Pat" Hurley, United States secretary of war from 1929 to 1933; Tulsa attorney, oilman, and Republican political leader.

[6]James Eli Watson, Republican United States senator from Indiana from 1916 to 1933; leader of conservative Republicans in the Senate.

[7]James Cannon, Jr., bishop in the Methodist Episcopal Church, South, from 1918 until his death in 1944. Cannon, an ardent "dry," appeared before the Senate Lobby Committee in early June of 1930 to answer questions concerning his political and prohibitionist activities.

Senator Grundy represented the main force behind the passage by Congress in June of 1930 of the Hawley-Smoot Tariff, the highest schedule of duties in the history of the country.

[8]James Joseph "Gene" Tunney, American pugilist who won the world heavyweight boxing championship in 1926 in a match against William Harrison "Jack" Dempsey, who had reigned as champion since 1919. Tunney held the title until his voluntary retirement in 1928.

[9]Jack Sharkey, American prizefighter who held the world heavyweight title from 1932 to 1933.

[10]Max Siegfried Schmeling, German boxer who held the world heavyweight championship from 1930 to 1932; the most successful profes-

sional boxer in German history. Schmeling won the heavyweight crown on a foul by Sharkey in the fourth round of their scheduled fifteen-round bout in New York City in June of 1930.

[11]Aimee Semple McPherson, phenomenally successful California evangelist who preached a Pentecostal, fundamentalist, faith-healing doctrine; founder of the International Church of the Foursquare Gospel, based in Los Angeles.

CHICAGO (June 22, 1930)

[1]George "Bugs" Moran, Chicago underworld figure who, with his associates, controlled the North Side of Chicago throughout much of the late 1920s, rivaling in power the "gangdom" of Al Capone.

[2]Graham McNamee, radio broadcaster for the National Broadcasting Corporation; the premier announcer during the period 1923 to 1927; the leading "master of ceremonies" of radio programs during the 1930s.

[3]James Hamilton "Ham" Lewis, Democratic United States senator from Illinois from 1913 to 1919 and 1931 until his death in 1939; noted for his splendor of dress.

[4]Samuel Insull, Chicago public utilities magnate with vast holdings throughout the Midwest. Overexpansion caused the collapse of his empire in the 1930s. Insull's favorite philanthropy was the Chicago Civic Opera.

[5]William Hale "Bill" Thompson, Republican mayor of Chicago from 1915 to 1923 and 1927 to 1931. A flamboyant figure, he attracted much attention during the 1927 mayoral campaign with his tirades against England.

[6]Raphael Floyd Phillips Gibbons, American journalist, author, and radio commentator; internationally-known roving reporter; the leading war correspondent of his generation.

[7]Robert Tyre "Bobby" Jones, American amateur golfer who was one of the all-time great players of the sport; winner of four United States Open Championships, three British Open crowns, and five United States amateur titles.

[8]Rufus Cutler Dawes, Chicago financier and utilities magnate; brother of Charles Dawes. Rufus Dawes served as president of the private corporation that planned and staged the Century of Progress Exposition in Chicago in 1933 and 1934.

BACON AND BEANS AND LIMOUSINES

Rogers delivered this radio address on October 18, 1931, during a national broadcast for President Herbert Hoover's Organization on Unemployment Relief. The text published herein comes from a transcription made from a tape on file at the Will Rogers Memorial in Claremore, Oklahoma. The tape in question is believed to be complete, but some discrepancies exist between it and copies of the speech that appeared in print as early as four days after the broadcast. Major textual variations between the tape and the address as it appeared in the *Beverly Hills* (California) *Citizen* on October 22, 1931, are noted below. The heading for the broadcast comes from *The Survey* magazine which printed the text of the address in its issue of November 15, 1931.

[1]Beverly Hills Citizen (BHC): *...you are using is the wrong kind, you will just have to...*

[2]BHC: *...and I don't know what cigarette will drag in your Adam's apple—unless you lay off apples...*

[3]BHC: *Mr. Owen D. Young and Mr. Gifford asked me to annoy on this program; you just heard Mr. Gifford, the biggest "hello" man in the world, a very high class man, but what a job he has got. Mr. Hoover just told him, "Gifford, I have a remarkable job for you, you are to feed the several million unemployed." "With what?" says Gifford. "That's what makes the job remarkable, if you had something to do it with it wouldn't be remarkable."*

[4]BHC: *...anybody anything, so that being such an improvement over Young's plan, why it's the one Europe is working under now.*

[5]BHC: *...by appearing with him, so I took the chance. So if we do all right today, there's liable to be a new team on radio. I told him not to get Mr. Coolidge in it, he would be selling some insurance.*

Mexico's President was about to resign, Spain's resigned, Chili has had a crate of 'em lately, so that leaves Mr. Hoover the "Dean of Presidents."

Mr. Hoover has done some splendid work for us lately. He rounded up the bankers and told 'em if they wanted to continue to get eight and ten per cent from the yokels they better start letting out some dough without the security of a right eye and three ribs—he told 'em to melt some frozen assets. A frozen asset is just a banker's mistake. Anyhow he sent 'em home renewing notes.

So now things are different, everybody is holding their own, in fact that's just what's the matter with the country, everybody is holding their own and won't let go.

We used to be told that depression was just a state of mind, but starvation has changed that impression. Depression is a state of health, it's moved from the mind to the stomach, and it ain't really depression either, it's just a return to normalcy; we are just getting back to earth and it don't look natural to us anymore—we are back to two-bit meals and cotton underwear and off the $1.50 steaks and silk under rompers. The trouble with us is America is just muscle bound from holding a steering wheel; the only place we are calloused from work is the bottom of our driving toe.

Now everybody has got a scheme to relieve unemployment. Now there is just one way to do it and that's for everybody to go to work. "Where?" Why, right where you are. Look around; you see a lot of things to do, weeds to be cut, fences to be fixed, lawns to be mowed, filling stations to be robbed, gangsters to be catered to. There is a million little odds and ends right under your eye that an idle man can turn his hand to every day. Course he won't get paid for it, but he won't get paid for not doing it. My theory is that it will keep him in practice in case something does show up—you can lay off so long that you can lose the habit. So keep practicing so work won't be a novelty when it does come. You eat just as much loafing as you do working, in fact more, you got more time.

The trouble with us is today we are in such bad shape that it takes us all day to tell about it, we keep yawning and yapping for the good old days of '26, '27, '28. Well, we just as well wake up, for those "cuckoo" times are not coming back any more. How we all escaped a lunatic asylum during that time is more than we know now. We paid a dollar down on everything under the sun that anybody had to sell. I had a fifty-cent equity in every lot in America.

Now, here we are worrying and reading in the papers about a hundred different problems...

[6]BHC: ...more equal division of the wealth the country produces. Now if our big men in the next year can't fix that, well, they just ain't big men, that's all. What does all this yapping about disarmament amount to, compared to your own people that haven't worked in two years.

What does prohibition amount to,...

[7]BHC: ...can't eat. Is Japan's and China's troubles more to us than our bread-lines? We got more wheat...

[8]BHC: ...the first nation...

[9]BHC: Now if there ain't something "cockeyed" in an arrangement like that, then this microphone in front of me is a mouse trap. It's simply a case of getting it fixed; all the feed is going into one manger and the stock on the other side ain't getting any of it, but we are better off than all these other nations that are hard up; they haven't got all this, we got it but we don't know how to split it up. I guess we will get it fixed, for everybody is aroused and thinking on it; we been so busy in the last few years getting radios and bathtubs and facial creams and straight eights, that we forgot to see if we had any bacon and beans. Now, a miracle can't happen and all these people get a job overnight; it's going to take time, so they must be fed and cared for perhaps all winter; every one of us that have anything got it by the aid of these very people. There is not an unemployed man in the country that hasn't contributed to the wealth of every millionaire in America. The working classes didn't bring this on; it was the big boys that thought the financial drunk was going to last forever, and over bought, over merged, and over capitalized.

Now, the people are not asking for money, they are asking for a job, but as there is no job, towns and cities can't say they haven't got the money, for the same amount of money is in the country as when these folks had their share—somebody's got it. Last winter we didn't realize the need, but this winter we got no excuse, it's been shown to us all summer. I have said for the last two years that things would pick up in '32.

[10]BHC: ...good on election years. They give us three bad years and one good one,...

[11]BHC: Elections are always just a year too late for the Democrats.

Now, don't wait for the government to feed these people; the taxpayer is feeding now about one-fourth of the people who are not doing anything much for 'em. I'll bet you that every town and city comes through. I have seen lots of audiences and heard lots of appeals, but I have yet to see one where the people knew the need, and the cause was there, that they didn't come through; even Europe, who hates us and thinks we are arrogant, bad mannered and everything else, they will tell you that we are liberal, dog-gone it, our folks are liberal. I don't know anything about "America being fundamentally sound" and all that after dinner "hooey," but I do know that America is "fundamentally generous."

[12]Walter Sherman Gifford, president of American Telephone & Telegraph Company from 1925 to 1948. From 1931 to 1932 Gifford headed President

Hoover's Organization on Unemployment Relief, a federal agency that sought to help local and state officials meet the unemployment crisis.

GOOD GULF SHOW, April 30, 1933

[1]The Revelers Quartet, one of the first "precision" singing groups on radio, featured in its early years Franklyn Baur and Lewis L. James as tenors, Elliott Shaw as baritone, and Wilfred Glenn as bass. The group accompanied Rogers on a benefit tour of the drought-stricken Southwest in early 1931.

[2]Franklin Delano Roosevelt, president of the United States from 1933 until his death in 1945. Elected as a Democrat in the midst of the Great Depression, Roosevelt instituted a broad program of reform and recovery known as the New Deal.

[3]Irvin Shrewsbury Cobb, American journalist, novelist, and playwright; close friend of Rogers. Although he wrote more than sixty books, Cobb is best known for his humorous stories set in his native Kentucky, among the first of which was *Old Judge Priest* (1915).

[4]Amon Giles Carter, publisher of the *Fort Worth Star-Telegram* from 1923 until his death in 1955; prominent philanthropist and civic leader.

[5]Lee Arwell, unidentified.

[6]Walter Winchell, syndicated columnist for the *New York Mirror* from 1929 to 1963. Winchell, one of the best-known journalists and radio commentators in the country, specialized in show-business gossip and political commentary. He often was the first to report the impending parenthood of famous celebrities.

[7]Harry Houdini, American magician, world-famed for his escapes from bonds of every sort—locks, handcuffs, straitjackets, and sealed containers. He died in 1926.

[8]Soon after taking office on March 5, Roosevelt declared a temporary national bank holiday to afford beleagured banking institutions an opportunity to solidify their resources and to prevent an absolute panic among depositors.

[9]James Ramsay MacDonald, prime minister of Great Britain from 1929 to 1935; Labour party leader.

Pierre Laval, premier and minister of foreign affairs of France from 1931 to 1932, from 1935 to 1936, and in 1942.

[10]Ogden Livingston Mills, United States secretary of the treasury from 1932 to 1933. A Republican attorney from New York City and former congressman, Mills became a bitter critic of the New Deal policies of the Roosevelt administration.

[11]Franklin Roosevelt was one of the few members of the politically and socially prominent Roosevelt family to be counted among the Democrats.

[12]Mohandas Karamchand Gandhi, Indian political and spiritual leader, known as the Mahatma, or Great Soul; principal leader of the Indian struggle for independence from Great Britain.

[13]George Woodward Wickersham, New York City attorney and chairman of a Hoover presidential commission that conducted an extensive investigation in 1929 of the federal system of jurisprudence and administration of laws. Its final report, which called for the continuation of prohibition while providing evidence that it could not be enforced, generated much criticism and discussion.

[14]The manufacture and sale of mild beer, or 3.2 beer, once again became legal in the United States in April of 1933, signaling the end of more than thirteen years of federal prohibition.

[15]Harry Chandler, publisher of the *Los Angeles Times* from 1917 until his death in 1944.

[16]Adolf Hitler, German dictator and founder and leader of the National Socialist (Nazi) party in Germany. Hitler's organization steadily gained support after its birth in 1921, basing its appeal on nationalism, anti-Semitism, and German world power.

Huey Pierce Long, Democratic governor of Louisiana from 1928 to 1932; United States senator from 1932 until his assassination in 1935; political "boss" of Louisiana; known as "the Kingfish."

GOOD GULF SHOW, August 13, 1933

[1]Edwin A. Halsey, secretary of the United States Senate from 1933 until his death in 1945. One of the most popular figures on Capitol Hill, he spent forty-seven years in service to the Senate. The title of colonel was honorary.

[2]Fred Andrew Stone, American stage and screen actor, famous for creating the role of the "Scarecrow" in the 1903 theatrical production of *The Wizard of Oz*; Rogers' dearest friend.

[3]Jimmy Durante, much-beloved, long-nosed American comedian with a lengthy career in vaudeville, nightclubs, motion pictures, theatrical productions, and television.

[4]The National Governors' Conference was held in California in late July of 1933. Rogers, who was a member of the state welcoming party, attended and hosted many of the official events.

[5]James Rolph, Jr., Republican governor of California from 1931 until his death in 1934.

Fred Bennett Balzar, Republican governor of Nevada from 1927 until his death in 1934.

John Gilbert Winant, Republican governor of New Hampshire from 1925 to 1926 and 1931 to 1934.

[6]James Aloysius Farley, American businessman and politician who served as chairman of the Democratic National Committee from 1932 to 1940 and as United States postmaster general from 1933 to 1936.

[7]Greta Garbo, Swedish film actress whose sultry sexuality and beautiful features made her one of the foremost star personalities ever to appear on the screen. She arrived in Hollywood in 1926, where she soon became one of the highest paid performers in films. An extremely private person, she retired suddenly in 1941 at the age of thirty-six.

[8]Marlene Dietrich, German-American film actress and singer. She scored her first success in 1930 as "Lola" in the German film *The Blue Angel*. She then came to the United States to star in such motion pictures as *Shanghai Express* and *Blonde Venus* in 1932.

[9]Janet Gaynor, American film star of the 1920s and 1930s who gained immense popularity in sentimental roles; winner of the Academy Award for best actress in 1927. Gaynor appeared with Rogers in the popular film *State Fair* in 1933.

[10]Lilian Harvey, British actress, singer, and dancer who starred in many

German-made motion pictures in the 1930s and a few Hollywood-produced films. Her greatest success came in 1931 in *Der Kongress Tanzt (Congress Dances)*.

[11]Clara Bow owned a ranch in Nevada that she operated with her husband, actor-turned-politician Rex Bell.

[12]Marie Dressler, American comedienne of silent films and early "talkies," formerly in opera, vaudeville, and burlesque. Before her death in 1934, she achieved box-office success as a character actress, specializing in roles of tough, elderly pessimists of wide girth and broad humor.

[13]Blue Boy, the mammoth prize-winning Iowa boar that "starred" with Rogers in the motion picture *State Fair* (1933).

[14]John Clinton Porter, Republican mayor of Los Angeles from 1929 to 1933. Porter and other American mayors visited France in May of 1931 as official state guests. At a reception in Paris, Porter, an ardent prohibitionist, snubbed his hosts by leaving the party when champagne toasts were offered.

[15]Peggy Hopkins Joyce, American vaudeville, stage, and screen actress whose six marriages and countless engagements brought her much publicity.

[16]Victor Herbert, Irish-American cellist and composer; conductor of the Pittsburgh Symphony Orchestra from 1898 to 1904. Herbert achieved his greatest success as a composer with his operettas, including *Babes in Toyland* (1903), *The Red Mill* (1906), and *Naughty Marietta* (1910).

[17]Dorothy Stone, American stage and motion-picture actress. The eldest daughter of Fred Stone, she co-starred with Rogers in the Broadway hit *Three Cheers* in 1928-1929.

[18]George Michael Cohan, American actor, playwright, and theatrical producer; composer of many popular, patriotic tunes and the writer of the book, music, and lyrics of twenty musicals.

[19]Kathryn Elizabeth "Kate" Smith, American singer and entertainer who won wide popularity in the 1930s and 1940s. A show-business legend, Smith continued to make occasional appearances in the 1980s.

[20]Jack Pearl, American vaudeville, stage, and screen star; creator of the famed "Baron von Munchausen" character. Pearl headlined one of the major comedy-variety radio shows of the Depression era.

GOOD GULF SHOW, June 17, 1934

[1]Norman Ernest Brokenshire, American radio announcer who began his broadcasting career in 1924 and is credited with many innovations, including special events broadcasts, "soap operas," and celebrity interviews.

[2]Charles "Buddy" Rogers, American motion-picture actor who appeared in films from 1926 to 1957; often remembered as the husband of silent screen star, Mary Pickford.

[3]Ed Wynn, American vaudeville, radio, and television comic who after an initial film failure in *Rubber Heels* in 1927 returned to Hollywood in the 1950s as a successful character actor. Wynn's radio show, "The Fire Chief," sponsored by Texaco, enjoyed brief popularity in the early 1930s.

[4]Portions of the text from *"And so I sure want to apologize,...."* through *"... and you're liable to geographically get 'em mixed up"* were garbled or deleted from the available tape of the broadcast. The text given herein is from

a transcription made soon after Rogers' performance. Hereafter, any similar-ly questionable passages will be noted as FROM TRANSCRIPTION.

[5]FROM TRANSCRIPTION: *Even 'Amos 'n Andy,' as wonderful as they are; . . . didn't even have a toothbrush.*

[6]Bill Hay, long-time announcer for the "Amos 'n Andy" radio show, well-remembered for his introduction, "Here they ah."

[7]Eddie Cantor, popular American comedian who starred in vaudeville, in motion pictures, and on radio for more than fifty years and who delighted audiences with his rolling eyes, lively movement, and inimitable singing voice. "The Eddie Cantor Show," sponsored in its early years by Chase & Sanborn coffee, was the most successful and popular program on radio dur-ing the 1930s.

[8]Ben Bernie, American comic and musician who appeared in vaudeville and on radio as "The Old Maestro." A pioneer in radio, Bernie enjoyed his greatest success with a weekly program that ran from 1931 to 1940.

[9]Primo Carnera, Italian boxer known as the "Ambling Alp" who reigned as world heavyweight champion from 1933 to 1934.

Maximilian Adelbert "Max" Baer, American heavyweight prizefighter who defeated Carnera in the eleventh round of their title bout on June 14, 1934. Baer lost the heavyweight crown less than a year later.

[10]Mussolini and Hitler met for the first time at Venice, Italy, in June of 1934. During their closed-door sessions, the two dictators apparently agreed to respect the independence of strife-torn Austria and to attain parity of ar-maments for Germany.

[11]Finland was the only country to repay the United States in full its debt from World War I.

[12]FROM TRANSCRIPTION: *Baer won, you know, maybe. . . carry him along.*

[13]Cordell Hull, United States secretary of state from 1933 to 1944; recip-ient of the Nobel Prize for Peace in 1945.

GOOD GULF SHOW, June 24, 1934

[1]FROM TRANSCRIPTION: *For those of you who are not familiar, . . . that has always has been suspicious of them.*

[2]FROM TRANSCRIPTION: *You know, such extermination has. . . is really unparalleled in history.*

[3]FROM TRANSCRIPTION: *You see a bounty or tax. . . bear that lost her cub, you know.*

[4]Paraguay and Bolivia waged war from 1932 to 1935 over possession of the Gran Chaco north of the Pilcomayo River. The two sides finally signed a truce in 1935 after more than 100,000 lives had been lost. A peace treaty in 1938 gave the greater share of the disputed territory to Paraguay.

[5]FROM TRANSCRIPTION: *. . . there's some kind of humor. . . Mr. Dillinger's birthday.*

John Herbert Dillinger, American bank robber and murderer who head-ed one of the most notorious gangs of criminals in the Midwest during the early 1930s. Captured in 1933, he escaped from an Indiana jail in March of 1934, prompting an intensive, nationwide manhunt. The end finally came on July 22, 1934, when he was ambushed and killed by federal agents outside a Chicago movie house.

GOOD GULF SHOW, July 8, 1934

[1]FROM TRANSCRIPTION: *In other words, do you need a prompter to tell you? Now from the comedian's standpoint, we like the audience.*

[2]Joe Penner, Hungarian-born American entertainer who hit stardom on radio in the 1930s. He was voted the outstanding comedian of that medium in 1934.

Jack Benny, renowned American comedian who starred first on the vaudeville circuit and then on radio and television. His highly successful radio show premiered in 1932 and, thereafter, dominated the airways until Benny's last live broadcast in 1955.

[3]"Brain Trust," a group of academicians who served as advisers and public servants in the Roosevelt administration.

[4]FROM TRANSCRIPTION: . . . *your applesauce straight, or an audience, see? If you. . .*

[5]Paavo Nurmi, Finnish long-distance runner; gold medal winner in the Olympic Games of 1920, 1924, and 1928.

[6]Hugh Samuel Johnson, American army officer and governmental administrator; head of the National Recovery Administration from 1933 to 1934; retired brigadier general in the United States Army.

Rexford Guy Tugwell, Columbia University economics professor and a leading member of President Roosevelt's "Brain Trust"; assistant secretary of agriculture from 1934 to 1937.

[7]Japan occupied Manchuria in 1931-1932 when Chinese military resistance there was weak. The seizure of Manchuria was, in effect, an unofficial declaration of war against China that led to full-scale combat in the mid-1930s.

GOOD GULF SHOW, March 31, 1935

[1]Harry von Zell, American radio announcer, actor, and master of ceremonies who began his long-term broadcasting career in 1926 with a station in California. Soon thereafter he went to New York City where he became one of the most popular announcers in the country.

[2]Hitler abrogated the military clauses of the Versailles Peace Treaty when he announced on March 16, 1935, that Germany would return to its pre-World War I policy of the conscription of all young men. The action appalled the French and British, but they did nothing except lodge protests and start negotiations with Germany on nonaggression pacts.

[3]Robert Anthony Eden, British foreign minister from 1935 to 1938, 1940 to 1945, and 1951 to 1955; later, prime minister of Great Britain.

[4]Bill, Jr., Will Rogers' eldest son, graduated from Stanford in 1935.

After leaving office, Hoover returned to his home at Palo Alto, California, where he began writing his memoirs.

[5]Republican leaders from the Midwest met near Kansas City in March

to criticize the Roosevelt administration and to plan a six-state "grassroots" conference, which was held two months later in Illinois.

[6]Italian and Ethiopian forces first clashed along the Italian Libyan border in December of 1934. Italy, whose leader, Mussolini, was determined to establish an empire in North Africa, thwarted all offers at conciliation and, finally, on October 3, 1935, launched a full-scale invasion of Ethiopia. The African nation fell within a year, despite sanctions against Italy imposed by the League of Nations.

[7]William Vincent Astor, American financier, publisher, investor, and philanthropist; director and principal stockholder of the shipping firm United States Line. President Roosevelt often took cruises aboard Astor's yacht, *Nourmahal.*

[8]John Nance "Jack" Garner, vice president of the United States from 1933 to 1941. A Texas Democrat, Garner previously had served several terms in Congress and two years as Speaker of the House.

[9]Byron Patton "Pat" Harrison, Democratic United States senator from Mississippi from 1919 until his death in 1941.

[10]National Recovery Administration (NRA), a major New Deal agency established in 1933 and empowered to make voluntary agreements with employers concerning hours of work, rates of pay, and the fixing of prices. A part of the act providing for the NRA was ruled unconstitutional in 1935.

[11]Arthur Capper, Republican United States senator from Kansas from 1919 to 1949; owner and publisher of the *Topeka Daily Capital, Capper's Weekly, Capper's Farmer,* and other publications.

[12]Gerald Prentice Nye, Republican United States senator from North Dakota from 1925 to 1945. An outspoken isolationist, Nye headed a senatorial committee that investigated the role played by United States arms manufacturers in the American entrance into World War I.

[13]Bernard Mannes Baruch, American businessman, statesman, and Democratic political adviser and financial contributor; confidant of several presidents.

[14]Henrik Shipstead, United States senator from Minnesota from 1923 to 1947. Originally elected to the Senate as a Farmer-Laborite, Shipstead later switched to the Republican party.

[15]William Edgar Borah, United States senator from Idaho from 1907 to 1940; maverick Republican progressive; chairman of the Senate Committee on Foreign Relations from 1924 to 1933 and wielder of much influence in the foreign affairs of the United States.

[16]Early in 1934 Long introduced his plan for national social and economic reform, the "Share-the-Wealth" program; it proposed a guaranteed annual income and a homestead allowance for every family.

GOOD GULF SHOW, April 7, 1935

[1]Raymond Charles Moley, American political economist and magazine editor. A central figure in Roosevelt's circle of advisers, Moley later became an energetic critic of the Roosevelt administration while serving as an editor of *Today* and *Newsweek* magazines.

[2]Reconstruction Finance Corporation (RFC), a governmental lending

agency established in 1932 to provide financing for banking institutions, life insurance firms, railroads, and farm mortgage associations.

[3]Francis Everett Townsend, California physician who conceived and promoted an old-age pension scheme known as the "Townsend Plan." Certain aspects of his proposal were embodied in the Social Security Act of 1935.

Charles Edward Coughlin, Catholic priest from Detroit who attracted a wide following with his frequent radio broadcasts in the 1930s assailing American financial leaders for having caused the Depression. Coughlin advocated such measures as silver inflation and the nationalization of banks, utilities, and natural resources.

[4]Samuel Goldwyn, Polish-American motion-picture producer who arrived in Hollywood in 1910 where he soon became one of America's leading filmmakers. In 1918 he formed Goldwyn Pictures Corporation, which later became a part of Metro-Goldwyn-Mayer.

GOOD GULF SHOW, April 14, 1935

[1]James Wolcott Wadsworth, Jr., Republican United States senator from New York from 1915 to 1927; United States representative from 1933 to 1951.

[2]Civilian Conservation Corps (CCC), a New Deal program established in 1933 to provide work and vocational training for unemployed single young men through conserving and developing the natural resources of the United States.

[3]Stephen Grover Cleveland, Democratic president of the United States from 1885 to 1889 and 1893 to 1897.

[4]William Allen White, influential owner and editor of the *Emporia* (Kansas) *Gazette* from 1895 until his death in 1943; recipient of a Pulitzer Prize in 1923; prominent Republican leader.

GOOD GULF SHOW, April 21, 1935

[1]Harold Le Clair Ickes, United States secretary of the interior and administrator of public works from 1933 to 1939.

Harry Lloyd Hopkins, American public official; intimate friend and adviser to Franklin Roosevelt; director of the Federal Emergency Relief Administration from 1933 to 1935; head of the Works Progress Administration from 1935 to 1938.

[2]Eugene Talmadge, Democratic governor of Georgia from 1933 to 1937 and 1941 to 1943; ardent states' rights advocate. During his second term as governor (1935-1937), his staff was forbidden by Harry Hopkins to disburse federal relief funds, and Talmadge became violently opposed to the New Deal.

[3]Henry Agard Wallace, United States secretary of agriculture from 1933 to 1940. Son of a prominent Iowa farm editor, Wallace served as vice president of the United States from 1941 to 1945.

[4]John Pierpont Morgan, Jr., chairman of the board of J. P. Morgan & Company, one of the most influential banking firms in the world. Morgan built an already sizable family fortune into a colossal financial and industrial empire.

[5]Theodore Roosevelt, Jr., eldest son and namesake of the twenty-sixth president. A former assistant secretary of the navy, Roosevelt was a noted writer, explorer, politician, and soldier.

[6]Anna Eleanor Roosevelt, wife of Franklin Roosevelt. Charming and outgoing, Eleanor Roosevelt greatly expanded the duties of a first lady by undertaking innovative and precedent-setting responsibilities.

GOOD GULF SHOW, April 28, 1935

[1]Henry Morgenthau, Jr., United States secretary of the treasury from 1934 to 1945.

[2]Henry Morgenthau, German-born American diplomat, attorney, and financial expert; United States ambassador to Turkey from 1913 to 1916 and to Mexico in 1920.

[3]A circus press agent placed a female midget in the lap of J. P. Morgan, Jr., during proceedings of a Senate stock market investigation in June of 1933. Although flabbergasted, the multimillionaire financier dismissed the publicity stunt good-naturedly.

[4]Mae West, platinum-wigged American leading lady of the screen who combined sexuality, suggestiveness, and humor in a successful film career that began in 1932 with *Night After Night*.

GOOD GULF SHOW, May 5, 1935

[1]Key Pittman, Democratic United States senator from Nevada from 1913 until his death in 1940; leading silver inflationist.

[2]Arthur Hendrick Vandenburg, United States senator from Michigan from 1928 until his death in 1951; an influential Republican leader in the upper house.

Curtis "Buzzy" Roosevelt, the eldest son of Anna Roosevelt, who was the only daughter of Franklin and Eleanor Roosevelt.

Upton Beall Sinclair, American novelist, social activist, and Pulitzer Prize winner. Sinclair, a socialist, ran unsuccessfully in 1934 as the Democratic candidate for governor. He campaigned on a platform of "End Poverty in California" (EPIC).

Alfred Mossman "Alf" Landon, Republican governor of Kansas from 1933 to 1937; unsuccessful candidate for the presidency in 1936.

Clark Gable, American leading man of the cinema who became known as the "king" of Hollywood actors. A stalwart of Metro-Goldwyn-Mayer studios for twenty-five years, Gable received an Academy Award in 1934 for his performance in *It Happened One Night*.

GOOD GULF SHOW, May 12, 1935

[1]Edgar Fogel Magnin, rabbi of Wilshire Boulevard Temple in Los Angeles

since 1915; lecturer in history at the University of Southern California from 1934 to 1955.

[2]Quintuplets were born on May 28, 1934, to Oliva and Enzire Dionne of Callander, Ontario, Canada. The multiple birth of the four girls and one boy attracted worldwide attention.

GOOD GULF SHOW, May 19, 1935

[1]Hiram Warren Johnson, United States senator from California from 1917 until his death in 1946; a leading member of the progressive wing of the Republican party.

[2]Frank Finley Merriam, Republican governor of California from 1934 to 1939; lieutenant governor from 1931 to 1934.

[3]Rogers was in Sacramento for the filming of *Steamboat Round the Bend*, one of two motion pictures that were released after his death in August of 1935.

[4]On May 16 the Roosevelt administration allocated more than one-half billion dollars for jobs in highway construction and repair. Texas received, by far, the largest share of the funds.

[5]William Gibbs McAdoo, Democratic United States senator from California from 1933 to 1939; United States secretary of the treasury from 1913 to 1918; candidate for the Democratic nomination for the presidency in 1920 and 1924.

[6]*Judge Priest* was based on a character created by Cobb. Rogers appeared in the title role of the film, which was released in 1934.

[7]John Ford, Irish-American motion-picture director who made nearly 200 features from 1917 until his death in 1975. He won Academy Awards in 1935 for *The Informer* and in 1940 for *The Grapes of Wrath*.

[8]Lincoln Theodore Monroe Andrews Perry, "Stepin Fetchit," black American comedian who appeared in several motion pictures with Will Rogers, including *Judge Priest* and *Steamboat Round the Bend*.

GOOD GULF SHOW, May 26, 1935

[1]The Patman bonus bill, providing for a $2.2 billion cash payment on the compensation certificates held by World War I veterans, passed Congress in early May of 1935. Roosevelt vetoed the measure, however, chiefly on grounds that the pay-out would spur inflation. The House overrode the veto on May 22, but the Senate sustained it one day later.

[2]Jesse Holman Jones, Houston publisher, political figure, and civic leader; chairman of the Reconstruction Finance Corporation from 1933 to 1939.

[3]Robert Marion La Follette, Jr., Progressive-Republican United States senator from Wisconsin from 1925-1947.

GOOD GULF SHOW, June 2, 1935

[1]Two kidnappers of nine-year-old George Philip Weyerhaeuser were ap-

prehended by federal agents on June 9, 1935. They later were convicted and sentenced to long prison terms. A third suspect was never captured.

[2]Daniel Calhoun Roper, American lawyer and politician; United States secretary of commerce from 1933 to 1938.

[3]The National Industrial Recovery Act, of which the NRA was a major part, was invalidated by the Supreme Court on May 27, 1935, in the case of *Schechter Poultry Corporation* v. *U. S.* The NRA fell under the purview of Roper's Department of Commerce.

[4]Roberta Campbell Lawson, an Oklahoman whose ancestry was one-eighth American Indian, was elected president of the General Federation of Women's Clubs in a hotly-contested election on June 10. She served as president from 1935 to 1938. Rogers mentioned her in his "Daily Telegram" of May 25, 1935.

[5]Francis Monroe "Frank" Hawks, American aviator who established numerous transcontinental and point-to-point speed records in the 1920s and 1930s. Early in 1931 Hawks flew Rogers on a benefit tour of the Southwest to raise money for drought victims in the region.

GOOD GULF SHOW, June 9, 1935

[1]Katharine Hepburn, American actress of the stage and screen; winner of four Academy Awards for best actress and nominated on eight other occasions. In 1935 she starred in the highly acclaimed *Alice Adams,* which also featured Fred Stone in his first film with sound.

[2]Frank Richardson Kent, American syndicated newspaper columnist from 1924 until his death in 1958; an executive with the firm that published the *Baltimore Sun.*

Mark Sullivan, American newspaper columnist and radio commentator who began his journalistic career as a muckraker but who later became a spokesman for conservative Republicans. Both Sullivan and Kent were frequent critics of Roosevelt's New Deal.

[3]Shirley Temple, American child film star who began to appear in leading roles in 1934, enjoying phenomenal popularity in a succession of winsome roles.

[4]Frank E. Tours, English-born American conductor and composer; director of Broadway shows. He wrote many successful songs, including "In Flanders Fields" and "Mother o' Mine."

[5]James Melton, American tenor who sang with the Revelers Quartet in the late 1920s and also enjoyed a successful solo career in opera, on Broadway, and on radio in the 1930s.

Allie Lowe Miles, American cosmetician, radio personality, and advertising writer.

Lew Lehr, American vaudeville, film, and radio comedian, noted for his newsreel commentary and his use of dialects.

Henry M. Neely, American writer and lecturer in astronomy, active in the field until his death in 1963; writer, director, and star of several radio shows during the 1930s.

INDEX

Abyssinia: *see* Ethiopia
acting: 23, 24
actors and actresses: 23, 24, 80-82, 88, 87, 155
advertising: 56, 65; on radio, 83, 88-89, 118-19; in newspapers, 111
Africa: 11, 37, 104
agriculture: 28, 44-45, 125
air mail: 8
alarm clocks: 78, 85, 128
Alaska: 11
Albany, N. Y.: 23
alcoholic beverages, consumption of: 89, 150
Allen, Frank G.: 54
Allied Powers, in World War I: 104-105
amateur theater: 23
ambassadors: 40, 41; *see also* diplomacy and diplomats
American Civil War: 39, 44, 158
American Federation of Labor: 28, 138
American Legion: 55, 138
American Relief Association: 12
American Revolution: 43, 55, 137, 167
Amherst College: 39, 40
ammunition manufacturers: 84, 107
"Amos 'n Andy" (radio show): 44, 66, 88-89, 108
ancestry: 38-39
announcers, on radio: 83, 87, 89
applause: 96-98, 100-101
archeologists: 122
archeology: 120-22
aristocracy, of Mexico: 41
Arkansas: 12
Armenians: 12
Armistice Day: 165
artists: 28
Arwell, Lee: 72

Aryan myths: 154
Astor, Nancy L.: 29-32; home of, 29, 30
Astor, W. Vincent: yacht of, 105, 132, 170
Astor, Waldorf: 29
athletes: 57
Atlanta, Ga.: 61
Atlantic & Pacific Tea Company: 89
Australia: 11
automobiles: 66, 72, 111; credit purchases of, 4; Ford models, 35, 38, 43, 44, 45, 46-47, 137, 144, 170; Star models, 43; Chevrolet models, 46, 144; deaths involving, 50; accidents involving, 133-34; Chrysler models, 144
aviation: 7-9, 15-16, 98; in Guatemala, 8-9; in Mexico, 8; military, 15; commercial, 49

babies: 89, 156-57
Baer, Maximilian A. (Max): 89-90
Balzar, Fred B.: 80
bands (musical): 96; on radio, 72
bank "holiday," national: 73
banking and bankers: 23, 113, 122, 148, 158
Baruch, Bernard M.: 107, 160
baseball: 103
beer: 75
Belgium, wartime starvation in: 12, 46
Benny, Jack: 97
Bernie, Ben: 89
Beverly Hills, Calif.: 49
Bible: 38, 51
bicycles: 144
big business: 127, 165
birth control: 76
Black Sea: 100
Blue Boy: 81